miami
& the keys

NATIONAL
GEOGRAPHIC

TRAVELER

miami
& the keys

by Mark Miller
photography by Matt Propert

National Geographic
Washington, D.C.

CONTENTS

Pages 2–3: Art deco lifeguard stations line the South Beach stretch of Miami Beach's Atlantic beachfront. Opposite: Hip cafés line the open-air Lincoln Road Mall, Miami Beach.

TRAVELING WITH EYES OPEN

Alert travelers go with a purpose and leave with a benefit. If you travel responsibly, you can help support wildlife conservation, historic preservation, and cultural enrichment in the places you visit. You can enrich your own travel experience as well.

To be a geo-savvy traveler:

- Recognize that your presence has an impact on the places you visit.

- Spend your time and money in ways that sustain local character. (Besides, it's more interesting that way.)

- Value the destination's natural and cultural heritage.

- Respect the local customs and traditions.

- Express appreciation to local people about things you find interesting and unique to the place: its nature and scenery, music and food, historic villages and buildings.

- Vote with your wallet: Support the people who support the place, patronizing businesses that make an effort to celebrate and protect what's special there. Seek out shops, local restaurants, inns, and tour operators who love their home—who love taking care of it and showing it off. Avoid businesses that detract from the character of the place.

- Enrich yourself, taking home memories and stories to tell, knowing that you have contributed to the preservation and enhancement of the destination.

That is the type of travel now called geotourism, defined as "tourism that sustains or enhances the geographical character of a place—its environment, culture, aesthetics, heritage, and the well-being of its residents." To learn more, visit National Geographic's Center for Sustainable Destinations at *www .nationalgeographic.com/travel/sustainable*.

miami
& the keys

ABOUT THE AUTHORS & THE PHOTOGRAPHER

Mark Miller earned a degree in American Social History from Stanford University, entered journalism as a newspaper copyboy, and subsequently reported for Reuters and the CBS Radio network, where he also produced documentaries. He has contributed to National Geographic Society books and publications, including *National Geographic,* since 1977, his assignments ranging across North America from Alaska to Florida's Dry Tortugas, as well as to the Caribbean and Europe. Miller lives in Los Angeles, where he is a partner of 12 Films, a documentary film production company.

Elizabeth Carter, a food journalist and experienced restaurant/hotel inspector, compiled the Travelwise for the original edition.

David Raterman updated and revised this book for the 2005, 2008, and 2012 editions. He has been a features correspondent for the South Florida *Sun Sentinel* since 2000. Raterman has written for many other publications, including *National Geographic Adventure* and *Writer's Digest* magazines.

Matt Propert is a freelance photographer and photo editor based in Washington, D.C. His work has appeared in many national and international publications and has been shown in major solo exhibitions. In addition to Miami and the Keys, Propert has photographed in Italy and throughout much of the Caribbean for the National Geographic Society.

Charting Your Trip

Millions of tourists flock to South Florida each year to take advantage of its sub-tropical climate and its miles upon miles of coastline. Beyond the sandy beaches, they indulge in Miami's blossoming arts scene, partake in outdoor adventures in Biscayne Bay or the Everglades, and unwind in the slower-paced Keys.

How to Visit & Get Around

Both Miami International Airport (MIA) or nearby Fort Lauderdale–Hollywood International Airport service Miami. Cruise ships provide the most luxurious form of transportation, and in the 2009/2010 fiscal year the Port of Miami served 4.15 million cruise-ship passengers. The Port of Key West handles approximately 850,000 each year.

Reaching Key West, at the tip of the Keys, about 160 miles southwest of Miami, by air requires a connection from MIA, or from Tampa and Orlando. You can also rent a car or take a shuttle, such as the bus provided by Greyhound, from MIA (see Travelwise p. 240). The shuttle from MIA to Key West takes approximately 4.5 hours, mostly along the scenic Overseas Highway (US 1).

Visitors in South Beach and downtown Miami will find many attractions within walking distance or ten-minute car rides (when there's no traffic). You can also utilize Miami–Dade County's extensive public transportation system (see Travelwise pp. 241–242). Within downtown Miami, that includes Metromover, whose driverless, computer-operated coaches transport passengers over short distances, and buses.

Outside of Miami, buses are the only public transportation for much of Dade County, including the island of Miami Beach. Buses are also the only public transportation in Key West.

If You Only Have a Week

A complete trip to Miami should include a mix of beach, culture, tourist attractions, and outdoor activities. Start **Day 1** with a visit to the wide, white oceanfront strand of Miami Beach. After you've swum, suntanned, and ogled some of the most beautiful people on the planet, partake of the hip sidewalk café life along Ocean Drive. In the evening stroll through South Pointe Park.

Day 2 should be for more relaxing. In the morning, return to the sand and surf of South Beach, and in the afternoon stroll along the nearby Lincoln Road Mall—noted for upscale boutiques and stylish restaurants and

Brown pelican, a common denizen of the Florida Keys

NOT TO BE MISSED:

bars—where you'll see fashion models and possibly a celebrity or two. Stop at Britto Central Art Gallery to see colorful pop art by Miami's most famous visual artist, the Brazilian Romero Britto. In the evening, dine at a casual Lincoln Road restaurant and finish the evening at a nightclub or two.

By **Day 3,** it's time for the cultural offerings of downtown Miami. In the morning, visit the two museums located at the Miami–Dade Cultural Center, the Museum of HistoryMiami and the Miami Art Museum. At the history museum, you'll learn about Tequesta and Seminole Indians as well as early pioneers. At the art museum, marvel at post–World War II works from through-out the Americas. Afterward, have lunch at one of the many upscale restaurants in the Shops at Mary Brickell Village. In the evening, take in a ballet or symphony performance at the Adrienne Arsht Center for the Performing Arts.

Start **Day 4** with a visit to Coconut Grove's Vizcaya Museum & Gardens. This spectacular Renaissance Italian villa and formal garden was completed in 1916, when being just a few miles south of downtown meant being in a separate world. Later, visit neighboring Coral Gables and stroll the Miracle Mile, marveling at the Mediterranean Revival architecture that gave forth the nickname "City Beautiful." Next, drive 3.5 miles to the nearby University of Miami and stop by the Lowe Art Museum, which features collections of Renaissance, baroque, American, Native American, Asian, and African works.

On **Day 5,** visit Zoo Miami, Florida's largest zoo and the United States' premier subtropical one. In the late afternoon, while driving back to central Miami, stop at Little Havana's Máximo Gómez Park, where you'll see Cuban Americans playing dominoes and inevitably discussing the Castro brothers. Top off the evening at the Versailles, a restaurant that is the social locus of all things Cuban in Miami.

Let **Day 6** be one for exploring Everglades National Park. At the Shark Valley entrance 25 miles west of downtown Miami, you can take a two-hour tram ride, join a ranger-led hike, or walk or bike on your own. You will see definitely alligators, birds, and other wildlife. Outside the park, on the Tamiami Trail

Online Information

With so much unreliable information on the Internet, it's best to stick with trustworthy sources. For attractions, check out the **Greater Miami Convention & Visitors Bureau** (www.miamiandbeaches .com) and the **Florida Keys tourism bureau** (www.fla-keys.com). For public transportation within Greater Miami, visit **Miami–Dade Transit** (www.miamidade.gov/transit). Newspapers such as the *Miami Herald* (www.miamiherald.com) and Key West's *Citizen* (www.keysnews.com) are good sources of information too.

Essential Facts

Virtually all visitors to Miami will be safe, but use caution in certain areas, such as Overtown and Opa-locka, and anywhere else if you're alone at night.

Most tourist sites are open seven days a week, but some are closed on Mondays or Tuesdays, as are some restaurants and bars.

Tipping should be approximately 15 to 20 percent of your bill in restaurants and bars. Without tips, servers make much less than minimum wage.

(US 41), plenty of billboards advertise airboat rides. These are a great way to enter the heart of a unique ecosystem, while having lots of fun.

Spend **Day 7** on two of Florida's keys, located just a few miles east of downtown Miami and accessed via the Rickenbacker Causeway. While away the morning at Virginia Key Beach and then visit the nearby Miami Seaquarium. This world-renowned marine attraction has orca and dolphin shows, and its massive aquariums showcase manatees and sea lions as well as fish in all shapes and sizes. In the late afternoon, travel five minutes to neighboring Key Biscayne and visit the lighthouse at Bill Baggs Cape Florida State Park. Its café with outdoor tables serves casual food, which is just right after a day spent outdoors and among sea life.

If You Have More Time

On longer visits, set up bases at three locations. The first is Miami (see the weeklong itinerary). The second is in the Upper Keys at a resort on Key Largo or Islamorada, and the third is Key West.

The Upper Keys are celebrated for water sports, so do those on **Days 8, 9, and 10.** Your hotel will have connections to operators, so it's best to ask at the front desk. Some resorts even host their own water sports. Go on a half-day scuba diving or snorkeling trip followed by a stand-up paddleboarding—a sport in which you stand on a flat surfboard and use a long paddle to maneuver—tour. The next day, go fishing in the morning and kayaking in the afternoon. And on a third day, treat yourself to a swim with dolphins at one of five locations. Afterward, feed the 100-pound wild tarpon that congregate at Robbie's Marina in Islamorada.

On **Day 11,** as you drive farther west on the Overseas Highway (US 1), stop on Big Pine Key to look for miniature Key deer in the National Key Deer Refuge. At the

Best Times to Visit

If you love water sports, then come during the hot, rainy summer. Otherwise you will probably prefer visiting Miami and the Keys during the dry, warm winter. Tourist season commences with the end of hurricane season—officially November 30—and ends in May. Tourist season is when festivals, such as Art Basel Miami Beach, Miami Book Fair International, and South Beach Wine & Food Festival, take place, as well as outdoor competitions like the ING Miami Marathon.

Note that spring breakers do not swarm to the beaches of Miami and Key West like in days gone by, but many will come. Spring break for most colleges is between the middle of March and the middle of April. If you're a grown-up who likes to party, plan on visiting Miami during Carnaval Miami (late February–early March), Miami Beach during Urban Beach Week (Memorial Day weekend), or Key West during Fantasy Fest (October). Or you may decide to avoid those revelers.

People nightly gather in Mallory Square, Key West, to enjoy street artists and the often fiery sunsets.

refuge's visitor center, pick up a map and follow it to Blue Hole, a former quarry where you'll probably see wild alligators 10 feet long. Stroll the nearby nature trail through a native tropical hammock. Spend the rest of the day exploring the keys off the highway's next 30 or so miles before arriving at the road's end, Key West, for dinner.

On the morning of **Day 12,** visit Smathers Beach, blessed with calm surf and backed by swaying palm trees. In the afternoon, survey the island via trolley-like bus. A popular stop is at the Harry S. Truman Little White House, which the U.S. President visited 11 times while in office. A 15-minute walk south stands the Hemingway Home & Museum, where the island's most famous writer crafted several of his stories. As dusk approaches, make your way to Mallory Square, where crowds nightly gather to watch the sunset while being entertained by street performers of all ilk. The sheer exotica on display will astonish you. Finish your day with a drink at either Captain Tony's Saloon or Sloppy Joe's, two beer joints connected to Hemingway.

On **Day 13,** visit the Mel Fisher Maritime Museum, where the museum's namesake placed much of the $400 million treasure he salvaged from shipwrecked Spanish galleons in the 1980s. Highlights are gold and silver ingots and a 77-carat emerald. Then visit Audubon House & Tropical Gardens, which showcases several of the naturalist's works, and stroll along nearby Caroline Street, which is picturesque with old-style Key West mansions

For **Day 14,** visit Dry Tortugas National Park, which is 45 minutes by seaplane and 2.5 hours by ferry from Key West. The park's main attraction is the 19th-century Fort Jefferson, but the scenic journey is just as rewarding. ■

History & Culture

Coral Gables City Hall, with its statue of the city's founder, George Merrick Opposite: Elkhorn Reef, Biscayne National Park, a snorkeler's paradise

Miami Today

In recent decades, Miami has become home to many Americans embracing the subtropical weather and to immigrants looking for a better life. It grew to 2.5 million people in 2010, a 10.8 percent increase over the previous decade, further enriching the city's mélange of ethnic groups. In fact, as a percentage of population, Miami has more foreign-born residents than any other U.S. city.

These newcomers have brought with them a desire for the arts, which led to stunning new performing arts centers in downtown Miami (Adrienne Arsht Center for the Performing Arts) and South Beach (New World Center) and to internationally renowned festivals. And unique ecosystems with a sunny climate have steered residents to outdoor adventures. While scuba diving and fishing remain the most popular, stand-up paddleboarding and kayaking are surging.

In 1994 some 34 heads of state from North, Central, and South America convened at the Biltmore Hotel in Coral Gables for what was called the Summit of the Americas. (Fidel Castro was conspicuously absent.) The meeting had a post–Cold War viewpoint—that the future of the three Americas includes increasing economic and cultural interdependence. Greater Miami played host to the summit not simply because the United States wished to offer the Biltmore's hospitality to the presidents and prime ministers, but because the metropolis already symbolizes that interdependence more than any other city in the Western Hemisphere.

> **The epic saga of Miami's Cuban community obscures the fact that the city has large and vital groups of expatriates from other southerly lands.**

The city inherited the mantle of "Capital of the Americas" as a result of politics—most notably, the historical accident that has kept Havana out of competition for the title since 1959—but mainly because of finance. Miami's money industry has ties extending south nearly to the pole, and the city is the leading import/export hub in the region, a brokerage house for a bewildering variety of products and commodities shipped through the region. Perhaps even more important is the largely successful merging of Anglo-American business and culture with the customs of the Americas to the south, which shows that while borders drawn by statesmen and enforced by arms are one thing, human ambitions and the historical momentum they generate are quite another.

The epic saga of Miami's Cuban community obscures the fact that the city has large and vital groups of expatriates from other southerly lands. Some arrived first class by air; others, like a good many Haitians, risked their lives in decrepit fishing boats. Some newcomers are among the richest and most influential people in Miami; others languish among the ranks of the poorest.

Miami's internationalism translates into a metropolitan sprawl with an astonishing diversity of ethnic neighborhoods where homeland language and customs are

South Beach's trendy Ocean Drive sidewalk restaurants pulse with life year-round.

Two Miami Scenes on the Rise

As Miami's population rapidly increases, the city is redefining itself. For tourists, this means that now they have more of two disparate pastimes: arts and gambling.

Las Vegas and Atlantic City are not renowned for high culture, and cities that are heralded as cultural gems do not usually allow gambling. Can the two coexist?

They're trying in Miami.

In recent years, legislation has allowed the county's dog and horse tracks and a jai-alai fronton to install slot machines and high-stakes poker tables. By 2012, the subject of opening massive Las Vegas–style casinos was being hotly debated.

Miami's arts scene is also expanding fast. In addition to two spectacular performing arts centers opening since 2006— Adrienne Arsht Center (see p. 69) and New World Center (see pp. 94–95)—the city is home to internationally acclaimed museums and festivals, including Art Basel Miami Beach, which debuted in 2002. Creating the works are local artists, many with studios in the burgeoning Wynwood Arts District (see pp. 69–70).

preserved in family life, cafés and restaurants serve indigenous fare, and shops and markets trade in the essentials and whimsies of the communities' particular traditions and heritage. Besides the city's historic Cuban and Jewish districts, Greater Miami has enclaves of African Americans, Bahamians, Colombians, Guyanese, Haitians, Jamaicans, Nicaraguans, Puerto Ricans, Peruvians, Trinidadians, Venezuelans, Russians, and Virgin Islanders, not to mention the indigenous Miccosukee Indians, whose world endures on a small reservation in the Everglades. The transitions are seldom obvious, for in Miami the process of assimilation is one of blending—as Little Havana, for example, has taken in a new generation of political refugees from Nicaragua.

With over 140 commercial banks, Miami is indeed an international financial capital, and it is not an exaggeration to call it the Capital of the Caribbean. To those more interested in culture, however, the city's other nickname, "Gateway to the Americas," is more evocative of Miami's peculiar appeal.

Introducing Miami

There is no American metropolis like Miami. Most of its residents consider themselves fortunate, despite a six-month threat of hurricanes, to live so close to South Florida's captivating wetlands and jungles and the bewitching Florida Keys.

Relative to other American urban areas, Greater Miami is a youngster, taking root only at the end of the 19th century. Its polyglot character reflects a heritage peculiar to this region—as an outpost of Spanish colonials, a vacation mecca, and a sun-drenched retirement haven for work-weary Northerners. Then came the exodus of Cubans following Fidel Castro's takeover, a phenomenon that quickly transformed a slow-paced, leisure-oriented city into the "capital of Latin America."

Miami is probably best known by stereotypes. Films, television, and hard-boiled fiction generally portray it as a flamingo-colored city of outlaws. For years, Miami Beach was known as God's waiting room, where elderly Jewish folk lived out their years in residential hotels. Other notions persist—of a nightlife capital where club-crawling hedonists pursue ephemeral pleasures (true); of drug trafficking (true); of anti-Castro sentiment (true); and of an excess of pink things (not true except perhaps in Miami

Beach's Art Deco District, where refurbished moderne and streamline hotels and apartments sport vivid pastels).

Greater Miami lies hard by some of the most inviting seashore in the Americas, caressed by gentle surf and balmy trade winds. In November, as autumn chills northern places, Miami's "high" season commences, bringing daytime temperatures in the low 80s, and overnight lows in the 70s. Warm days and nights year-round are what makes South Miami Beach the closest thing to a 24-hour city in the land. Biscayne Bay, which separates Miami from Miami Beach's barrier Island, is a sailor's delight, with dozens of small islands left in a wild state. Along its shore, public parks preserve thousands of forested acres and grassy beaches. Communities such as Coconut Grove and Coral Gables explain why some 700 people move to Florida every day: neighborhoods of gardened homes, tree-shaded boulevards, appealing civic architecture and grand plazas, and tropical gardens lapped by azure waters—the apotheosis of the Florida Dream.

The most enjoyable sojourns here indulge the senses. Take time to experience what state officials proudly call "The Real Florida"—the beaches, reefs, and shoreline jungles of Biscayne Bay, and the dreamy wilds of the Everglades, a place unlike any other on Earth, where you can rent a canoe and explore a primordial water world so serene, the loudest sound is often the beating of your heart. Taste New World cuisine, immerse yourself in warm Gulf Stream waters, dig your toes into the sand that crunched beneath the boots of Florida's first European visitor, Juan Ponce de León, and idle away a day on a shore so paradisiacal it seemed to the Spanish adventurer proof certain that his long-sought Fountain of Youth lay close at hand. ■

Enormous cruise ships ply Biscayne Bay in Miami, recognized as the cruise capital of the world.

Miami Districts

Along with its beaches and hotels, Miami is home to a diverse range of ethnic communities and intriguing architectural styles. No one quite agrees on the names of Miami's major districts, let alone their boundaries, but here, in brief, are its main areas.

For many of Miami's Cuban Americans, Little Havana is a microcosm of their homeland.

Downtown: You can't miss downtown's skyline, one of America's most handsome, especially at night when spotlights paint skyscrapers in vivid colors. It is anchored by commercial and residential high-rises, the appealing Adrienne Arsht Center for the Performing Arts, and Bayside Marketplace, a popular shopping, dining, and entertainment complex on Biscayne Bay.

Little Havana: A political and economic beachhead for arriving Cubans since 1959, now seeing Latinos from elsewhere, Little Havana lies just southwest of downtown. Shops and restaurants include Nicaraguan, Mexican, and Colombian enterprises. Miami's Cuban population has expanded from here, but this remains the sentimental heart of the community.

Upper Eastside: Miami's northeastern reach flanks Biscayne Boulevard (US 1) north of downtown. An ethnically mixed district, its charm lies off the boulevard's deteriorating motel row in distinctive neighborhoods such as Bayside and Morningside, whose Mediterranean Revival and bungalow-style residences, built before 1940, grace palm-lined avenues.

Little Haiti: Just west of Upper Eastside, this fragment of the Caribbean is decorated with Haitian art and commerce. Its Buena Vista neighborhood has more Mediterranean-style residences. Adjoining is Miami's Design District (around N.E. 40th Street), whose showrooms, galleries, and furniture and fabric stores cater to designers and architects; and the fast-growing Wynwood Arts District (around N.W. 2nd Avenue), which features some 60 art galleries.

Allapattah: This working-class neighborhood of 41,500 (about 82 percent Hispanic), northwest of downtown, includes Miami's industrial, medical, and government buildings. Locals shop in the wholesale outlets that are supplied by garmentmaking factories. Cooks favor the Produce Market, Miami's largest. Photographers roam the Miami River here for picturesque exotica—funky bistros, old ships, auto repair shops, even rusty iron junkyards.

Overtown: Situated between Allapattah and downtown, this predominantly African-American community of about 10,000 struggles to overcome unemployment, homelessness, and crime. Community pride and civic programs have helped instill hope for rejuvenation. Overtown's theme park celebrates Miami's African-American heritage, an inspiring saga too often obscured by the community's day-to-day travails.

Flagami: Jutting west from Little Havana near the international airport, its contrived name a salute to Miami's first railroader, Flagami's grid of houses and small businesses is a middle-income, Anglo-American and Hispanic community of about 52,000. Its supper clubs and lounges draw patrons citywide, and windsurfers take advantage of the lakes in its Blue Lagoon district.

Coral Gables: In Coral Gables the classic beauty and grandeur of historic Spain mix with the vibrancy of a large American metropolis set in the tropics. With more than 46,000 residents, including many rich Latin émigrés, and more than 140 multinational corporations, the city has grown into Latin America's unofficial business capital in the U.S. Additionally, the private University of Miami's main campus is located here.

Coconut Grove: Sophisticated, comfortable, culturally diverse, and overgrown with vegetation, "the Grove" is one of Miami's most appealing suburbs. Its bohemian flair invites comparisons with New York's Greenwich Village and London's Chelsea. The 20,000 people who live here are proud of it. Many of its most luxurious addresses are condominiums overlooking Biscayne Bay, where wooded shores seclude some of South Florida's most sumptuous residences.

Coral Way: This area north of Coconut Grove embraces the neighborhoods of Brickell, Coral Gate, Douglas, Parkdale-Lyndale, Shenandoah, Silver Bluff, and the Roads. The Brickell district holds some of America's most critically acclaimed condominium designs. Older houses in Shenandoah and Silver Bluff display a diversity of handsome architecture.

Miami Beach: There are no 2 square miles anywhere like these on the American Riviera, a dazzling sweep of sand and Gulf Stream–warmed blue shallows flanked by some 800 art deco buildings, and some of the nation's most determinedly posh hotels. Here also is a preeminent nightclub scene, whose photogenic habitués decorate dance floors by night and sidewalk café tables by day.

History of Miami

Miami has been coveted by the Spanish and the English, served as a haven for runaway slaves, and inspired everything from a railroad magnate's ambitions to some of the country's most imaginative architecture. It has been home to pirates, Prohibition rumrunners, and celebrities, to hurricanes, Seminole wars, and a burgeoning tourist industry.

Prehistory

It is believed that the first Miamians were the Tequesta, hunter-gatherers and fisherpeople who settled at the mouth of the Miami River and on Biscayne Bay's coastal islands as early as 10,000 years ago. The Miami River—El Rio Nombrado de Agua Dulze on Spanish maps—ran clear, and at least one great freshwater spring gushed from the floor of shallow Biscayne Bay, creating upwelling offshore

The Spaniards dedicated St. Augustine, their first settlement in Florida, in 1565.

fonts and making it possible, even up to the late 1800s, to dip a cup into the sea and drink from it. Perhaps because of this phenomenon, the notion arose that "miami" is Tequesta for "sweet water"—*agua dulze*—as fresh water was once called. Others trace the name to the Seminole language and translate it as "big water." Hunting parties into the Everglades brought back deer, bears, and wild pigs. Men fished from dugout canoes for shark, sailfish, porpoises, stingrays, and manatees. Women and children gathered clams, conchs, oysters, and turtle eggs from the river-banks and beaches.

Yet the Spaniards left a more fateful legacy: Old World diseases against which Miami's native populations had no immunity.

Europeans started to write accounts of this region in the 1500s, but the Tequesta's sheltered world saw few changes until one day in 1566, when they encountered their first European, Pedro Menendez de Aviles, appointed by Spain as the first governor of "La Florida." He arrived with a company of soldiers and a Jesuit priest bent on saving heathen souls. Brother Francisco Villareal promptly founded a mission but failed to imbue the Tequesta with Christian fervor. Yet the Spaniards left a more fateful legacy: Old World diseases against which Miami's native populations had no immunity.

First European Explorers

In April 1513, Christopher Columbus's lieutenant, Juan Ponce de León, landed somewhere north, near present-day St. Augustine, around Easter Sunday—*la pascua florida* in Spanish, perhaps why the explorer named his "island" La Florida. The next half-century saw mistreatment of Florida's native peoples at the hands of the conquistadores.

Menendez's visit to the Miami Tequesta in 1566 was a peacemaking overture—he would soon sign a treaty with the Calusa, whose domain included the Keys. He traded with cloth and hardwares, more valuable to the tribes than the gold bars and Spanish shipwreck survivors given in return. He put up watchtowers from the Carolinas to Biscayne Bay to warn treasure galleons of lurking pirates, and he enlisted the Tequesta as allies, ending their enslavement of shipwrecked Spaniards. La Florida joined Spain's New World empire, though the swampy peninsula appeared to offer little more than turtle eggs and mosquito bites, and was valued mainly for its strategic location above the main sea lane of the Gulf of Mexico.

By the mid-1700s, St. Augustine was still a beleaguered garrison of about 2,000, its economy dependent upon supplying the military. Spain's mission system was a failure. Meanwhile the Spanish crown was refusing to allow desperately needed trade with the English colonies, barring non-Catholics from becoming colonists, and failing to convince entrepreneurs to bet their futures on La Florida. Capital flowed instead to Mexico and Cuba.

The 1763 treaty ending the French and Indian War delivered La Florida to the British, whose settlement schemes also foundered. Following the American Revolution, Great Britain traded Florida back to Spain for possession of the Bahamas, and in 1784 the Spanish instituted a new settlement program. A 175-acre tract on Bahía Biscaino was granted to Pedro Fornells, and an Englishman named John Egan was awarded 100 acres on the north bank of the Rio Nombrado, making the unlikely pair Miami's first documented residents.

Beginning of American Settlement

What kings and ministers decree is one thing; what people do is another. Americans began to see their destiny in terms of expansion, and resented European adventurers on the continent. In Spain's corridors of power, sober minds saw La Florida's sale to the United States as the logical option, but logic was losing ground to greed, a force more handily exploited by mercantile minds than bureaucratic ones. Pirates had turned the south coast and the Keys into a no-man's-land of tropical treachery, where cutthroats preyed on American ships, convincing Washington that a Spanish Florida meant anarchy. Meanwhile, Spain's policy of giving sanctuary to escaped American slaves enraged Southern planters, who sent raiding parties from Georgia. In 1811, a band of Yankee irregulars attacked St. Augustine and set about razing plantations until British warships chased them off. The outbreak of the War of 1812 obliged Madrid to let Great Britain take up positions in Florida, further arousing American ire; its outcome stripped La Florida of British naval protection. American adventurers—more pirate than patriot—continued to raid Spanish settlements. In 1821, its options evaporated, Spain ceded the Florida peninsula to the United States, and the Stars and Stripes flew over the new Florida Territory.

In 1821, its options evaporated, Spain ceded the Florida peninsula to the United States, and the Stars and Stripes flew over the new Florida Territory.

By 1825, Cape Florida, on Key Biscayne, had a lighthouse, although mariners complained that its beacon was so ineffectual there was greater danger they would run ashore while searching for it. Congress passed the Homestead Act, opening up Florida to settlers. The dark side of this policy was the strong-arm removal of Indians from their lands and forced relocation to reservations in the West. Their futures bleak, thousands united under the Seminole banner. In 1835, the settlers went to war, led by Maj. Francis Dade, for whom today's Dade County (of which Miami is the seat) is named. For the next 22 years, Florida was a guerrilla war zone.

Miami's Beginnings

Miami languished through the Civil War as an uncontested Confederate backwater, but after the South's defeat, it sprang back to life. In 1870, an Ohioan named William Brickell built a home and trading post on the Miami River. A fellow Clevelander, Ephraim Sturtevant, acquired land on Biscayne Bay. Clearing mangrove tangles a few miles south, settlers established a post office where mail was postmarked "Coconut Grove." Word of South Florida's tropical weather spread, luring adventurous travelers to Miami's first inn, the Bay View House, built on a rise now embraced by Peacock Park. The Biscayne Bay Yacht Club started up in 1887, and the following year a school opened. It was not until 1891, however, that the area found a civic leader with a vision for its future. Ephraim Sturtevant's daughter, Julia Sturtevant Tuttle, had visited in 1875 and returned from Ohio as the widowed mother of a son and daughter. She purchased 640 acres—1 square mile—on the north bank of the river and moved into the abandoned buildings of Fort Dallas. Surveying the shoreline, she determined to develop it into a major city.

A key requirement was a rail link to the rest of America. Tuttle sought out Henry Flagler. His Florida East Coast Railway had reached West Palm Beach some 70 miles

By 1912, Henry Flagler had extended his Florida East Coast Railway to Key West.

north, but Miami struck him as an unworthy destination. A freak freeze during the winter of 1894–1895 changed his mind. Most of Florida's citrus trees were stunted, but Miami's escaped the chill. The story is that Tuttle and her friends, William and Mary Brickell, brought healthy orange blossoms to the mogul, declaring Miami a meteorological oasis of sunshine and warmth. The ploy worked; on April 15, 1896, the first of Flagler's trains steamed into town. Flagler opened the luxurious Royal Palm Hotel for tourists lured south by promotions of "America's Sun Porch." He built houses for workers, dredged a ship channel in Biscayne Bay, and donated land for public schools. In July 1896, voters approved the city's incorporation. There was talk of naming it Flagler, but the 368 who cast ballots codified a name then more than two generations old, and Miami became an official Florida city.

Miami & the Spanish-American War

The city was barely two years old in April 1898, when the United States took up arms against Spain over the issue of Cuba's independence. During the three months of the "Splendid Little War," as Secretary of State John Hay called it, Miami (population about 1,200) grew up fast. Initially the Army rejected the city as a base for training an invasion force, a decision bemoaned by every local businessman from Flagler on down. The mogul became an enthusiastic supporter, dismissing the onset of Miami's sweltering summers by assuring Army brass that a "constant sea breeze" guaranteed "the comfort of officers and men." There was no "pleasanter location on the Atlantic Coast." At his own expense, he broke ground for "Camp Miami." It was an offer impossible to refuse. Soon more than 7,000 recruits were living in canvas tents set up in what today is downtown Miami near the Freedom Tower, sweltering in wool uniforms. Officers were put up at the airy Royal Palm.

For Miami merchants, it was indeed a splendid little war. Drugstores switched from selling lemonade by the glass to delivering it by the barrel; larger enterprises saw proportionate jumps in revenue. In North Miami, a hard-drinking red-light district flowered. But Flagler's lie that Miami had an "inexhaustible supply of purest water" evaporated in the heat of typhoid fever that killed 24 recruits. Hundreds were felled by dysentery, and the mosquito-tormented soldiers nicknamed the base "Camp Hell." Flagler assured Washington that their "discomforts" were "grossly exaggerated." Luckily, the war ended, and Camp Hell was disbanded after a mere six weeks.

The military's sojourn in Miami, however, accelerated the city's development by clearing land, laying track, paving streets, digging wells, and constructing buildings. Even more important in terms of Miami's future was the war reporting that introduced the hitherto little-known city to the nation. Thousands of young men returned to far more prosaic hometowns with a lingering sense of wonder and an unsatisfied curiosity.

Modern Miami

For all its progress, as the 20th century dawned Miami was still little more than a strip of civilization sandwiched between Biscayne Bay and the Everglades wilderness 3 miles west. But America's demand for residential land increased, triggering development fever and conservationist fervor, two forces that immediately

Pan Am's Clippers

One of the most romantic eras in American air travel came to an end in Coconut Grove on August 9, 1945, when the last scheduled Pan American Airways "clipper"—a four-engine Boeing 314 flying boat—taxied away from Dinner Key Marina (see p. 123) and took to the air. Few had expected the big flying boats to become obsolete so quickly. Pan Am's first clipper (a Sikorsky S-40) had only taken to the skies in 1931.

But World War II sped up change, and after the war, places that once seemed so remote, from Brazil to Burma, now had airfields that opened them up to visits by more economical planes that took off and landed on land. The reign of the "flying boat" was over.

A Sikorsky flying boat is towed behind Pan American's new marine air terminal in the mid-1930s.

clashed and have figured in Miami-area politics ever since. Draining of the Everglades commenced in 1906. A decade later Royal Palm Park was dedicated, planting the seed of Everglades National Park. Carl Fisher, a wealthy industrialist from Indiana, crossed the new 2-mile wooden bridge to "Ocean Beach," a spit of sand and coral rock paralleling Miami's shoreline across Biscayne Bay. Gazing at the wilderness of bay cedar, sea grape, mangrove, sea oats, and prickly pear cactus, he had a vision of hotels, golf clubs, and polo fields, a pleasure mecca incorporated in 1915 as Miami Beach.

By 1920, Miami's population stood at nearly 30,000—a 440 percent increase over the 1910 census. Word spread that an investment in Florida land guaranteed fabulous returns—that today's swamp was tomorrow's subdivision. Thousands moved to Miami and its soggy environs, setting off the frenzied buying and selling of the Florida land boom. In 1925 developers sought permits for 971 subdivisions. Nearly 175,000 deeds were recorded in new sister communities like Coral Gables, Miami Shores, Hialeah, Miami Springs, Boca Raton, and Opa-locka. The boom ended the following year with tax scandals and a devastating hurricane. The 1929 stock market collapse administered the coup de grâce.

Miami's location, however, continued to entice visionaries such as Fisher, and Juan Trippe, founder of Pan American Airways, once known for its "clippers" (see sidebar opposite). By 1935, Trippe's flying boats linked Miami to 32 Central and South American countries, bathing the city in the romantic glow of the glamorous new world of transoceanic aviation. World War II transformed the city back into a military town, turning hotels into barracks; beaches were used for drill, preparing 550,000 troops for combat. As with the Spanish-American War, thousands of young men and women would remember their time in the sun, and many would come back to stay.

Cuban Exodus

The postwar years were good to Greater Miami. The influx of newcomers continued, and tourism increased exponentially, spurring construction booms that produced pleasure palaces like Miami Beach's 1,504-room Fontainebleau, whose glittery opulence symbolized the region's status as the capital of hemispheric hedonism. The city appeared to have matured into a community best known for retirees and sun-seeking tourists, but history was about to deal it a wild card in the person of Fidel Castro. As the year 1958 came to a close, the 32-year-old rebel commander's guerrilla war waged against longtime Cuban dictator Fulgencio Batista sent the strongman fleeing into exile.

Castro's transformation of Cuba into a Communist state commenced with public executions and moved swiftly on to the confiscation of private industry and property. By the summer of 1960, the island's social elite and mercantile class began to leave in droves, most aboard one of the half dozen daily "Freedom Flights," a 250-mile hop from Havana to Miami. There were no round-trips on this route.

Cuban refugees living in Miami protest against Castro's regime at a rally in 1994.

When the first refugees arrived, Miami's population was about 700,000. For every resident of Hispanic heritage—estimated then to number around 50,000—there were three African Americans, and about ten more in the demographic category of "All others," most of them white. By the mid-1970s Miami's Cuban refugee population stood at more than 300,000; today, Cuban Americans account for about 675,000 of Greater Miami's almost 2.5 million residents. Indeed, Miami is where more than half of all Cubans in the United States have chosen to live.

The profound transformation worked on Miami's character by the Cubans' exodus, however, was less a result of numbers than of their backgrounds. Many were business people, professionals, or entrepreneurs whose enterprises ranged from small shops to sugar plantations, rum distilleries, and cigar factories. Many had worked in government and law enforcement, or taught in schools and universities. There were those for whom Castro's policies held the most draconian possibilities, and they arrived determined to reestablish themselves.

> **The profound transformation worked on Miami's character by the Cubans' exodus, however, was less a result of numbers than of their backgrounds.**

Their efforts reenergized the city while re-creating neighborhoods reflecting the culture of prerevolution Cuba. Streets were renamed after Cuban martyrs, moribund Cuban social clubs were revitalized, and trade organizations were set up. Cuban-owned small businesses, a mainstay of pre-Castro Cuba, sprang up all over Miami. Cuban grocery stores opened, while other stores added Cubano versions of coffee, cheese, and bread to their shelves to serve their new clientele. The refugees' need for places to live generated a boom in housing renovation and construction. Cuban restaurants delighted tourists by offering an exotic alternative to Miami's familiar kosher delis, seafood emporiums, and traditional steak houses.

Miami in the New Millennium

Today, more than 50 years after starting to flee the island, Cuban Americans dominate Miami's roster of notables. "We have a City of Miami mayor and police chief who are both Cuban, and so is the mayor of Miami–Dade County," Pablo Canton, administrator for the city's Little Havana Net Enhancement Team, said in 2012. "A lot of prominent people are Cuban here, a lot of entrepreneurs. A large medical clinic is Cuban owned, Miami–Dade College's president is Cuban. Since the start of the influx of Cubans after the Castro revolution, our impact on Miami has been tremendous."

Cubans remain the region's single largest Latin American group, making up about 50 percent of the total Hispanic population, which accounts for more than half of Miami–Dade County's residents. In recent years, however, the influx of non-Cuban Hispanic immigrants has turned talk of Miami's "Cubanization" to its "Latin Americanization." The change is evident even in Little Havana, where store windows display Salvadoran corn pancakes, and restaurant waitresses are likely to be from Honduras or Peru. In contrast to a decade ago, the music and talk broadcast by Miami's highest rated station is not Cuban, but Colombian—proving that the notion of the melting pot here remains a vital part of American life. ∎

Florida's Cuisine

With Miami becoming the crossroads of Cuba, the Caribbean, and Latin America, the ethnic diversity has caused its own culinary revolution—a fusion of tastes. And the star of this cuisine is Florida's own bounty: Florida's chefs finally have become aware of the gastronomic cornucopia growing in their own backyards, after decades of dishing up international and California fare as early bird specials.

Throughout Miami and the Keys, chefs make use of Florida's natural bounty to create their menus.

The result is a cuisine that bursts with tropical flavors and vibrant combinations, with the upbeat Latin American tempo bringing style, and the Caribbean Basin contributing most in terms of ingredients and inspiration. Salt cod, tamarind, guava, plantains, conch, and even the hottest chili pepper known, the Caribbean scotch bonnet, are all considered everyday fare. Superb local raw ingredients also play a part: seafood from the Atlantic Ocean and Gulf of Mexico; exotic natives such as stone crabs, snapper, catfish, frogs' legs, alligator, blood oranges, and hearts of palm; along with the luxuriant subtropical climate that supports a year-round growing season.

Following herewith are just some of the stars of Florida's cuisine, the catchwords of which are "fresh" and "healthy."

Florida Natives

Given its tropical climate, Florida is blessed with an unparalleled bounty of native foodstuffs of both the animal and plant variety, many of which make for interesting menu reading. Here are just a few of them:

Alligator—Farm raised, not from the wild. A smooth, very lean meat that can be tough if not carefully prepared and cooked—best battered and deep-fried. Alligator stew is an old Florida specialty.

Citrus fruits—Largest cash crop in Florida, producing more than 80 percent of the nation's limes, 50 percent of the world's grapefruits, and 25 percent of the world's oranges. In addition, Homestead, a farming community near Miami, has become the nation's exotic fruit capital, noted for lychees, passion fruit, mameys (looks like an elongated coconut and tastes like baked sweet potato), and mangoes.

Conch (pronounced conk)—A Bahamian specialty, a giant edible sea snail, firm textured, similar to abalone, shrimp, and scallops. Their huge, flaring conical shells that you can blow as a horn or put to your ear to hear the ocean need no introduction. High in protein, low in fat, and usually served as an appetizer, perhaps in a ceviche or in a chowder, or battered and fried as fritters.

Florida catfish—A specialty of Lake Okeechobee, northwest of Palm Beach, where it is filleted, sprinkled in cornmeal, and deep-fried. However, more and more Florida catfish is farmed.

Florida lobster—The formidable looking spiny lobster is a crustacean with giant antennae, a barb-covered carapace, but no claws. All the meat is in the tail. Abundant in Florida waters, it's smaller and sweeter than the bi-clawed Maine lobster. In season from the end of August to April.

Florida mangoes—Short season, roughly May–August, but used in salsas and chutneys year-round. Hundreds of varieties grow in yards and along roadsides during the season.

Frogs' legs—Hunted wild in the Everglades. Prized as much by backwoods fishermen as by gifted chefs for meat that is tender, succulent, mild-flavored, and sweet.

Key lime—Small, yellow, and indigenous to South Florida and the Florida Keys. Key lime pie is the region's most famous dessert. In its authentic form, it is sweetened with condensed milk and has a yellow, puddinglike filling with a graham cracker crust.

Stone crab—In season from October to April. The claws are the only part you eat; crabbers clip one of the two claws and toss the crab back into the water so it can grow a new claw in 12 to 18 months. Traditionalists serve the claws with melted butter or mustard sauce, but Florida's new generation of chefs is experimenting with novel ways to serve this delicacy.

Swamp cabbage or hearts of palm—Once the mainstay of the pioneer diet. Popular in rural areas, and with creative chefs.

Fresh Fruit

Florida's cuisine includes fresh fruit as a major component of meals, and the more exotic the better. You will find them served in fruit salads and salsas, chutneys and slaws, compotes and desserts. They're mixed into breads, ice cream, and mousses, pureed into sauces and spreads, and even fermented

Red peppers and fried bananas, typical of Cuban dishes popular throughout Miami

into delicious wines. Key limes (see above), kiwis, mangoes (see above), and kumquats are among the better known stars of this innovative cuisine, while less familiar exotics include the following:

Acerola—The "Barbados cherry" tastes like a tart strawberry. Just one packs between 20

A cluster of near-ripe papayas

and 50 times the vitamin C of an orange.

Atemoya—Heart-shaped or round, its pale green, bumpy skin holds a juicy, white pulp with the taste of a piña colada.

Bignay—With a sweet-tart taste resembling white grapes, loaded with vitamin A, the bignay is a popular source of homemade quality wine.

Black sapote—A green-skinned cousin of the persimmon, sometimes called chocolate pudding fruit because of its rich, sweet, chocolate-brown flesh. Often served alone with a dash of vanilla or lemon juice, and used in mousses and to flavor ice cream.

Calomondin—Resembling a tiny orange, related to the kumquat, it has an edible peel and a taste not unlike a lemon. Popular in preserves.

Carambola—Also known as the star fruit for its shape when sliced crosswise, this golden fruit lends itself to artistic presentations. Depending on the variety, its crisp flesh hints of apple, grape, and citrus, sometimes sweet, sometimes tart.

Ciruela—A decorative red or orange fruit sized and shaped like a plum tomato. Its cream- or red-colored flesh reminds some of peanuts.

Guava—Common around Greater Miami, this oversize member of the berry family comes in many shapes and varieties whose skin may be white, yellow, green, or pink. (The yellow kind are usually the sweetest.) Its flesh reminds some of strawberry; others say pineapple or lemon. Miami menus are sweetened by guava nectar, preserves, sauces, and desserts. You can buy it canned or in tubes of paste. Take it home with you to try baking your own *pastelitos*.

Jackfruit—The world's biggest tree fruit can weigh in at 80 pounds. Bumpy-skinned and oval-shaped, yellow or brown when ripe, its flesh suggests melon, mango, and papaya. Sometimes cooked like a vegetable, its chestnut-flavored seeds are roasted and used as seasoning.

Monstera—A cucumber-shaped fruit that sheds pale green scales as it ripens. Its custard-like flesh has a sweet acidic taste hinting of ripe bananas. Often used in desserts or eaten fresh.

Muscadine grape—A Florida native, larger than most grapes, with pale green, brown-speckled skin and a musky, fruity, tannic flavor. It is used for making juice, preserves, and a local wine called scuppernong.

Papaya—In the Greater Miami area, the most common papaya variety is the small, yellowish pear-shaped Solo. Its sweet, aromatic flesh reminds people variously of peaches, apricots, or berries. Is frequently served sliced with a spritz of lime juice, and in salads, salsas, and desserts.

Sugar apple—Also known as sweetsop, the skin of this nubby, heart-shaped fruit can be mauve, yellow-green, or red. Regardless, it bursts open as the fruit ripens, revealing citruslike segments of creamy, sweet flesh (sometimes white, sometimes yellow). This fruit is often blended into ice cream. (Ask for this specialty when you visit King's Ice Cream on Calle Ocho; see p. 58.)

INSIDER TIP:

Try to take advantage of honeybell season if you visit Miami in winter. This juicy, Florida-grown, tangerine-grapefruit hybrid is only available at fruit stands in January.

—CAROLINE HICKEY
Editor, National Geographic Books

Florida Fish

With the Atlantic Ocean and the Gulf of Mexico to choose from, Florida's chefs can feature any number of fish as the catch of the day. Look for the following in particular:

Amberjack—A large, firm-fleshed, deep-water fish with a mild flavor similar to grouper.

Cobia—A large warm-water fish that resembles a shark. Has a mild-flavored, firm flesh that works well in chowders and ceviche.

Dolphin—A white-meat saltwater fish—not the sea mammal—also known as mahimahi.

It tastes at its best simply either blackened or plain grilled.

Grouper—A large, firm, sweet, white-fleshed fish; it can weigh up to 80 pounds.

Kingfish—A dark-fleshed fish popular with Cubans and Central Americans. This is the traditional fish used for making *escabeche* (pickled fish).

Mullet—The number one cash fish in Florida, caught in great quantities off the west coast. Rich and oily, ideal for smoking.

Pompano—A flat, silvery fish that's highly prized for its mild-flavored fillets.

Snapper—This fish flourishes in the shallow waters off the Keys. Florida's most popular fish, sweet, mild flavored, and tender.

Tuna—Both the 500- to 600-pound yellowfin tuna and the 20- to 40-pound blackfin tuna are caught off the Florida coast.

Wahoo—The name is Hawaiian and means "sweet." A particularly prized Florida game fish, it is dark, with a firm bite and a robust, dulcet flavor. The tropical fish belongs to the mackerel family, but it has a gray/white flesh.

EXPERIENCE: Annual Miami Food Festivals

Delight your taste buds at a number of food festivals, where you can sample the best Florida cuisine Miami has to offer, often to the accompaniment of live music. From countless food booths lining Miami's Calle Ocho (S.W. 8th St.) to celebrity chef events at the South Beach Wine & Food Festival, there's something for everyone, and all of it featuring local Miami color. Don't miss these four:

Calle Ocho Festival—This March affair is part of Carnaval Miami, a massive nine-day celebration of Latino food and culture extending 23 blocks through Little Havana. *Tel 305/644-8888, www.carnavalmiami.com.*
Great Taste of the Grove—Held in April, this two-day food and music fest features

Coconut Grove's most popular restaurants offering samples of their finest foods. *Tel 305/444-7270, www.thegreattasteofthe grove.com.*
South Beach Wine & Food Festival—Each February, this three-day annual celebration presented by the Food Network attracts TV personalities and tens of thousands of visitors. Events are priced separately; many sell out well in advance. *Tel 305/625-4171, www.sobefest.com.*
United Way Miami Wine & Food Festival—Held in February at various locations around Miami, this annual four-day festival celebrates wine, spirits, beer, and all sorts of food. Top local sommeliers, brewers, and chefs lead the way. *Tel 305/646-7111, http://miamiwinefestival.org.*

Arts & Culture

Do you enjoy authentic Caribbean festivities? You'll find everything here from Cuban block parties to Haitian nightclubs, from *moros y cristianos* (black beans and rice) with fried plantains to local blue crabs drenched in butter and garlic. For more traditional tastes, there are Western art galleries, orchestras, ballet, and off-Broadway productions, not to mention fishing tournaments.

Fine Arts

Owing to the aggressive forays of Spanish adventurers in the New World commencing in the 16th century, South Florida's European-American history is a lengthy saga relative to other regions in North America. The lineage of Miami's cultural institutions runs back nearly as far, to the first missions established by Catholic priests who dreamed of imbuing Florida's native people with Christian faith and customs, and teaching them to speak and read Spanish so that they might someday be relied upon as kindred souls and loyal subjects of Madrid. It proved an unrealistic ambition, at least in those days, but the friars' determination presaged a tradition among Miami-area settlers to found institutions of civilization in the tangled tropical jungles as soon as they could, as proof, perhaps mainly to themselves, that they had subdued the wilderness surrounding them.

Miami's successive influxes of ethnic groups added a variety of culturally and ethnically themed museums, libraries, and memorials found in few other American cities.

The first artist of any note to work in Florida was America's great painter of wild birds, John James Audubon, who briefly explored the Keys in the 1830s. It was not until the arrival of railroads in the later years of the 19th century and the land booms of the early 20th century, however, that the Miami area acquired a moneyed class from which came its founding patrons of the arts. These families gave their names, their money, and often their private holdings to endow small yet elegant collections such as Miami's Bass Museum of Art, a treasury of old master paintings, sculptures, textiles, period furniture, objets d'art, and ecclesiastical artifacts generally regarded as the finest of their kind in southeast Florida.

Like many leading American pioneers in far-flung places, these patrons promoted the establishment of schools and colleges whose roles in the community went beyond education to celebrate and nurture their community as well. Thus, within the walls of Greater Miami's leading learning institutions—the University of Miami, the Wolfson Campus of the Miami–Dade College, and Florida International University, most notably—you'll find some of the region's premier public art collections.

Miami's successive influxes of ethnic groups added a variety of culturally and ethnically themed museums, libraries, and memorials found in few other American cities. The flowering of Greater Miami's Jewish community, for example, is celebrated at Miami Beach's Jewish Museum of Florida. The continuing exodus of Cubans from

Xavier Cortada, a prominent Cuban-American artist, at his Miami Beach studio

their island home has transformed Miami into a surrogate Havana, where galleries, libraries, museums, restaurants, and nightclubs focus almost exclusively on Cuban art, literature, history, cuisine, and music. The arrival of other Caribbean émigrés, most notably Haitians, is reflected in the shops of Miami's Little Haiti district, and in the rise of ethnic theater companies, often itinerant troupes without a stage of their own, and the growing presence of Caribbean music on Miami's radio stations.

Miami's awareness of its political and financial roles as the unofficial capital of the Caribbean (some would say of Latin America as well) is the reason the city's downtown Miami Art Museum at the Miami–Dade Cultural Center is devoted to Western Hemispheric art since World War II, and why the Wolfson Campus of the Miami–Dade College, once primarily a showcase for innovative Miami area artists, maintains a noted collection of international works in its InterAmerican Art Gallery. It is a phenomenon reflecting the city's status as a cultural crossroads.

Elizabeth Caballero

Miami can claim one of opera's rising stars, Elizabeth Caballero—a soprano that the New York Times has described as having a "pearly tone, exacting technique and brazen physicality." A Cuban American, Caballero immigrated to Miami as part of the Mariel boatlift in 1980 when she was three years old. She performed in the show choir at Hialeah–Miami Lakes Senior High School and majored in vocal performance at Miami–Dade College. Before hitting it big on stage, she once worked in Florida Grand Opera's box office. Although now performing all over the United States and abroad, she regularly returns to Miami and is committed to at least one FGO opera per year.

Open the Tropical Life section of the Miami Herald (which publishes a Spanish-language edition, El Nuevo Herald) and you'll find notices spanning the spectrum of the region's cultural colors: a panel discussion by Holocaust scholars and survivors; an exhibition of African-American artists working in Miami; a symposium on Eastern European issues; galleries featuring folk art produced in Miami by Caribbean newcomers. If there is a theme that unifies all this diversity, it is one of hope and faith in the future. Even Miami Beach's famed art deco hotel architecture is much more than merely an ornamental vogue. Originally built for sojourners from the Northeast, many of whom had fled European oppression, the buildings' jaunty upbeat styles, owing little to the past, still seem optimistic about this great metropolis's destiny, and that of the people who choose to live here.

Performing Arts

The sense of being at a geographic threshold that so many people feel upon arriving in Miami—a place where embarkation to faraway places hangs in the air and hints at exotic possibilities—has encouraged an unusually exuberant creative tradition in the region's roster of performing arts troupes. In the beginning, the impetus for putting up concert halls and theaters was civic pride among Miami's founding families, who wanted their cousins in the long-established cities of the Northeast to take seriously their outpost of progress under the palms. As elsewhere in young communities in the late 19th century, in Miami it was more often the custom for friends to gather in a parlor around a piano and entertain themselves by singing Broadway tunes, reciting poetry, and acting out plays.

Miami pulses with music, from South Beach bars to Little Havana clubs to the New World Center.

Ambitions soon extended beyond citrus growing, shipping, fishing, city building, and railroading, however, to garnish the growing settlement with more than homespun performances. An official brass band was formed to welcome travelers who rode the rails south to the sun. On occasion, Miami's wealthiest winter visitors invited musicians south for private concerts in estates such as Coconut Grove's palatial Vizcaya. Some of the performers, seduced by the region's balmy weather and Miami's exotic fringe of azure sea, dazzling white sand, and gently rustling palms, saw not only a delightful comfort to be enjoyed, but opportunity to go from a back seat in an orchestra at home to the podium.

The influx of Northerners into the Miami area, many of them newcomers of European heritage and thus as fond of opera and classical music as Miami's native-born Yankees were of ragtime and vaudeville, created audiences in the city who might not be wealthy but were sophisticated in their appreciation of the performing arts. Opera singers, string quartets, and orators were invited down from the Northeast to perform—invitations made all the more attractive by the prospect of exchanging winter chill for tropical sunshine. As often as not, these talented visitors stayed to become pioneers of the musical or thespian variety.

Greater Miami has proved to be as nurturing to start-up companies as it is to orchids. Miami City Ballet held its inaugural performance in Miami in 1986; today it is one of the ten best-funded troupes in the United States (with an annual operating budget of $14 million) and enjoys the support of more than 14,000 season subscribers. In 2006 the opera moved to the Adrienne Arsht Center for the Performing Arts, an acoustically advanced hall with dramatic common areas.

The great odyssey of Cubans to South Florida, along with the city's proximity to the cultures of the Tropic of Cancer, is reflected in the variety and quality of its troupes. The *Miami Herald*'s Tropical Life section on any day demonstrates the remarkable diversity of performances, from flamenco ballet to dancers interpreting the music of Eastern Europe, the Caribbean, West Africa, Israel, and Central and South America. On weekend evenings in Miami's Little Havana district, a half dozen clubs throb to the big-band sound of pre-Castro Cuban jazz, and contemporary music by young Cuban-American musicians fusing the styles of both cultures.

For the same reasons, including long-standing cultural links with the Northeast in general and New York City's theater industry in particular, Greater Miami's playhouses draw on a small army of seasoned, well-schooled actors and an astonishingly fecund cadre of playwrights. The result is a year-round calendar of significant new works, as well as polished productions of perennially popular musicals and plays reflecting the region's kaleidoscopic creative multiculturalism.

A large number of Greater Miami's performing arts organizations have websites enabling you to peruse upcoming playbills and, in many cases, buy tickets online (see Travelwise pp. 262–263 for more details).

> **The great odyssey of Cubans to South Florida, along with the city's proximity to the cultures of the Tropic of Cancer, is reflected in the variety and quality of its troupes.**

Other Cultural Attractions of Note

Subtropical weather and the Caribbean influence have filled Greater Miami's calendar with a never ending pageant of festivals and cultural performances. Their variety reflects the region's diversity: concerts, operas, ballets, flower shows, fishing tournaments, marathons, and more. Its signature events are Miami Book Fair International, Art Basel Miami Beach, and South Beach Miami Wine & Food Festival.

Be sure to explore ethnic districts on foot if your schedule permits doing so—they're full of exotica. Book and music stores sell the songs and stories of the Caribbean, Africa—even prewar Europe—and offer uniquely personal insights into the unusual bloodlines of this one-of-a-kind American metropolis.

The region's unusual tradition of whimsical experimentation in architecture is seen in few other American cities, and is a continuing phenomenon inspired by the hopefulness and optimism so many feel here. Take the time to visit some of Greater Miami's distinctive neighborhoods, such as the Wynwood Arts District, and adjoining communities such as Coral Gables and Opa-locka.

Pick up one of Miami's informative daily or weekly newspapers and open its pages (and your mind) to the unfamiliar. Here, if the trade winds bring a purple sky that rains on your beach party, you still have plenty of places to go and countless things to do.

The best source for festival information is the *Travel Planner*, updated annually and distributed free by the Greater Miami Convention & Visitors Bureau. You can view it online or order a copy at the bureau's website *(www.gmcvb.com)*. ∎

One of America's best known, least understood metropolises—
a place unlike any other city in the United States

Miami's Central Districts

Detail of mural, Miami Art Museum

Miami's Central Districts

Although flamboyant island-bound Miami Beach tends to garner more attention than its mainland sister city, the heart and soul of what makes Greater Miami a truly international metropolis and the commercial center of South Florida lie in Miami's central districts. Here you'll find some of the region's oldest neighborhoods, often a short walk from the highest concentrations of immigrant newcomers, creating the city's exotic juxtapositions of cultures.

Seen from across Biscayne Bay, Miami's downtown skyline twinkles under a darkening sky.

Here, too, are most of the financial interests that use Miami as a base for hemispheric operations, and the power base of Miami's determined, passionately political Cuban-American leadership.

South Florida's Crown Jewel City

The steady influx of immigrants to the city—through legal or illegal channels—makes accurate population counts difficult, but most assessments suggest that fewer than a quarter of central Miami's residents

remain in the category of non-Latin whites who originally settled the community. Estimates of the central districts' non-Cuban Caribbean citizenry—primarily Haitians, Puerto Ricans, Jamaicans, Bahamians, and Dominicans—currently range in the vicinity of a quarter-million, creating an inner city tableau in which one out of every three faces is Caribbean.

Miami's central districts hold some of the city's best known tourist attractions (Bayside Marketplace, Little Havana) and cultural institutions (Miami–Dade Cultural Center, Adrienne Arsht Center for the Performing Arts), most of its most significant archaeological sites (Miami Circle), prime examples of the fanciful residential "theme" architectures that characterize the entire region (Opalocka, Morningside), and expansive parks (Bicentennial Park, Bayfront Park) and racetrack venues (Hialeah) that serve as meeting grounds for many of Miami's residents in search of relaxation and entertainment.

Miami's heart also wears South Florida's social problems on its sleeve: minority unemployment and despair, homelessness, and pockets of economic blight. But Miami has a long record of overcoming hardships, and everywhere in Miami's central districts you'll find new construction and renovation work under way, propelled perhaps less by the region's resilient economy than by Miamians' conviction that their city is destined to become a cosmopolitan and influential hemispheric capital.

Miami's Street Plan

A note on navigating Miami's central districts: The city's streets are generally numbered according to an east–west, north–south orientation. Although you will almost certainly encounter exceptions,

---

NOT TO BE MISSED:

Watching a jai-alai game at the Casino Miami Jai-Alai 44

A delicious meal of Cuban specialties at Versailles 56

The fierce domino action taking place in Máximo Gómez Park 62

Seeing traditional cigarmaking at El Crédito Cigar Factory 63

Taking in a performance at the Adrienne Arsht Center for the Performing Arts 69

Gallery-hopping in the Wynwood Arts District 69–70

The Rubell Family Collection's audacious artwork 70–71

---

most avenues, courts, places, and roads run north–south, while most streets, drives, lanes, and terraces run east–west. The division between east and west is Miami Avenue; Flagler Street divides north from south. Street prefixes reflecting the compass rose—N., S., E., W., N.W., N.E., S.W., and S.E.—are assigned according to the road's position relative to the intersection of Miami and Flagler.

Avenues, beginning with First, count upward the farther west and southwest they lie from Miami Avenue. Streets, starting with First, are numbered progressively according to their distance from Flagler Street. Downtown Miami is largely arranged according to a grid of right angles, permitting easy around-the-block recoveries from missed turns while exploring by car. But beware: Many streets, avenues, boulevards and the like are numbered but also have names, and sometimes more than one (for example, in Miami, S.W. 13th Street is also known as Coral Way, and US 1 is known as Biscayne Boulevard in the north, Brickell Avenue in the center, and South Dixie Highway in the south). ∎

Painting Miami

Downtown's skyscrapers are illuminated in color after dark to celebrate a season or a holiday, salute a charity or foreign dignitary, encourage a local athletic club, or just inspire a sigh. There are 40 permanently illuminated high-rises in Miami. Some, such as the Bank of America Tower, change colors up to 100 times a year. Red and orange probably mean a salute to the Miami Heat basketball team. Orange and aqua are the colors of the Miami Dolphins football team.

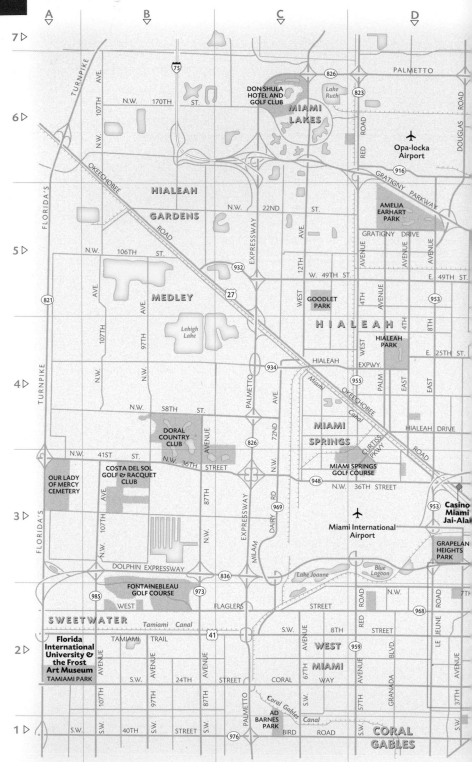

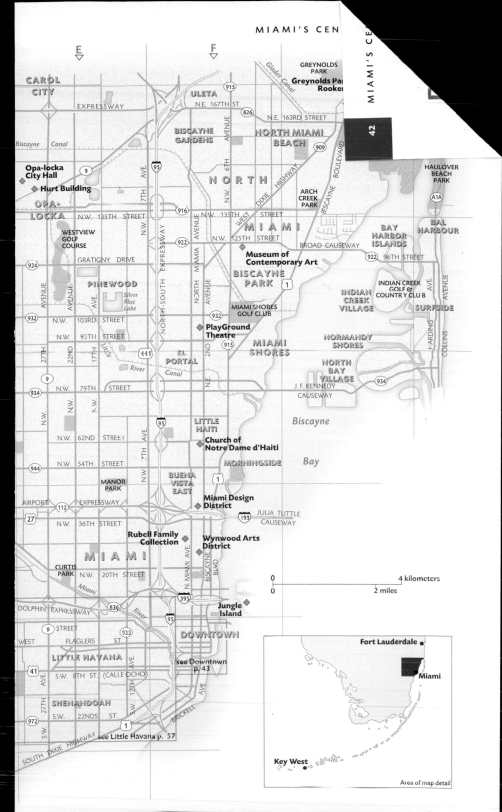

E

F

CAROL CITY

EXPRESSWAY

Biscayne Canal

ULETA

N.E. 167TH ST.

915

826

N.E. 163RD STREET

GREYNOLDS PARK

Greynolds Par Rooker

BISCAYNE GARDENS

N O R T H

NORTH MIAMI BEACH

909

Opa-locka City Hall

9

Hurt Building

OPA- LOCKA

N.W. 135TH STREET

916

N.W. 135TH STREET

M I A M I

N.W. 125TH STREET

BROAD CAUSEWAY

ARCH CREEK PARK

HAULOVER BEACH PARK

A1A

BAY HARBOR ISLANDS

BAL HARBOUR

WESTVIEW GOLF COURSE

GRATIGNY DRIVE

922

Museum of Contemporary Art

922

96TH STREET

SURFSIDE

924

PINEWOOD

Silver Blue Lake

BISCAYNE PARK

1

INDIAN CREEK GOLF & COUNTRY CLUB

INDIAN CREEK VILLAGE

932

N.W. 103RD STREET

N.W. 95TH STREET

932

MIAMI SHORES GOLF CLUB

932

N.W. 95TH STREET

PlayGround Theatre

915

MIAMI SHORES

NORMANDY SHORES

441

EL PORTAL

River

Canal

NORTH BAY VILLAGE

934

934

N.W. 79TH STREET

J. F. KENNEDY CAUSEWAY

95

N.W. 62ND STREET

LITTLE HAITI

Church of Notre Dame d'Haiti

Biscayne

944

N.W. 54TH STREET

MORNINGSIDE

Bay

MANOR PARK

BUENA VISTA EAST

1

AIRPORT

112

EXPRESSWAY

27

N.W. 36TH STREET

Miami Design District

195

JULIA TUTTLE CAUSEWAY

Rubell Family Collection

Wynwood Arts District

M I A M I

CURTIS PARK

N.W. 20TH STREET

Miami

0   4 kilometers

0   2 miles

DOLPHIN EXPRESSWAY

836

River

395

Jungle Island

9

STREET

933

95

WEST

FLAGLERS

ST.

DOWNTOWN

LITTLE HAVANA

41

S.W. 8TH ST. (CALLE OCHO)

see Downtown p. 43

SHENANDOAH

972

S.W. 22NDS ST.

1

see Little Havana p. 57

SOUTH DIXIE HIGHWAY

Fort Lauderdale

Miami

Key West

see Downtown p. 43

see Little Havana p. 57

Area of map detail

Downtown Miami

Opinions of downtown Miami differ. Grand when seen from a distance, the financial district's skyscrapers turn out to be not particularly people-friendly when confronted close up. Travelers can be disoriented (and disappointed) by the downtown area's seeming lack of a center or a unifying social current. There is no Boulevard St.-Germain here, no Upper West Side to stroll on weekends; and come evening, downtown sidewalks become deserted and not the safest place to wander—but the area has interest nonetheless.

At lunchtime, downtown Miami's office workers flock to Bayfront Park for some relaxation.

Miami's downtown is generally said to fall between N.E. 15th Street and S.E. 14th Street, and run from the Biscayne Bay waterfront to I-95. Within this 28-block-wide embrace lies a district that can be rewarding to those who explore it on foot. Here are the museums of the Miami–Dade Cultural Center, the hustle and bustle of Bayside Marketplace, and the serenity of Bayfront Park, among other sights.

The Downtown Scene

You'll find street vendors selling brewed coffee and Caribbean-style pastries, cakes, juices, and fruit drinks. Spanish-language music radio blares from the entrances of low-priced empo-riums occupying sidewalk-level storefronts (many specializing in consumer electronics, lug-gage, clothing, and jewelry and catering mainly to a year-round traffic of Latin American shoppers), creating a peculiar blend of North and Latin American retailing. Venture a few blocks west of Biscayne Boulevard (the main north–south thoroughfare closest to the waterfront) and you find yourself in a cultural mélange— Haitian here, Jamaican there, now Puerto Rican, now Central or South American—

MIAMI

Area of map detail

0	500 meters
0	500 yards

Freedom Tower
American Airlines Arena
Port of Miami
PORT BOULEVARD
Arena/State Plaza Station
N.W. 5TH STREET
N.E. 5TH STREET
College North Station
BISCAYNE
N.W. 1ST AVENUE
NORTH MIAMI AVENUE
N.E. 1ST AVENUE
N.E. 2ND AVENUE
College/Bayside Station
BOULEVARD
Bayside Marketplace
Government Center Station
Miami-Dade Cultural Center
First Street Station
BAYFRONT
N.E. 1ST STREET
Alfred I. duPont Building
EAST FLAGLER STREET
Gusman Center
Walgreen's
41
PARK
Miami Avenue Station
S.E. 1ST STREET
Ingraham Building
Bayfront Park Station
Third Street Station
Knight Center Station
Riverwalk Station
Biscayne Bay
S.W. 2ND
Miami River
1
41
Fifth Street Station
Miami Circle Park
BRICKELL KEY
BRICKELL PARK
Mandarin Oriental Hotel
SOUTH
41 S.W. 7TH STREET
Eighth Street Station
Greater Miami Convention and Visitor's Bureau
41 S.W. 8TH STREET
MIAMI AVENUE
BRICKELL AVENUE
Xavier Cortada Art Gallery
Mary Brickell Village
Tenth Street Promenade Station
Brickell Banking/Commercial District

EXPERIENCE: Attend a Jai-alai Game

The sport of jai-alai (pronounced HIGH-lie) is billed as the "world's fastest game"; players (pelotaris) throw its hard ball at nearly twice the velocity of the fastest pitches in baseball. Attending a game (which usually run four to five hours) can be a memorably exotic adventure for the uninitiated, and a great passion for aficionados, of which Miami has many. America's premier jai-alai venue, **Casino Miami Jai-Alai** (map 40 D3, 3500 N.W. 37th Ave., tel 305/633-6400, www.fla-gaming.com, $) is five minutes east of Miami International Airport in a handsome building completed in 1926 and housing a 4,000-seat main auditorium (called a fronton).

Also known as pelota, the game is more than three centuries old, originating in Spain's Basque country. It's played on a court of three granite walls about 176 feet long and two stories high. The players strap boomerang-shape baskets (cestas) to their hands and fling the balls against the walls, often running up them in displays of athletic agility, while fans cheer and wager throughout the 14-round performances. Spectators watch from theater-style seats behind a protective wire fence. The fronton has a cocktail lounge, gift shop, and snack bar, as well as a low-stakes poker parlor. The fronton is open to adults only, except for Sunday matinees, when children can attend with adults.

Miami–Dade Cultural Center

⓶ Map p. 43

✉ 101 W. Flagler St.

a mix of frenetic shops, hole-in-the-wall lunch counters, and Cuban cafeterias (cafés) serving powerful café Cubano by the cup, on the sidewalk.

Downtown Miami is polyglot; Spanish is ubiquitous and Creole is heard often, as are Hebrew and Brazilian Portuguese. On some streets, Rastafarians brush elbows with Orthodox Jews, and their sidewalk shops occasionally adjoin. It is a city evolving toward a cosmopolitan character that holds a vision of a uniquely American future.

Walk east on Flagler Street from its intersection with Miami Avenue, and you will find handsome relics of Miami's past, architectural jewels such as the Walgreen's drugstore chain's streamline moderne flagship (now a La Epoca store) at N.E. Second Avenue and, beside it, the ornate 1926 Florentine Renaissance

Ingraham Building, its lobby a study in art deco. Some call the 1939 Depression moderne Alfred I. duPont Building, at 169 E. Flagler Street, Miami's answer to New York's Rockefeller Center. (The exquisite murals arching above the ornate lobby were inspired by Florida's history and the era's dogged determination to believe in a better future.) At 174 E. Flagler you'll encounter the Olympia Theater at the Gusman Center for the Performing Arts, which occupies a movie theater built in 1926 by the Paramount Pictures studio in the style of a Mediterranean courtyard (see sidebar p. 47), now a prime venue for screenings during Miami's annual film festival.

The cacophonous throng of humanity swirls around downtown until midafternoon, then quickly thins as shadows of high-rise buildings lengthen. By evening the only people you're likely to see here are tourists looking lost.

Miami–Dade Cultural Center

Downtown's long-discussed lack of a center was addressed in the late 1970s and 1980s by a much-debated redevelopment project that amounted to a total makeover of its western flank. The centerpiece (and most successful aspect) of this ambitious undertaking is the 3.3-acre Philip Johnson–designed Miami–Dade Cultural Center complex between First and Flagler Streets, home to the Miami Art Museum, the Museum of HistoryMiami, and the city's premier repository of books and historical documents, the Miami–Dade Public Library. Johnson's creation was labeled "neo-Mediterranean," and in fact the tiled plaza has the ambience of a public place alongside that Old World sea. Chairs and benches offer peaceful respite away from downtown street and sidewalk traffic.

Miami Art Museum:

Though the museum's imposing facade might suggest an omnibus approach, its collection showcases international art, from the perspective of the Americas, from World War II to the present. Exhibitions change regularly and their quality is high, with a growing reputation; in the museum's large pleasant galleries you will certainly see some things you recognize from books and art postcards, but there are also many surprises—unfamiliar works by modern

Miami Art Museum

✉ 101 W. Flagler St.

☎ 305/375-3000

🕐 Closed Mon. & major holidays

💲 $$; $$ combo ticket with Museum of HistoryMiami also available

**www.miamiart
museum.org**

A large sculpture adorns a park at Government Center, just north of the Miami–Dade Cultural Center.

Thousands upon thousands of books line the shelves of the Miami–Dade Public Library.

Museum of HistoryMiami

✉ 101 W. Flagler St.
☎ 305/375-1492
🕐 Closed Mon. &
   major holidays
💲 $$; $$ combo
   ticket with
   Miami Art
   Museum also
   available

**www.history
miami.org**

masters and artists surely destined for similar recognition in the future. This is an especially fine archive of work from Central and South America, the Caribbean islands, Europe, Asia and the Middle East, and also from South Florida.

Note: In late 2013, the art museum is slated to move to a new, larger location in the Museum Park complex being built at Bicentennial Park, across the street from the Adrienne Arsht Center for the Performing Arts (see p. 69).

Museum of HistoryMiami:

The task is formidable: to chronicle in a comprehensible way some ten millennia of human life along these shores. The museum does it brilliantly, using traditional and state-of-the-art interactive exhibitions and installations, such as an old Miami streetcar. You

can explore the galleries on your own or on a guided tour (check schedules when you arrive). Exhibits depict Miami and its environs centuries before Europe knew of the New World. In the **Folklife Collection** you can trace the human odysseys that brought so many cultures to the Florida peninsula, right up through this century's Jewish and Cuban communities.

One popular exhibit recounts the unusual influence that railroads had in bringing Miami and the rest of South Florida into the American cultural mainstream. The emphasis of the museum is on helping visitors understand the social forces that produced this region's unusual history and unique character.

In addition to its exhibits, you can visit HistoryMiami's Archives and Research Center, which houses more than a million

INSIDER TIP:

Enjoy live music and wine at the Museum of HistoryMiami's Wine Down Wednesday (5 p.m.–8 p.m., $$), held the first Wednesday of each month.

—JANE SUNDERLAND
National Geographic contributor

images of South Florida and the Caribbean region. These include historic maps, photographs, illustrations, and postcards. Written archives available to the public include family letters, diaries, and transcripts of oral history recordings as well as rare books and magazines, early city directories, old tourist brochures, and newspaper clippings from the early 1900s to the 1960s. With Miami sprouting out of the coastal wetlands in just the past century, much of it can be followed by reading up on its

construction history. The center's Woodrow W. Wilkins Archives of Architectural Records are superb.

The exhibitions include some shows designed to be especially appealing to younger visitors. Call ahead to reserve a place on group tours in languages other than English, and for walking tour prices and times.

Miami–Dade Public Library:

You need not be a scholar to appreciate and enjoy this handsome flagship library of the Miami–Dade Public Library System, which holds more than four million books and artifacts, though many scholars do research here, often in the special collections.

There's art as well in the first floor auditorium and in the lobby on the second floor. While on the first floor, look up at the domed ceiling of the cupola to see trompe l'oeil clouds and a pungent quote from Shakespeare's *Hamlet* on words and

(continued on p. 50)

Miami–Dade Public Library

✉ 101 W. Flagler St.
☎ 305/375-2665
🕐 Closed Sun. July–Sept.

www.mdpls.org

Olympia Theater

Miami theatergoers have visited Olympia Theater for decades, first for silent movies and vaudeville acts, then for musical performers like Elvis Presley, B. B. King, and Luciano Pavarotti, and today for ballet, opera, symphonies, and movies—with sound. Built in 1926, its elaborate Moorish architecture includes majestic turrets and golden balconies as well as an evening sky with sparkling stars and billowy clouds.

Today officially known as the Olympia Theater at the Gusman Center for

the Performing Arts (*174 E. Flagler St., 305/374-2444, www.gusmancenter.org*), the Olympia is now a performance and rental hall; the theater receives grants that underwrite performances of companies such as Miami Lyric Opera, Florida Classical Ballet, and the Miami Symphony Orchestra. It is also the flagship venue for the Miami International Film Festival held in March. Outside of performances, visitors may walk around the theater's front lobby (*closed Sun.*). Check the website for a complete schedule of events.

Downtown Miami by Metromover

Making two scenic loops on the city's free, elevated Metromover trains takes less than an hour and will enable you to reconnoiter the whole of downtown—the area between the bay and N.W. First Avenue, and the north–south stretch bounded by N.E. 15th and S.W. 14th Streets—and get a clear sense of the Central Business District's layout, making subsequent trips through the grid less confusing.

A computer-controlled Metromover train traverses downtown Miami.

NOT TO BE MISSED:

Bayfront Park • Freedom Tower • Adrienne Arsht Center for the Performing Arts • Brickell Avenue

Taking the air-conditioned, driverless, computer-operated coaches is easier and often cooler than roaming downtown on foot. Be sure to take the easy-to-read Miami–Dade County Transit Map with you to track your journey (available free at the Government Center station at 138 N.W. Third Street, at all visitor information centers, and at www.miamidade.gov/transit); it is an essential guide to the county's wide-ranging transit system, including the Metromover. There are two Metromover loops, and you should take both for a comprehensive tour.

Inner Loop

The Inner Loop circles the business district, and permits transfer to a spur running north near the bayfront to N.W. 15th Street. On your way there you will pass **Bayfront Park**

(see pp. 50–51). Just north of the College/ Bayside station (after you switch trains) is the **Freedom Tower,** rising above Biscayne Boulevard; it was completed in 1924, and once served as home to the long-gone *Miami News.* Offices here processed requests for political asylum during the first wave of Cuban immigration (see pp. 22–25). Its neighborhood is transitioning from being down-at-the-heels to modern and dynamic. The highlight is the 14-story, 20,000-seat bayfront **American Airlines Arena** (see sidebar p. 53), whose opening ceremony was a Gloria Estefan concert on December 31, 1999. The Miami Heat professional basketball team plays here. Its unusual design, a whirlwind of concrete and steel, is the work of Miami's high-profile architectural firm, Arquitectonica.

Just past the Park West station the route skirts **Bicentennial Park.** To the north is the massive **Port of Miami,** serving Miami's heavy cruise ship traffic, with shops and restaurants. As you glide over Interstate 395, which crosses Biscayne Bay to Miami Beach over the MacArthur Causeway, look inland to check out the beautiful new **Adrienne Arsht Center for the**

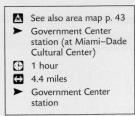

- See also area map p. 43
- Government Center station (at Miami–Dade Cultural Center)
- 1 hour
- 4.4 miles
- Government Center station

Performing Arts (see p. 69), a two-block-square opera, ballet, and symphony complex that opened in 2006. Ahead are the current **headquarters of the** *Miami Herald* and its Spanish-language alter ego, *El Nuevo Herald.* (Note: The fate of the 1963 Herald Building is up in the air: Recently sold, it is slated for demolition some time after 2013 to make way for a proposed gambling resort, but preservationists are attempting to gain it landmark protection.)

Brickell Avenue Outer Loop

Your destination is **Brickell Avenue** (see pp. 52–54), home to Miami's financial district, near Brickell and S.W. 14th Street. (Transfer to the Financial District train at the Third Street station.) Once a boulevard of grand estates, Brickell is still trod by moguls; not railroaders anymore, but financiers inhabiting the office and luxury condominium towers shading the street. South of the Riverwalk station there is a good view up and down the **Miami River,** where the Tequesta first settled. You can even see the grass covering the **Miami Circle** (see p. 54), a 2,000-year-old, 38-foot-wide Indian ruin that was discovered in 1998. The few older wooden houses along the way are survivors of Miami's first suburb. The train reverses

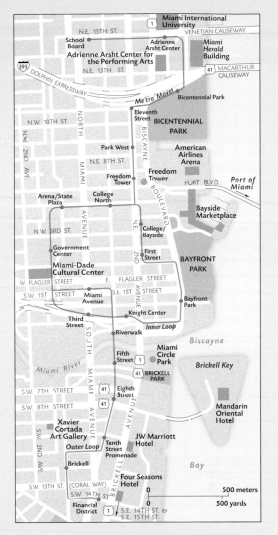

direction at the Financial District station.

If you have a half hour to spare, take a pleasant walk through a neighborhood of posh condos. Walk east from the Metromover's Financial District station to the bay along 14th Street—here designated S.E. 14th Street, as all local streets east of Brickell below the Miami River are S.E. Follow S.E. 14th's arc south to S.E. 15th Street, which loops west back to Brickell, a few blocks south of the Financial District station.

South Florida's Starring Role in Crime Fiction

With one of the country's most transient urban populations, murky swamps, and steamy subtropical climate, plus extreme wealth and glamour, Miami has developed a canon of colorful crime fiction. Notable among the genre's authors using South Florida as a backdrop are *Miami Herald* alumni Edna Buchanan, Carl Hiaasen, and even humorist Dave Barry, as well as Elmore Leonard, James Grippando, and Thomas Harris.

In recent years, Jeff Lindsay's Dexter character has scared readers and TV viewers alike. Through half a dozen novels and several seasons on Showtime, the serial killer/police bloodspatter analyst has appeared all over Miami and its neighborhoods. And when you look at Biscayne Bay, try not to think of him discarding bodies there.

Bayfront Park
🅐 Map p. 43
✉ Bet. S.E. 2nd &
N.E. 2nd Sts.

Bayside Marketplace
🅐 Map p. 43
✉ 401 Biscayne
Blvd.
☎ 305/577-3344
www.baysidemarket place.com

meaning, both works of public art by the distinctive California-based modernist Edward Ruscha (pronounced roo-SHAY).

A big draw at the library are the changing exhibitions in the auditorium, usually of photographs and paintings relating to Miami's past and present. Many photos are drawn from the library's **Romer Collection** (archived in the Helen Muir Florida Collection), a resource of 17,500 prints and negatives documenting Miami history. (You can find some wonderful images of old Miami online at *www.mdpls.org/databases/Romer_Site/search_romer.asp.*)

Don't be embarrassed to duck inside the library simply for the relief of its air-conditioning. The library also has Wi-Fi; ask the librarians for help on accessing it.

Bayfront Park

In 1926, this rolling, tree-shaded green flanking Biscayne Boulevard was built up with fill dredged from Biscayne Bay. It hasn't always been a peaceful retreat: In 1933, an assassin fired his revolver at Franklin Delano Roosevelt here, missing the newly elected president but fatally wounding Chicago mayor Anton Cermak. Pleasanter political memories are evoked by the **Claude and Mildred Pepper Fountain.** (Congressman Pepper, who died in his 90s, ended his long career as a champion of the rights of America's aged.)

The fountain is a magnet for the romantic, particularly on warm evenings. The imposing figure from another time guarding the park's eastern edge is that of Cristóbal Colón, better known as Christopher Columbus. The **statue of Columbus** is a 1953 gift to Miami from the Italians, Colón's countrymen.

The **Challenger Memorial**, a stark and subdued double helix, rises at the park's southeastern edge. Created by Japanese sculptor Isamu Noguchi, the sculpture honors the seven astronauts who died in 1986 when NASA's space shuttle *Challenger* exploded soon after its launch from Cape Canaveral. Noguchi, an inspired minimalist, presided over the park's 1987 makeover. The intricate brickwork of

Biscayne Boulevard, reminiscent of promenades on the beach in Rio de Janeiro, is the work of Brazilian landscape architect Robert Burle Marx.

Bayfront Park still hosts a cross section of Miami life—families on picnics, Caribbean steel drummers, strolling lovers, tourists, elderly chess players, and people

Bayside Marketplace

The Bayside Marketplace, arguably the biggest tourist magnet in all of Dade County, lies just north of Bayfront Park, sprawling over 16 waterfront acres. Its 150-odd retail shops, outdoor cafés, and stand-up eateries overlook a harbor that at times seems as busy as Hong Kong's.

Old Miami's rough-and-tumble waterfront has evolved into Bayside Marketplace's glittery bazaar.

exercising dogs. The **Tina Hills Pavilion,** an open-air amphitheater, often reverberates with music, and every night a laser light show pierces the Miami sky with glowing beams of vivid electronic colors. Even if nothing is happening, you will remember the views of Biscayne Bay and the Port of Miami from the park's waterside promenade.

A large parking garage adjoins the marketplace, putting you within a minute's walk of such attractions as Miami's Hard Rock Café.

The marketplace's low-key friendliness attracts a lot of people who come simply to dawdle, browse, and nibble their way around the large food court. Pull up a stool and order a frozen daiquiri or a rum-spiked slurry

Brickell Avenue
🅰 Map p. 43

The Shops at Mary Brickell Village
🅰 Map p. 43
✉ 901 S. Miami Ave.
☎ 305/381-6130
www.marybrickell village.com

of ice and fruit, and watch the boats and the people and life go by. Outlets for national chain stores like Victoria's Secret, the Gap, and Brookstone are popular with shoppers. The marketplace features daily afternoon concerts, and even laser shows for special occasions. The complex stays open late—by American standards (to 8 p.m. Sun., to 10 p.m. Mon.–Thurs. & to 11 p.m. Fri.–Sat.; some restaurants & bars may close later), and has the safe and cordial ambience of a small-town fair.

INSIDER TIP:

One of the interesting things about Miami is the elevated Metromover. At the Brickell station (1001 S.W. 1st Ave.), look up to see the artwork in the coffered ceiling.

—KAY KOBOR HANKINS
National Geographic designer

Harbor Offerings: The harbor is home to charter companies offering on-the-water tours of Biscayne Bay. One of the most interesting operates the 85-foot-long topsail schooner *Heritage of Miami II* (tel 786/663-1199, www.heritage schooner.com, $$$$$, tours at 11:30 a.m., 1:30 p.m., 3:30 p.m., & 5:30 p.m. year-round, plus 7:30 p.m. in summer), a 47-ton steel-hulled reproduction of the 19th-century cargo and passenger carriers that voyaged between

here and Havana. The *Heritage* hoists her rust-red sails (when wind and weather permit) for 75-minute round-trips south to the palatial shores of Coconut Grove and back. During your cruise, the captain will point out interesting landmarks and tell tales of Miami's colorful past.

Brickell Avenue

The street that commemorates William and Mary Brickell's role in elevating Miami into a full-fledged city (see p. 23) starts just south of the Miami River and runs to Coconut Grove. (To the north, by the river, it is S.E. Second Avenue; near Coconut Grove it veers inland to merge with S. Miami Avenue, both avenues losing their identities to then become S. Bayshore Drive.)

Prior to World War I, Brickell Avenue was a bucolic horse-and-carriage lane to the coral rock cottages and houses all but submerged in Coral Grove's unrestrainable undergrowth. But things were about to change, for a new generation of enthusiastic supporters was at work, nationally advertising Miami's virtues—the curative power of "tropical" climes, quick riches in real estate speculation, smarter children as a result of sun-warmed young brains. The campaign lured many, including wealthy sojourners who built spacious homes and mansions along Brickell Avenue.

The location was desirable: close to Biscayne Bay, yet far enough inland for the mangrove thickets and native Florida jungle to block winds and break tidal

American Airlines Arena

Miami's largest entertainment and sports venue, American Airlines Arena *(map p. 43, 601 Biscayne Blvd., tel 786/777-1000, www.aaarena.com)*, was inaugurated on New Year's Eve, 1999. Opening onto Biscayne Boulevard and Biscayne Bay and seating 19,600 people, it hosts concerts by a variety of top acts such as Gloria Estefan, Kanye West, and the Rolling Stones, as well as ice shows and circuses. The Miami Heat basketball team *(tel 786/777-HOOP, www.nba.com/heat)* plays at the arena. There's plenty of parking, and yachts can dock at the marina behind the arena.

Greater Miami has additional sporting venues for other professional sports teams too, including baseball's Miami Marlins *(tel 305/626-7378, http://miami.marlins.mlb.com)*, football's Miami Dolphins *(tel 305/943-6300, www.miamidolphins.com)*, and hockey's Florida Panthers *(tel 954/835-PUCK, www.floridapanthers.com)*.

surges from hurricanes. Brickell Avenue became known as Millionaire's Row, particularly after the completion in 1916 of Vizcaya (see pp. 116–119), an oceanside Xanadu built in Coconut Grove by industrialist James Deering. Only a few such places remain, squeezed between fancy luxury condominiums and blocklike Bankers Row office towers put up during the corporate carnival of Miami's giddy 1970s and '80s. Check out the Atlantis condo, with its whimsical red spiral staircase, or Villa Regina's rainbow hues. The business boxes now house international banks whose assets serve as load-bearing columns in the economies of the Caribbean and the Southern Hemisphere.

The Shops at Mary Brickell Village:

On the western side of Brickell Avenue stands the Shops at Mary Brickell Village, a new collection of boutiques and eateries set in a compact, shaded environment. Retailers include Sowinski Jewelers, Edward Biener Eyewear, Joanna Paige (shoes), and several upscale clothiers. To recuperate during an hours-long shopping jaunt, stop at one of the many restaurants, such as **Perricone's Marketplace and Café** *(tel 305/373-8449, www.perricones.com)*, which serves fine Italian food indoors as well as outdoors in a lush setting. Or visit **Fadó Irish Pub & Restaurant** *(tel 786/924-0972, www.fadoirishpub.com/miami)*, a popular spot with an interior imported from Dublin.

Along the Miami River:

Locals needing a riparian respite often come down to the casual, open-air, moderately priced, and well-reviewed seafood specialty house **Bijan's on the River** *(64 S.E. 4th St., bet. S.E. 2nd & S. Miami Aves., tel 305/381-7778, www.bijans.biz)*. Nearby, at 66 S.E. Fourth Street, is a cottage built in 1897, one of 14 Dade County pine houses commissioned by railroader Henry Flagler, who rented them out for $15 to $22 a month.

Miami Circle Park

🔺 Map p. 43

This survivor was moved here in 1980 from its original site on S.W. Second Street, where a parking garage now stands.

Despite lying hard by Miami's white-collar, high-dollar Financial District, much of the Miami River's downtown stretch looks like a location for a Humphrey Bogart movie about drug smugglers, or the setting of a picaresque novel of backwater rogues living in ways that would no doubt distress the polite society of the million-dollar condominium set downstream.

INSIDER TIP:

At Miami Circle Park, near the mouth of the Miami River at Biscayne Bay, visitors get a sense of strategic importance. Miami's earliest inhabitants lived there, and today high-rises surround it.

—BOB CARR
Executive director, Archaeological and Historical Conservancy

(Miami life imitates art in this instance; several years ago, as city officials dedicated the new Brickell Avenue drawbridge and citizens applauded, Drug Enforcement Administration agents were storming a freighter passing below.)

Miami Circle Park

Stand by the Tequesta Indian statue on the Brickell Avenue Bridge and gaze southeast to the open area surrounded by high-rises. This is where the Miami Circle, a 2,000-year-old Indian ruin 38 feet in diameter, can be found.

Discovered in 1998 when an apartment building was razed, the circle contains 24 large holes and many smaller ones, all carved in limestone, and on the east is what appears to be a human eye. Archaeologists speculate that it was the site of a chief's house or a village center for an unknown tribe, dating back hundreds of years. From the 150,000 artifacts discovered at the site, including dolphin skulls, pottery shards, shell tools, and exotic materials such as basaltic axes from Georgia, archaeologists believe it was continuously occupied until contact with the Spaniards 400 years ago, although its use had dwindled to just ceremonies. Before the circle's discovery, archaeologists believed South Florida's indigenous peoples were nomadic.

The Brickell Point Site (another name for the circle) was listed on the National Register of Historic Places in February 2002 and designated a national historic landmark in 2009. Although the circle remains covered in dirt to protect it, interpretive panels and educational brochures provide explain its importance. Inaugurated in 2011, the Museum of HistoryMiami (see pp. 46–47) offers infrequent guided tours ($$$$$) of the site. A more reliable option is a free, self-guided audio tour. Use your smart phone to listen to the audio narrative at *www .historymiami.org/visit/miami-circle/ audio--video-tours.* ■

Little Havana

This 30-block neighborhood, centering around S.W. Eighth Street (Calle Ocho), is to Miami what Little Italy is to New York: an ethnic beachhead where immigrants began the American chapter of their saga, cushioned by familiar traditions.

Cuban Americans play dominoes next to a mural depicting Latin American statesmen.

Little Havana begins near Brickell Avenue's Banker's Row and runs west, crossing the Miami River and petering out in residential neighborhoods around Florida International University near Sweetwater. Many of Little Havana's better known attractions are on or near S.W. Eighth between S. Miami Avenue and S.W. 27th Avenue. (Calle Ocho refers to S.W. Eighth Street in particular and the surrounding Little Havana district in general, as Wall Street denotes all of Lower Manhattan's financial district.) The Cubans were followed here (continued on p. 59)

Little Havana's Changing Faces

As new immigrants arrive and Cuban Americans assimilate further into mainstream America, Little Havana is becoming more cosmopolitan. Over the past decade, many Cuban Americans have moved into Greater Miami cities like Hialeah, Miami Gardens, and Homestead, with other Spanish speakers taking their place, particularly from Colombia, Guatemala, Honduras, Nicaragua, and Puerto Rico. So although Little Havana's faces are changing, its population is still predominantly Hispanic—93 percent, according to the 2010 U.S. Census.

Calle Ocho Walk

If you can look at Little Havana and empathize with its evident nostalgia for a way of life lost to its residents some 40 years ago, you will forgive Calle Ocho's aesthetic shortfalls— the occasionally bogus "Caribbean" decoration, the hand-lettered signage—and admire its sanguine humanity.

The Cuban flag adorns the Woodlawn Park grave of Carlos Prío Socarrás, president of Cuba 1948–1952.

To start your walking tour in the heart of Little Havana, take Metrobus No. 8 from Miami Avenue and Flagler Street near the Miami–Dade Cultural Center. A good place to get off the No. 8 for your stroll east is at Calle Ocho's intersection with 36th Avenue.

As you amble east along S.W. Eighth Street, you will see sidewalk cafés (*cafeterias*) and lunch counters (*fondas*) where locals sip *café Cubano*, an espresso-style jolt, from shot glass–size paper cups. Consider making a dinner reservation for later in the evening at **Versailles ❶** (*3555 S.W. 8th St., tel 305/444-0240, www.versaillesrestaurant .com; see p. 245*), which draws patrons from all over town. The fare is traditional (rich, spicy,

NOT TO BE MISSED:

Versailles • El Brazo Fuerte • Hoy Como Ayer • King's Ice Cream

and sweet), including everything from *arroz con pollo* (rice with chicken) to roast pork to flan in oversize portions. Versailles is the Cuban community's most endearing restaurant, and political events tied to Elian Gonzalez and the latest Cuban rafter have often taken place here. But Anglos will also enjoy the festive ambience of a pre-Castro Havana, and everyone enjoys

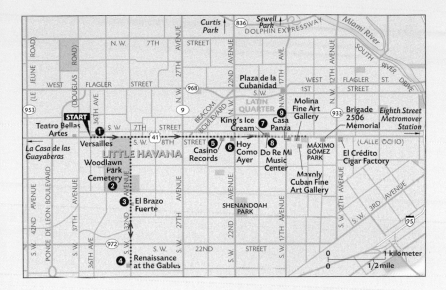

the walls of mirrors and etched glass that
enable indirect people-watching.

Two blocks east, at the corner of S.W.
8th Street and 32nd Avenue, lies the gothic
Woodlawn Park Cemetery ②, which has a
black marble tribute to the Unknown Cuban
Freedom Fighter and the graves of three
former Cuban presidents. The cemetery, which
opened in 1913, also has a memorial to the
victims of South Florida's tragic 1935 hurricane,
the Category 5 Labor Day storm that ravaged
the Florida keys and points north, claiming over
400 victims in its path.

Along S.W. 32nd Avenue

Follow S.W. 32nd Avenue south for several
blocks to get a feel for Little Havana off its
main street. Women pushing babies in strollers carry string-tied pink boxes from *dulcerías*
(pastry shops). On S.W. 32nd Avenue you
will find plenty of dulcerías to tempt you.
One of the best is **El Brazo Fuerte ③** *(1697
S.W. 32nd Ave., tel 305/444-7720, www.ebf
bakery.com)*, where, save for the fresh bread
and Cuban crackers, virtually everything is
sugar-coated, caramelized, or topped with
meringue. Try a *pastelito*, whose sweet dough

> | 🄰 | See also area map p. 33 |
> | ► | Intersection of S.W. 8th St. & 36th Ave. |
> | 🕐 | 3 hours |
> | ↔ | 6.75 miles |
> | ► | Metromover's 8th St. station |

is stuffed with meat, guava, or cream cheese,
or one of the custard Napoleons called
señoritas, or *masareales*, guava pastries so
sweet they can make you light-headed.

Lunch carts, called *fritangas*, selling roasted
meat *(carne asada)* with tortillas, beans, and
rice, are wheeled along mostly by Nicaraguan
newcomers. Usually on their bill of fare are
baho, a meat-and-vegetable stew, and *nacata-
mul*, a tamale filled with rice, pork, potatoes,
green olives, and prunes and wrapped in
a banana leaf. For something cool, order a
guarapo, sweetened by a syrupy extract from
sugarcane stalks, or a *cocofrio*, whipped up from
coconut milk.

For nouvelle Cuban cuisine, you can
try **Renaissance at the Gables ④** *(2340
S.W. 32nd Ave., tel 305/445-1313)*, which
features live entertainment Friday through
Sunday nights.

Musicians take to Calle Ocho during Little Havana's Viernes Culturales monthly festival.

Calle Ocho Music & Food

Back on Calle Ocho, head east and watch for **Casino Records ❺** (2290 S.W. 8th St., tel 786/394-8899); it displays recordings according to their country of origin. Just a little bit farther east is **Hoy Como Ayer ❻** (2212 S.W. 8th St., tel 305/541-2631, www .hoycomoayer.us), where on Thursday, Friday, and Saturday nights various Latin bands perform the music of yesteryear. Dark, hot, and thumping with Latin beats and sexy patrons, this is one of Little Havana's most popular bars. Even Mick Jagger and Bono have reportedly visited.

Next, stop in at **King's Ice Cream ❼** (1831 S.W. 8th St., tel 305/643-1842) to order a scoop of something mysterious, like guanabana or mamey, or maybe something slightly more familiar, like coconut or mango. Nearby, at No. 1829, is the **Do Re Mi Music Center ❽** (tel 305/541-3374), a shop of Cuban music, including reissues from pre-Castro decades, when Havana nightclubs reverberated with big-band jazz. Calle Ocho is Miami's top bazaar for music from Latin and South America, and also from Spain.

Flamenco dancers perform at tiny **Casa Panza ❾** (1620 S.W. 8th St., tel 305/643-5343), a place known for superb Spanish fare. The festivities carry on late into the night, or rather well into the morning, seven days a week.

Continuing east on Calle Ocho, you soon reach **Máximo Gómez Park** (see p. 57), nicknamed Domino Park for the game that is played here by visitors, most of whom are old men. A couple blocks farther on stands the **Brigade 2506 Memorial** (see pp. 59–60), a poignantly simple tribute to the scores of Cuban exiles who lost their lives in the Bay of Pigs invasion in 1961.

Finish your walk at the Metromover's Eighth Street station (59 S.E. 8th St.), a mile and half or so farther east on Calle Ocho. (If your feet are tired, catch the No. 8 bus to the Brickell Metrorail station, then the No. 48 bus from there to the Eighth Street station.)

Retrace your route if you are returning to Versailles for dinner. Just west of the restaurant, the **Teatro Bellas Artes** (3713 S.W. 8th St., tel 305/325-0515) is known for its Saturday midnight revue of beautiful, lip-synching cross-dressers who sway to Latin pop hits.

INSIDER TIP:

Don't miss Little Havana's Viernes Culturales, an amazing monthly cultural festival with salsa dancing in the streets and strolling musicians, among other things.

—MATT PROPERT
National Geographic photographer

by Central and South American immigrants, notably Nicaraguans, Salvadorans, and Dominicans. Their restaurants are interspersed among long-established Cuban bistros, fruit stands *(puestos de frutas),* and shoeshine stands *(limpiabotas).* Sidewalk coffee windows *(cafetines)* serve up appetizing *media noche* sandwiches and espressolike *cafecitos* that pump up enthusiasm for *juegos de domino,* sidewalk domino games played by men in Panama hats.

Some critics have called Calle Ocho's downscale business strip seedy, and they feel its virtues as a tourist attraction have been oversold. Newcomers expecting a Disneyland version of Old Havana or an ethnic enclave with the exotic density of San Francisco's Chinatown will be disappointed.

Still, Little Havana's vibrancy can be beguiling, especially on weekends, when aficionados of Latin music and dancing throng its clubs and gourmands its best restaurants. And gentrification may take root with the 2012 debut of the Miami Marlins' new stadium, a $634 million architectural gem, complete with vibrant artwork from local pop artist Romero Britto (see sidebar p. 94).

Brigade 2506 Memorial

Some monuments age quickly, but where Calle Ocho crosses S.W. 13th Avenue—the latter better known in Little Havana as Memorial Boulevard—even

Brigade 2506 Memorial
- 🅰 Map p. 57
- ✉ S.W. 8th St. & S.W. 13th Ave.

Viernes Culturales
- ✉ Centering on S.W. 8th St. bet. S.W. 12th Ave. & S.W. 16th Ave.
- 🕐 Held the last Friday of each month.
- **http://viernes culturales.org**

Plotting Castro's Overthrow

During 1960 and 1961, Manuel Artime went often to the unremarkable little ranch-style house on Poinciana Avenue, between Le Jeune and Douglas, just inside Miami's city limits. Shaded by trees and secluded behind a high fence, it was rented by a tall man who wrote spy novels in his spare time. His name was E. Howard Hunt, a CIA agent with whom Artime and his comrades, including former Cuban officials, were designing a government to replace Fidel Castro's regime. Years later, Hunt recalled with amusement a neighbor lady who, noting the late-night gatherings of men always without women, gossiped to others her suspicions about his sexual orientation. "She got me a date with her recently divorced daughter," said the operative, who would later spend 32 months in prison for his role in the Nixon-era Watergate break-in. "Inasmuch as I was married, which of course I couldn't reveal to my neighbor, I guess the daughter—when I didn't make any advances—confirmed her mother's suspicions. Which was fine. It was an additional layer of cover, you could say." The house is now gone.

EXPERIENCE: Little Havana's Annual Block Party

If your Miami visit falls in late February and early March, you will have the opportunity to experience Carnaval Miami International, the nation's largest Hispanic cultural festival. Carnaval Miami's nine-day calendar of concerts, parades, and contests, including a golf tournament held on the verdant and challenging Biltmore Hotel course in Coral Gables, ends with Little Havana's swirling Kiwanis Club-sponsored block party, a celebration of art, dance, music, and food that crowds Calle Ocho with thousands of people between 4th and 27th Avenues.

If you attend the block party, consider taking the Metromover to the Eighth Street station. It's a bit of a hike west to the center of the festival, but you will avoid the hassles of traffic and parking. Miami's No. 8 Metrobus leaves from the intersection of Miami Avenue and Flagler Street (just east of the Miami–Dade Cultural Center complex; see p. 45) and proceeds into the heart of Little Havana. A good place to get off on Calle Ocho is its intersection with 36th Avenue, where you will find people waiting for tables outside the popular **Versailles** (3555 S.W. 8th St., tel 305/445-7614; see pp. 56–57).

For information about the event, call 305/644-8888 and follow the recorded menu of instructions, or you can try the Salsaweb Internet Company website (www.carnavalmiami.com).

---

after more than five decades, a simple stone monument with an eternal flame stirs strong emotions. If there had been additional troops of equal determination backing up the 2506th brigade, the outcome might well have been different. However, within three days the force of about 1,300 Cubans who had committed themselves to overthrowing Fidel Castro found themselves terribly alone, especially in the hours after landing near Cuba's south coast Bahia de Cochinos (Bay of Pigs) on April 17, 1961. Newspapers were soon calling the adventure a fiasco.

It began in Miami, among Cubans determined to free their island from Castro's two-year-old grip. Encouraged, trained, and bankrolled by the CIA, and convinced that the American government was solidly behind them, they felt assured of air support and other aid. (During the 1960 presidential campaign, John F. Kennedy had proposed that America support Cuban exiles in an invasion.)

Most of the counterrevolutionaries had little or no combat experience or training. Many hit the beach wearing T-shirts and tennis shoes, carrying out-of-date rifles. The Cuban populace failed to rise up in support of them; the expected air support didn't come. Castro, a rifle in one hand and a cigar in the other, led his troops to battle. Ninety-four of the brigade were killed, the rest given 30-year prison sentences. Some two years later, they were back in Miami, ransomed by $62 million in public and private funds. (Among the survivors was the father of pop star Gloria Estefan.) The inscription on the memorial recalls "the Martyrs of the Invasion Brigade of April 17, 1961."

Three Cuban Art Galleries

During the past decade Little Havana has been invigorated by art and artists. Although there's no singular "Miami" style, the emerging movement often evokes nostalgia for a lost Cuba, or other Latin American country. Once a month, on the last Friday, the streets of Calle Ocho reverberate with the creative energy of **Viernes Culturales/Cultural Fridays.** Held from 7 p.m. to 11 p.m., it's an open-air gallery and celebration with more than a hundred artists of various media, as well as musicians, food vendors, and 3,000 attendees.

The **Xavier Cortada Art Gallery** exhibits works by the eponymous artist, one of Miami's premier artists. Cortada's style is an amalgamation of Cuban Modernism, a form of expressionism, and black outlines and bold tropical colors. His subjects range from the American dream to old Cuba, and from AIDS to sports and more. Besides in his studio and gallery, his work has been exhibited at the White House, the Florida Supreme Court, and the Miami Art Museum; it can also be found on street murals throughout Little Havana.

Maxoly Gallery is another place to find South American art. It specializes in Spanish colonial, early republic, vanguard, and contemporary paintings. A front gallery offers the work of emerging Latin artists and a back gallery presents Cuban masters.

At the **Molina Fine Art Gallery,** visitors can study or purchase the Cuban artist Luis Molina's colorful oil paintings and prints. Molina is celebrated for his Afro-Cuban folklore pieces that feature mulatto farmers as well as parrots, roosters, and other animals found on farms. Santeria, the religion in which African gods and goddesses mix with Catholic saints, is an important element in many of his works. Molina also participates in "Voices For Freedom," a movement that supports the dozens of intellectuals who were imprisoned by Fidel Castro in 2003.

Xavier Cortada Art Gallery
- Map p. 43
- 104 S.W. 9th St.
- 305/858-1323
- Open daily, but call to confirm

www.cortada.com

Maxoly Gallery
- Map p. 57
- 1600 S.W. 8th St.
- 305/631-0025
- Closed Sun.

www.maxoly.com/artgallery

Molina Fine Art Gallery
- Map p. 57
- 1634 S.W. 8th St.
- 305/642-0444

www.molinaartgallery.com

A Cup of José

If you like your coffee caffeinated, don't leave Miami without stopping by a Little Havana sidewalk *cafeteria* (café) for a shot of *café Cubano*. This coffee is major league stuff, brewed with sugar added to the grinds, then sweetened even more by adding sugar to the viscous espresso that results. If you ask for coffee in English, odds are you will be served a *colada*, an espresso in a cup barely large enough for your thumb. For something more like the standard Norteamericano "cuppa Joe," order *café con leche*, traditionally one part Cuban-style coffee to two parts milk.

Máximo Gómez Park

 Map p. 57

✉ S.W. 8th St. &
S.W. 15th Ave.

Tower Theater

✉ 1508 S.W. 8th St.

☎ 305/643-8706

www.mdc.edu/tower

Máximo Gómez Park

If you happen by Calle Ocho and S.W. 15th Avenue, and stay a while to watch the domino games played here, you will probably find the subject of Cuba's past and future being discussed amid the clatter of the wooden tiles of this popular Cuban pastime. More famous than impressive, this little enclosure, better known as Domino Park, is a beloved icon of Little Havana's founding generation.

The players are generally older men in billowing hot-weather shirts called guayaberas, watched over by a tableau of Southern Hemispheric leaders depicted in the surrounding mural, added after the real-life versions gathered in Miami for the 1994 Summit of the Americas.

At the southwest corner of W. Flagler Street and S.W. 17th Avenue, on the redbrick **Plaza de la Cubanidad,** a fountain bears the inscription *"Las palmas son novias que esperan"* (The palm trees are lovers who wait). So said José Martí, the 19th-century Cuban poet revered for his resistance to Spanish colonial rule. The palms still symbolize the yearning for an island free of despotism.

Tower Theater

Located at the intersection near Máximo Gómez Park in Little Havana, this movie theater played a role in the lives of many Cuban exiles arriving in Miami after 1959. Built in 1926, and remodeled in 1931 and 2000, this art deco structure features a classical chase light marquee and a 40-foot illuminated steel tower on the roof.

In 2002, the City of Miami authorized Miami–Dade College to manage and operate the theater. The college continues the

Cigarmakers, like these at El Crédito, were once read to by a colleague to help pass the time.

The Right Way to Smoke a Cigar

"The true smoker," decreed Auguste Barthélemy, author of *L'Art de fumer, ou la pipe et le cigare* (1849), "abstains from imitating Vesuvius."

- Clip the end closest to the label with a cigar cutter or sharp knife.
- Avoid damaging the wrapper leaf
- To light the cigar, hold it horizontally and rotate the end over a match or butane flame until evenly burning.
- Place the cigar in your mouth and lightly draw smoke.
- Don't inhale; cigar smoke is meant to be savored and then released.
- Hold the cigar firmly in the mouth but don't clench it in your teeth.
- Avoid wetting the "foot" excessively with saliva.
- Smoke slowly, no more than two puffs a minute, lest the cigar become overheated and sour.
- A cigar should last between 30 and 90 minutes—about 50 puffs in all—spending more time in your hand than in your mouth.

—Courtesy of Barnaby Conrad III, author of *The Cigar* (Chronicle Books, 1996)

Tower Theater's rich tradition by promoting the arts in all their forms within South Florida's multicultural, multiethnic, and international community.

El Crédito Cigar Factory

On February 3, 1962, President John F. Kennedy banned all trade with Cuba, his motive being to deprive communist Fidel Castro's cash-strapped economy of $35 million in annual income and to hobble Cuban efforts to export revolution in the Americas.

The embargo crippled Florida's cigarmaking industry, which then depended exclusively on Cuban tobacco. Warehouses held only a ten-month supply, after which some 6,000 people stood to lose their jobs. (The day before announcing the embargo, Kennedy, a cigar aficionado, sent an aide around Washington to buy up choice Cuban brands.) Many of South Florida's cigarmakers went bust. Among

the survivors was Calle Ocho's El Crédito Cigar Factory, where the cigars are rolled by hand, cut with rounded blades, wrapped tightly, and pressed in vises—just as they have been since the firm was founded in 1807 in Havana.

Here, at Miami's premier factory, you can see some two dozen employees, using plastic presses, quietly roll cigars using Dominican tobacco (grown, it is said, from Cuban seeds), producing highly rated smokes such as El Crédito's La Gloria Cubana. There's a store at the factory where you can buy cigars individually or in bulk. In 2008, El Crédito celebrated its 40th anniversary in Miami's Little Havana.

Miami River

The Miami River's meander through Little Havana is picturesque, as the placid stream is frequently navigated by tugboats, small Caribbean freighters, fishing boats, and luxury cruisers, its banks busied by

El Crédito Cigar Factory
- Map p. 57
- 1106 S.W. 8th St.
- 305/858-4162 or 800/726-9481
- Closed Sun.

Miami River
- 41 E3

Art lovers attend an exhibition opening at the Frost Art Museum, a showplace of 20th-century art.

boatyards, fisheries, warehouses, and marinas. Here a thriving bohemian creative community lives afloat in houseboats.

Early 20th-century draining cut the Miami off from its source in the Everglades, then near today's 32nd Avenue bridge; canals now supply it with water. East of 24th Avenue, the river follows its age-old path. The public parks along it are favorite destinations of strollers and bicyclists, who linger here to watch the occasionally exotic traffic on the water below. One of the most charming parks is **Sewell Park,** a somnolent palmy hideaway that slopes down on the south bank near the 17th Avenue bridge. There are picnic tables and Miami's only public boat-launching ramp just upstream at **Curtis Park** on the north bank

(take N.W. 20th St. west to N.W. 22nd Ave.).

If this part of town appeals to you, consider a stay at the Miami River Inn (118 S.W. S. River Dr.; see p. 245), a bed-and-breakfast on South River Drive. The inn is a cluster of nicely restored, early 20th-century, clapboard houses, wooden-floored architectural jewels set around a garden.

Frost Art Museum

This museum, on the campus of the public Florida International University, first started in 1977 as a student gallery. Three decades later, its new building, designed by Yann Weymouth, who served as chief design architect for the Louvre Museum under I. M. Pei, holds one of the Southeast's most smartly

INSIDER TIP:

During freshman orientation, students are told about spinning "Marty's Cube" in the Frost Art Museum's sculpture park for good luck. Give it a try.

—MADIANA ECHAVARRIA
Student, Florida International University

curated showplaces for Latin American and 20th-century American works. (Several times in recent years, readers of Miami's alternative *New Times* newspaper have voted it among Miami's best.) The collection of Cuban and Florida artists is one of the most interesting you will find anywhere in the state.

Treat yourself to a stroll in the 26-acre sculpture park, which holds monumental pieces by Jacques Lipchitz, Anthony Caro, Alexander Liberman, and Tony Rosenthal, among other masters. A visit to the museum's website reveals the exceptional richness of its holdings, due in large measure to the generosity of several major American collectors. If you visit Miami's Little Havana district, make this museum one of your stops—it's a 20-minute drive west on S.W. Eighth Street, Little Havana's main boulevard. ∎

Frost Art Museum

🏛 40 A2

✉ Florida International University's University Park Campus, S.W. 107th Ave. & 8th St.

☎ 305/348-2890

🕐 Closed Sun. a.m. & Mon.

http://thefrost.fiu.edu

Must-try Cuban Foods & Drink

Cuban foods and drinks have become an integral part of many southern Florida residents' diet. Be sure to sample some of the following Miami standards for a taste of Havana:

Adobo—A marinade of sour orange juice, garlic, cumin, and oregano.

Arroz con pollo—Rice with chicken served with spices. Restaurants tailor this Cuban staple into countless variations.

Boliche—Pot roast with, among other ingredients, chorizos, green olives, and lots of garlic.

Café con leche—The Cuban variation of "coffee with milk" is an espresso served with a side of steamed or just hot milk.

Cuba libre—A classic mixed drink, the "free Cuba" marries white or dark rum with lime juice and cola.

Cuban sandwich—Lightly buttered Cuban bread with roast pork, Serrano ham, Swiss cheese, dill pickles, and mustard. The sandwich is pressed and heated.

Empanada—Dough wrapped around beef, chicken, or cheese and deep fried.

Enchilado—Seafood in Cuban-style Creole sauce.

Flan Cubano—Cuban flan. This custard dessert is made with caramel and sometimes coconut.

Mariquitas—A side dish of plantain chips.

Mojito—A couple of these tall white-rum-and-sugar cocktails with crushed mint leaves will get your head spinning.

Mojo—Wonderful sauce with garlic and sour orange or lime juice.

Pastel de tres leches—A super sweet sponge cake made with three types of milk.

Pastelito de guayaba—The sweet guava fruit is the main ingredient in this quintessential Cuban dessert that resembles a turnover.

Vaca frita—Literally translated as "fried cow," this dish consists of shredded beef marinated in fresh orange juice and lime juice and served with sautéed onions. You can substitute chicken for the beef.

Architectural Fantasies

As America entered the 1920s, Florida found its first widely known architecture in Mediterranean Revival. Like the fabled sea it is named for, the style reflects many cultures: Tuscan, Venetian, Spanish, Andalusian, Moorish, even Roman, while borrowing accents from ancient Greece and Renaissance France and producing bungalows that resemble baby palazzos.

A courtyard in George Merrick's Spanish architecture–inspired 1926 Biltmore Hotel, Coral Gables

Miami, a city that prided itself on being practically forced upon an inhospitable landscape of swamp and dune, wanted an architecture rooted in imagination.

Mediterranean Revival

The signature of Mediterranean Revival was "oldness." Exterior walls were stained to mimic those of Rome. Roof and floor tiles duplicated those in Sicily. For architects, the style was a chance to dream in wood and stucco. The ultimate objective was to seduce through artifice—a millionaire's residence might look like a ruined Spanish monastery.

Beams were immersed in saltwater, burned with acid, and scored with chisels. Iron objects were dented, concrete was soaked in bicarbonate of soda. Miami's quest for bogus antiquity wrote the book on painting and plastering techniques still used today. Factories opened to supply designers with "period" furniture, ironwork, tiles, and even leaded glass windows. "Oriental" rugs and "medieval" tapestries were woven. Many chic Miami homes appeared to be furnished with salvage from Spanish convents.

The best of Miami's residential dream merchants created nearly theatrical environments. The interior of a lawyer's office became the suite of a 16th-century Venetian noble, a banker's living room that of a Spanish *ranchero*. The vogue flamed through the Roaring Twenties and guttered out in the Depression, when architects fell under the thrall of moderne and streamline, which seemed to symbolize the new technologies that might deliver America from its economic abyss.

Arabian Nights Whimsy

At about the same time that Mediterranean Revival bloomed, the vision of Miami's other indigenous architecture stirred the mind of airplane designer turned developer Glenn Curtiss, inventor of the pioneering Curtiss Jennie biplane. Anointed a warrior of the air in 1910 for piloting what amounted to a box kite with a lawn mower engine from Albany to New York City, he used his celebrity status to attract investors. The flyer and his architect, Bernhardt Muller, shared a weakness for the Arabic folk tales popularized in English as *The Arabian Nights*. In Hollywood, an Arabian Nights vogue had produced *A Princess of Baghdad* in 1916, *Aladdin and the Wonderful Lamp* in 1917, and *Ali Baba and the 40 Thieves*

in 1918. Women fainted in 1921 when Rudolph Valentino flashed his dark eyes in *The Sheik*, and even male hearts skipped a beat in 1924 when Douglas Fairbanks, Sr., bounded across rooftops in *The Thief of Baghdad*. In Russia, the ballet master Sergei Diaghilev created *Scheherazade*; in America his countryman Nikolai Rimsky-Korsakov composed a symphonic suite by the same name. The mass appeal of this international phenomenon was not lost on Curtiss.

What he and Muller envisioned in the mid-1920s was, in essence, a theme park with permanent residents. They chose a site northwest of Miami that the Seminole Indians called Opatishawockalocka ("wooded hummock"), removing the tongue-twisting tishawocka part to create the "Arabic-Persian" name Opa-locka. Their headquarters, today Opa-locka's City Hall, looked like the palace of a Saudi king. Every building had to have "romance." A bank was rendered as a ruined Egyptian temple; a gas station was designed with a dome and minarets. Ali Baba Avenue, Sharazad Boulevard, and Aladdin Street were lined with domed, single-story, two-bedroom homes. Buyers came running. Architectural buffs still do.

Finished in 1917, Coconut Grove's Plymouth Church recalls the Spanish mission style.

North Miami

North of Flagler Street in downtown Miami, street names acquire the prefix "North." Those on the bay side of Miami Avenue are considered to be in the Northeast; those on the Everglades side are designated Northwest. But the reality is that the borders between Miami's various compass-point districts are not precise, nor (save for the convenience of map readers) do they need to be.

Apartment high-rises line the very northern reaches of Biscayne Bay beyond Oleta River State Park.

If you were asked to draw the northernmost boundaries of North Miami, you would probably get little argument if you traced a line west from Biscayne Bay in the environs of Aventura, Golden Beach, and Golden Shores, following the Dade–Broward county line to Florida's Turnpike, and then following that toll highway as it heads southwest, passing between Hialeah and the Everglades, and then runs due south to Sweetwater. Inside this quarter-circle arc lies northwest Miami. It begins at I-95 and runs west for about 9 miles,

where subdivisions and industrial strips finally give away to farmland "reclaimed" from the Everglades.

Hialeah and Opa-locka are the northwest's best known communities. The former is a patchwork of residential development and commercial land, its name associated by most people who do not live in Florida with the Hialeah racetrack. Just north of Hialeah is Opa-locka, whose fanciful Moorish architecture arose from a developer's fascination with the *Arabian Nights,* Richard F. Burton's retelling of ancient Middle Eastern fables. West of Opa-locka Airport you will find Miami Lakes, where the Everglades' forced retreat left a plain of ponds shimmering amid upscale golf courses and private residential developments.

Miami's northeastern quadrant is much smaller and much more residential, its houses ranging from modest bungalows to high-rise condominiums overlooking more golf courses and the yachty northern backwaters of Biscayne Bay and the Atlantic. You need a car to get to North Miami's far-flung parks, museums, neighborhoods, and curiosities, but the effort will dispel your first impression that its sole attractions are golf and powerboating.

Adrienne Arsht Center for the Performing Arts

In 2006, the Arsht Center became the crown of the Miami arts scene. Built downtown at a cost of $473 million and covering two city blocks, it is the showcase of world-renowned architect Cesar Pelli.

Miami's most spectacular building is also the state's largest performing arts center. Its venues include the Sanford and Dolores Ziff Ballet Opera House (2,400 seats), the John S. and James L. Knight Concert Hall (2,200 seats), the Peacock Studio Theater, and the Carnival Studio Theater.

The ballet opera house and the concert hall are stepped masses clad in light-colored Sardinian granite, punctuated by large glass and steel curtain walls that add to their contemporary, crystalline expression. Inside the ballet opera

house, a 40-foot acoustic dome hangs over the audience, while in the concert hall, a spiraling acoustic canopy suspends over the stage.

The Florida Grand Opera, Miami City Ballet, and New World Symphony are resident companies, and smaller ones regularly perform here as well. Broadway Across America and the Cleveland Orchestra visit each year.

The center offers free one-hour tours at noon on Mondays and Saturdays. Visitors walk through the theaters, including backstage and into stars' dressing rooms while learning about the center's architecture and history and hearing anecdotes about performers such as Bernadette Peters, Itzhak Perlman, and Gloria Estefan.

INSIDER TIP:

In Wynwood, vivid art murals blanket once graffitied warehouses, and the neighborhood now hosts Miami's most important contemporary art galleries and collections.

—XAVIER CORTADA
Artist, Xavier Cortada Art Gallery

Wynwood Arts District

In recent years Miami's Midtown has exploded with art galleries, as well as coffeehouses, restaurants, and bars overflowing with creative energy, particularly in the Miami Design District and Wynwood. Previously a neighborhood of abandoned factories

Adrienne Arsht Center for the Performing Arts

- Map p. 49
- 1300 Biscayne Blvd.
- 305/949-6722

www.arshtcenter.org

Wynwood Arts District

- 41 F3
- Bet. Biscayne Blvd. & I-95, & N.W. 20th St. & N.W. 36th St.

www.wynwood miami.com

www.artcircuits.com

Rubell Family Collection

41 F3

95 N.W. 29th St.

305/573-6090

Closed Mon.

$$

www.rfc.museum

and warehouses, Wynwood was embraced by struggling artists yearning for success.

As artists began to flourish, so did this inner-city neighborhood. Artists turned many of their large, affordable living units into studios and galleries so that today Wynwood has 60 galleries open to the public. The majority feature contemporary art. Although you'll find sculptures, digital art, and other artistic mediums, paintings are predominant.

The Rubell Family Collection specializes in contemporary art, featuring established masters and emerging stars.

You'll also see a wealth of graffiti and other street art in Wynwood created by young artists. Some of that graffiti art has even been exhibited in museums.

The main strip of galleries, N.W. Second Avenue, offers a pleasant stroll for buyers and browsers of objets d'art. Be sure to visit the nearby **Fredric Snitzer Gallery** (2247 N.W. 1st Pl.), which showcases emerging local artists, including Hernan Bas whose

works have also been exhibited in the Rubell Family Collection (see below). Others galleries of note are the **Alejandra Von Hartz Gallery** (2630 N.W. 2nd Ave.; Latin American paintings), **Bernice Steinbaum Gallery** (3550 N. Miami Ave.; women and minority works), and **Alberto Linero Gallery** (2294 N.W. 2nd Ave.; sculptures and paintings from Latin America and other regions).

Wynwood's Art Walk takes place on the afternoon of the second Saturday of each month. Vendors open their booths, galleries, and studios to visitors, and musicians and dancers perform outdoors. The neighborhood also hosts half a dozen art fairs each year; most take place in the winter, which doubles as tourist season.

Rubell Family Collection

Another rich archive of art is the extraordinary treasury of contemporary art collected by Don and Mera Rubell, which some critics insist is among the most significant contemporary fine art collections in the world. (The Rubells, originally from New York, also own Miami Beach's stylishly upscale Albion Hotel.)

The collection bills itself as exhibiting "provocative works from the 1960s to the present," and delivers by featuring the likes of Jeff Koons, Keith Haring, Cindy Sherman, Jean-Michel Basquiat, Paul McCarthy, and Charles Ray, along with notable newcomers. It is certainly the most audacious private collection open to the public in Miami, with its works being displayed in a very large split-level warehouse-like industrial space in the Wynwood Arts District. What you'll find is a museum of works representing virtually every artist who has achieved note in the last two decades.

As the writer Tom Wolfe noted in his book *The Painted Word*, modern art sustains a contentious intellectual offshoot by its astonishing ability to evoke emotion and provoke debate about what is art—evidenced in the Rubells' museum by a formidable library of writings about the phenomenon.

Miami Design District

As often happens in American cities, artists in search of economical studio space sparked the revival of the part of Northeast Miami that runs roughly from N.E. Second Avenue to N. Miami Avenue and between 36th and 41st Streets. Only in the last decade have the flower-decorated streets shed a reputation for sidewalk peril, particularly at night, but like New York's East Village, it has acquired a corps of painters and sculptors, media artists and photographers who anchor it against any further drift toward decay.

In the late 1910s and 1920s, this neighborhood was known as Decorators Row, where interior designers and decorators came to showrooms that catered only to the trade. Today you can visit the district's antiques stores, fabric outlets, furnituremakers, and manufacturers' showrooms. Fortieth Street, between N.E. Second

Arch Creek Park

North Miami's Arch Creek Park *(map 41 G6, 1855 N.E. 135th St., 305/944-6111, closed Mon.–Tues.)* teems with natural beauty and human history. A small museum on the grounds educates visitors on the park's centerpiece attraction, a natural limestone bridge that was part of an important Tequesta and then Seminole Indian trail. During the Seminole Wars the U.S. Army traveled over it, as did pioneers and their stagecoaches in later years. The museum also features a wide variety of Indian and pioneer artifacts.

A half-mile figure-eight trail winds through the park, affording views of the native wildlife and tropical hammock vegetation. The park also has a butterfly garden and picnic shelters.

and N. Miami Avenues, has a reputation for elegant whimsy and exotica; let your tastes and interests guide you. If you're fond of antiques, visit the **Susane R Lifestyle Boutique** *(93 N.E. 40th St., tel 305/573-8483, www.susaner.com)* or **Artisan Antiques Art Deco** *(110 N.E. 40th St., tel 305/573-5619)*. In between showrooms are little hole-in-the-wall cafés where designers debate the merits of, say, Corbusier or the Bauhaus group. The flowered court of the **Michael's Genuine Food & Drink** *(130 N.E. 40th St., tel 305/573-5550)* offers a respite from street traffic, and so does the **Maitardi** *(163 N.E. 39th St., tel 305/572-1400, www.maitardimiami.com)*, with its shaded 4,000-square-foot outdoor terrace where northern Italian meals are served.

Most galleries and showplaces close at sundown. However, on the second Saturday evening of

Miami Design District

🏛 41 F3

✉ Bet. N.E. 2nd Ave. & N. Miami Ave., & N.W. 36th St. & 41st St.

www.miamidesign district.net

Morningside

⚑ 41 F4

Museum of Contemporary Art

⚑ 41 F5

✉ 770 N.E. 125th St.

☎ 305/893-6211

🕐 Closed Mon., Wed. a.m., & Sun. a.m.

💲 $

www.mocanomi.org

every month, from 7 p.m. to 10 p.m., design district galleries, shops, studios, and bistros, along with those in neighboring Wynwood (see pp. 69–70), hold open houses, often scheduled to coincide with the openings of artists' shows.

INSIDER TIP:

Be sure to visit the centuries-old Ancient Spanish Monastery, relocated to Miami from Spain, complete with Old World ambience. It has gorgeous gardens and stonework.

—MATT PROPERT
National Geographic photographer

Morningside

The revitalization of the Design District coincided with an interest in Miami's older residential neighborhoods, particularly those built during the city's boom era of the 1920s and the early Depression years. Almost forgotten were the bungalow enclaves of the Morningside subdivision flanking Biscayne Boulevard.

The 1920s' Jazz Age had a penchant for fantasies in architecture. It was not enough merely to build a home; it had to have a theme. Two leading styles of the period were mission revival, emulating the Spanish colonial churches of far-off California, and Mediterranean Revival, a catchall for imitations of homes built near

that fabled sea. These vogues were in full bloom across America when the building of Morningside commenced.

Morningside's theme homes have escaped the heavy hand of urban renewal, and today they are cherished by design-conscious homeowners. A few years back, restoration zealots lobbied successfully to have Morningside declared a historic zone. Among its notable homes are the Mediterranean Revival-style house at 5731 N.E. Sixth Avenue and an early example of the mission style at 5940 N.E. Sixth Court, both private residences.

You can drive Morningside easily enough, although traffic barriers along Biscayne Boulevard block automobiles from entering some of these pretty streets. It is probably most convenient to park somewhere along Biscayne Boulevard and explore on foot. The subdivision is not terribly large, extending from the bay shore west to around Biscayne Boulevard, and running north–south from N.E. 60th to N.E. 50th Streets. (The Museum of Contemporary Art—see below—occasionally offers guided architectural walking tours that include the Morningside area.)

Museum of Contemporary Art

Locals refer to the 23,000-square-foot Museum of Contemporary Art by its initials, "MoCA," and Miamians are especially fond of this already well-established museum, which opened in 1996.

The main gallery has an appealing studio-warehouse look, the kind of space artists covet. The big room represents the major leagues, drawing work from far and wide; a smaller separate space generally exhibits the newest of the new, often from local artists. Inside is contemporary fine art representing the world's avant-garde movements, which occasionally includes the usual multimedia installations and photography that expand the definition of art. The mainstay of the collection are paintings and sculptures, however. Among modern art icons, Mark Handforth is well represented.

MoCA's major exhibitions have examined the work of diverse art world legends such as Mexican artist Frida Kahlo, her husband Diego Rivera, and the internationally renowned Frank Stella. Whether or not the artists are to your taste, MoCA's unifying thread is quality and earnest intent. The museum is also committed to showing the work of Latino artists and filmmakers, whose works are screened, along with other avant-garde cinema, in MoCA's appealing courtyard.

Even if your time is limited, do try to visit the excellent gift shop, which holds a thoughtfully chosen inventory of art books, exhibition catalogs, and postcard reproductions of works in MoCA's permanent collection. Also check the schedule of guided architectural walking tours of North Miami's neighborhoods. The strolls explore some of Greater Miami's more appealing residential streets, particularly those in the Morningside district (see page opposite).

Ancient Spanish Monastery

Built in the 12th century, this building is by far the oldest edifice in North America, though it originally came from Spain.

After some 700 years as part of a Cistercian monastery, the Cloisters of the Monastery of St. Bernard of Clairvaux fell on hard times and were used as a

(see page opposite)

Ancient Spanish Monastery

- 🅰 41 G6
- ✉ 16711 W. Dixie Hwy. bet. N.E. 167th & 171st Sts.
- ☎ 305/945-1461
- 💲 $$
- 🕐 Closed Sun. a.m. & for special events; call to confirm opening hours.

www.spanish monastery.com

The 800-year-old Ancient Spanish Monastery survived dismantling and an improbable transatlantic journey.

Oleta River State Park

🏃 41 G6

✉ 3400 N.E. 163rd St./Sunny Isles Blvd., E of Biscayne Blvd.

☎ 305/919-1844

💲 $$

www.floridastate
parks.org/oletariver

granary and stable. Newspaper mogul William Randolph Hearst purchased the building in 1925 for $500,000, intending it for his California coastal house, Xanadu. He had it dismantled and shipped to New York in 11,000 numbered crates packed with straw. The straw spoiled everything. Customs officials believed it carried germs causing an epidemic of hoof and mouth disease. They uncrated the stones and burned the straw, but got the pieces and boxes hopelessly mixed up. Hearst walked away in disgust. The crates lay in a Brooklyn warehouse for 26 years, until 1952, when new owners had the pieces reassembled here as a tourist attraction at a cost of $1.5 million. A decade later the Episcopal Church acquired the monastery as a house of worship, a museum of early Gothic and Romanesque architecture, a

repository of ecclesiastical artifacts, and a place of peace and rest. In the gift shop hangs "La Gracia" by Spanish master painter Julio Romero de Torres.

The Spanish monastery is a popular wedding spot, so its grounds are often crowded with fancily clad guests on Saturday and Sunday afternoons.

Oleta River State Park

Though surrounded by intensive residential development, most visibly North Miami Beach's posh Bal Harbour community, this park offers an opportunity not merely to retreat from the world for a while, but also to drive, walk, or cycle among mangrove forests and serpentine lagoons.

If you stroll, you will encounter wading shore birds, and there is a good chance (especially early and late in the day) of seeing the snout

Miami's Russian Community

The Soviet Union's citizens included Moscow bureaucrats, Siberian shamans, Central Asian Muslims, Buddhist monks, Persian-speaking homemakers, and myriad other groups, and the makeup of northern Miami's "Russian" community mirrors this diversity. South Florida's tennis phenom Anna Kournikova is the one best known to Americans but Philip Kirkorov, Russia's top pop singer, also lives here much of the year.

Tatiana Night Club/Restaurant (1710 E. Hallandale Beach Blvd., tel 954/454-1222, www.fltatianarestaurant.com), a lively cabaret with sword eaters, jugglers, and beautiful dancing girls in sequined bikinis, is the Russian community's entertainment focal point. Its meals are delicious, and they recall the homeland: pickled Russian

vegetables, meats from the Caucasus, caviar from Azerbaijan, chicken Kiev from the Ukrainian capital, and Siberian pelmeni (ravioli). Tatiana serves Russian vodka, Armenian cognac, and Georgian wine.

For a different taste of the Eurasian landmass, visit the "Russian plaza," a beach shopping center filled with Russian-owned bookstores, travel agencies, and a deli called **Kalinka** (18090 Collins Ave., tel 305/705-9333). Ask the staff to recommend a dish, and be aware that Russian coffee is similar to Turkish coffee.

Drive north on Collins Avenue and turn left on Hollywood Boulevard to find **Chocolada Bakery & Café** (1923 Hollywood Blvd., tel 954/920-6400), another popular Russian hangout. Live music nightly.

A preeminent night out for Miami's Russians: dinner, dancing, and cabaret at Tatiana Night Club

of a porpoise rising from the water. The odds of spotting that strangest of aquatic Florida mammals, the lumbering manatee, are not so high, but these sweet-natured creatures, perched on the brink of extinction, often escape the estuary traffic in the park's quiet coves.

You can rent a bicycle here and cruise the 1.5-mile biking path, as well as the 10 miles of mountain bike trails, or rent a canoe or stand-up paddleboard and explore the 0.75-mile canoe trail. Locals come to lunch alfresco and read in the shade of nine picnic-area pavilions (available on a first-come, first-served basis or may be rented by reservation), wade into the warm water off the park's 1,200-foot-long sandy beach, and drop fishing lures from a sturdy fishing pier that reaches nearly 100 feet offshore.

It's difficult to imagine, looking at the far skyline of high-rise condos, that 150 years ago this little peninsula teemed with bears, deer, panthers, bobcats, wolves, and alligators, along with the then plentiful manatees in the surrounding waters. By the 1890s, pineapple and vegetable farms stood here near a village called Ojus. That's all vanished now.

Greynolds Park

Franklin Roosevelt's Civilian Conservation Corps is credited with rendering the site of a rock-mining company (owned by one A. O. Greynolds) into one of Miami's most popular public commons. The company left a pile of junked machinery (including railroad ties and a steam engine) for the CCC boys, who buried it under rock and sand, creating a 40-foot mound still topped by the observation tower they built, and turned the quarries into a lake, where paddle boats can now be rented. A Seminole Indian trading post operated here in the late 1800s, but that has gone now, and what is left is an emporium of outdoor recreation—golf links, a fitness course for joggers, picnic tables, and many places to throw

Greynolds Park

🏔 41 G7

✉ 17530 W. Dixie Hwy., N. Miami Beach

☎ 305/945-3425

💲 Free on weekdays, $ on weekends for motorists only

Let It Ride

Greater Miami has had a gaming scene, in some form or another, for decades. Pari-mutuel betting in Miami was legalized in 1932, and three years later slot machines followed suit until they were outlawed after just two years.

Horse racing at Gulfstream Park

At the height of gaming, more than 300 establishments from Fort Lauderdale to Key West had forms of it. They included bookie operations catering to sailors and locals, bolita (aka "numbers") that was popular with Cuban immigrants, and even full casino gaming, although much was illegal. Video slot machines became legal in 1992, and in 2008 table games opened when the Seminole Indians in neighboring Broward County signed a compact with the state of Florida. As more land-based gambling options developed, day cruises to waters outside local jurisdictions folded so that today none dock at the Port of Miami.

In recent years, the gambling situation in Miami–Dade has been highly fluid, with voters in 2008 passing a referendum to allow slot machines at the county's jai-alai fronton and dog and horse tracks; Broward County and the Seminole legalized the slots in 2005. By 2012, politicians were wrangling over plans to allow upscale destination-casino resorts, which would drastically expand the gambling landscape.

Here are some of Miami's more prominent casino and racetrack venues:

Magic City Casino *(450 N.W. 37th Ave., tel 305/649-3000, www.magiccitycasino.com)* opened its doors in October 2009. The facility offers seasonal greyhound racing and has an outdoor amphitheater that hosts nationally acclaimed performers.

At the **Casino Miami Jai-Alai** (see sidebar p. 44), visitors also can bet on simulcast pari-mutuel sports shown on big-screen TVs throughout the Crystal Card Room.

Calder Casino & Race Course *(21001 N.W. 27th Ave., tel 305/625-1311, www.calderracecourse.com)* features horse races from January to April.

Gulfstream Park Racing & Casino *(901 S. Federal Hwy., Hallandale Beach, tel 954/454-7000, www.gulfstreampark.com)*, a "racino" on the Broward side of the border with Miami–Dade County, presents the highest caliber of horse racing in South Florida. It hosts an annual Florida Derby that is a one-million-dollar precursor to the Kentucky Derby.

Historic **Hialeah Park** *(2200 E. 4th Ave., Hialeah, tel 305/885-8000, www.hialeahparkracing.com)*, a Glenn Curtiss creation (see p. 67), is a 1925 decorative old-style Thoroughbred horse racing track that sprawls across nearly 230 acres.

Greater Miami gambling is dominated by the **Seminole Hard Rock Hotel & Casino** *(1 Seminole Way, Hollywood, tel 866/502-7529, www.seminolehardrockhollywood.com)*, a massive complex with an entertainment district, bars, and shops set on the Seminole Tribe's Hollywood reservation.

Half an hour west of downtown Miami, **Miccosukee Resort & Gaming** *(500 S.W. 177th Ave., tel 877/242-6464, www.miccosukee.com)* is best known for its high-stakes bingo hall. The tribally owned complex includes a golf course.

INSIDER TIP:

Use the Opa-locka Express Circulator bus to tour Opa-locka. It's free, and its two routes go past many architectural gems, including City Hall.

—JANE SUNDERLAND
National Geographic contributor

a blanket. The green has a roosting population of wading birds and owls, a rare thing in Greater Miami, attracting bird-watchers to what was formerly the **Greynolds Park Rookery.** Mountain bikers speed around the 1.6-mile-long bike path, but it's also a pleasant circuit for leisurely pedaling.

Opa-locka

In a way this improbable phenomenon of Moorish make-believe is a sad memorial to the wonderfully fanciful visions of Glenn Curtiss (see pp. 66–67), who hoped to take his place as the supreme caliph of Florida entrepreneurs. He aspired to live among the rich, but the city for which he is best known is very poor—an economic ghetto populated mostly by African-American families and recent Caribbean and Latin American immigrants. But what a place it is, the fantasyland Curtiss christened the "Baghdad of Dade County."

Due north of Miami International Airport and due west of I-95 Interchange 13, its domes, minarets, crenelations, pointed horseshoe arches, and crescent motifs rise above uninspired buildings put up since the city's optimistic start some 85 years ago.

If nothing else, visit the **Opa-locka City Hall,** where Curtiss based his operatic production under blue and white domes, since repainted mauve and gold—the rest of the building is also now a shade of gold. In this imitation mosque-palace (designated a thematic resource on the National Register of Historic Places), architect Bernhardt Muller sketched hundreds of renderings of what was hoped would be the "most beautiful city on the East Coast," planted with poinciana, bamboo, eucalyptus, and more than 2,500 coconut palms. Appropriately, the building maintains a special shelf for its collection of books telling

(continued on p. 80)

Opa-locka
🗺 41 E6

Opa-locka City Hall
🗺 41 E6
✉ 777 Sharazad Blvd.
☎ 305/688-4611
🕐 Closed Sat.–Sun.

OPA-LOCKA EXPRESS CIRCULATOR
The Opa-locka Express Circulator (*www.opalockafl.gov*) operates Monday through Friday, 6 a.m.–7 p.m., along two routes. Both routes share a stop at the Tri-Rail Opa-locka Station.

EXPERIENCE: Take a Crash Course in Spanish

Want to brush up on your high school Spanish or at least learn the basics? Although you need longer than a typical vacation in and around Miami to learn the Romance language, **Berlitz** (*1200 Brickell Ave., tel 888/561-7174, www.berlitz.us/ miami*), **Inlingua** (*1101 Brickell Ave., tel 305/579-0096, www.inlingua-if.com/in lingua/locations-miami-florida/miami-brickell .aspx*), and **CCLS Miami** (*3191 Coral Way, Coral Gables, tel 305/529-2257, www.cclscorp .com/locations*) can set you up with intensive classes or private lessons. They'll tailor to your schedule, whether it's an hour a day for a few days or total immersion from 9 a.m. to 5 p.m. for two weeks. Classes start at $250 a month for standard group lessons and $3,990 per week for total immersion.

Little Haiti

This enclave of roughly 29,000 immigrants, predominantly Haitians, 3 miles north of Miami's Central Business District, was once Lemon City, a mercantile district surrounded by citrus orchards. Today the neighborhood is a hodgepodge of shoestring merchandising, as much a response to the needs of residents trying to survive here as it is a bid to attract tourists, who, owing to Little Haiti's overblown reputation for crime, tend to pass it by.

A vendor at Little Haiti's ad hoc weekend open-air market displays her bounty of tropical fruits.

Lying east of I-95, Little Haiti runs to just a few blocks inland from Biscayne Bay. Its main boulevard is N.E. Second Avenue, and the enclave extends (roughly) from the Miami Design District around N.E. 36th Street to the vicinity of the El Portal neighborhood around N.E. 85th Street. It is a fascinating area: hand-lettered signs in French Creole and English; folk art murals; women in wide-brimmed straw hats and pretty cotton smocks; the smoky aroma of pork and garlic roasting in hole-in-the-wall eateries; and old clapboard houses from Lemon City's maritime days, splashed in vivid colors—yellow, blue, green, magenta, flamingo.

Several thousand Haitians risked the Gulf Stream crossing in open sailboats to escape the cruelties and deprivations of the despotic regimes in their homeland. Yet contrary to occasionally misleading media portrayals, Miami's Haitian newcomers are seldom illiterate or unskilled. Like most immigrants, they boast better résumés than countrymen who stay behind, and often represent Haiti's middle and upper classes. Most who come to Miami are actually secondary émigrés, moved south after years in Haitian enclaves in the Northeast, and are usually college-educated and fluent in English. From them Little Haiti draws its business and community leaders, and much of its hope for the future.

Little Haiti's Central District

The heart of Little Haiti centers on N.E. 54th Street, between N.E. Second and Miami Avenues. You could spend a day browsing among the kitsch, the food, and the exotica, advertised by illustrated handmade signs that are themselves worth collecting. All the while, you'll hear Haitian *compas*—a melodic, hard-driving Caribbean music immensely popular in Little Havana and Little Haiti nightclubs—drumming from storefronts.

As you approach N.E. 54th Street's junction with Miami Avenue, look for the **Veye Yo (Watch Them).** Little Haiti's political center offers evening lectures, typically about Haitian politics and immigrant concerns. (If they're in Creole, someone will translate for you.)

On weekends, the intersection of N.E. 54th Street and N.E. Second Avenue often becomes an open-air food market selling just about anything eaten on the Caribbean isles. Sadly, a long effort to sustain a permanent Caribbean Marketplace at N.E. Second Avenue and N.E. 60th Street has faltered, even though in 1991 its facsimile of Port-au-Prince's century-old Iron Market won an award for its innovative design and striking color scheme. For the time being it stands nearly empty. Behind the marketplace is the new **Little Haiti Cultural Center** *(212 N.E. 59th Terr., tel 305/960-2969, www.miamigov.com/lhculturalcenter).* This Afro-Caribbean facility offers a black box theater, dance studios, and art galleries and studios.

Near the marketplace, on N.E. Second Avenue, is the **Church of Notre Dame d'Haiti,** once the cafeteria of a Catholic girls' school. Its vivid panels of stained glass illustrate the saga of Pierre Toussaint (1746–1803), a pious Haitian who escaped slavery to become consul of Haiti, a spiritual leader, and a candidate for Catholic sainthood. On another wall is a mural portraying the odyssey of Haitian refugees to America.

From the Church of Notre Dame d'Haiti, it's only a short walk to the **Mapou Cultural Center** *(5919 N.E. 2nd Ave., tel 305/757-9922, www.libremapou.com/cultural).* Owner Jan Mapou has created a focal point for Haitians in Miami to keep alive their language, dance, theater, literature, and other arts. You can buy souvenirs, paintings, and books translated from Kreyòl to English and vice versa.

Haitian Cuisine

One of the best things about Little Haiti is its cuisine, utterly casual but as tasty as any in the Caribbean. There is nothing nouvelle or New World about it; the sizzling fish and pork dishes are authentic recipes from Haiti. There are several inviting places to eat, including color-splashed cottages with tables in their backyards. The food at these restaurants is informal, inexpensive, and tasty, and most patrons are locals who eat nearly all their meals here. Creole names make the dishes sound more mysterious than they are: *lambi* is conch, and *griot* is fried pork. Almost everything else on the menus is familiar—fried fish and chicken, pickled vegetables, and the ubiquitous Caribbean side dishes of rice, beans, and fried plantains.

Buena Vista East

Little Haiti's Buena Vista East is another of Miami's older themed neighborhoods. The architectural styles are eclectic, fanciful, and familiar, as most derive from the Mediterranean vogue of the 1920s.

Botanicas

These aromatic shops supply the pharmacopoeia and accoutrements of voodoo and Santeria, religions arising among West Africa's Yoruba peoples and spread to the Caribbean by the slave trade. The shops provide believers with the medicinal herbs, candles, effigies, images, and other paraphernalia required for rituals. If you enter one, be aware that botanicas are not curio shops, nor are they intended for tourists. Consider yourself in a religious setting and act accordingly. Resist any impulse to laugh at what you find—crucifixes fashioned from bones, voodoo dolls bristling with stickpins. To many living in Little Haiti, this is sacred stuff.

Hurt Building

🅜 41 E6

✉ 490 Opa-locka Blvd.

Tri-Rail Opa-locka Station

✉ 480 Ali Baba Ave.

Miami Springs

🅜 40 C4

the tales of *The Arabian Nights*.

Two other must-sees are the **Hurt Building,** a smaller fantasy of arches, domes, and minarets, and the **Tri-Rail Opa-locka Station,** a beautiful 1927 edifice with exterior tilework and a crenellated roofline.

Due to economic setbacks in this city, crime of all kinds is rampant. It is best to visit the city during the day.

The PlayGround Theatre

Among the last great art deco buildings built in South Florida is Miami Springs' PlayGround Theatre *(map 41 F5, 9806 N.E. 2nd Ave., tel 305/751-9550, www .theplaygroundtheatre.com)*. This is one of the few surviving Paramount Pictures showplaces that were once the studio's exclusive outlets, and were built in most major American cities. Paramount commissioned Miami architect Harold Steward to design it in the late 1930s, but the war postponed its completion until 1946. The movie theater is now a performing arts center, but its exterior still evokes the bygone era of America's great cinema palaces.

Miami Springs

Miami's recent past is dominated by the schemes of entrepreneurs whose names appear often on street signs: Flagler, Brickell, Tuttle, and, of course, Curtiss, who has both a drive and a parkway named in his honor. But save for a group of historically conscious homeowners of the pueblo revival-style homes Curtiss built in Miami Springs, most residents have no idea that their little community

abutting Miami International Airport's north fence sprang from an early 20th-century aviator's imagination.

The pueblo style of red-tiled roofs, thick adobe walls, and wide shade porches had been sweeping the country like a wildfire. To Glenn Curtiss, the validity lay in the vogue, and so the curtain rose on Miami Springs—the Santa Fe of the subtropics.

Miami Springs is best toured with a car and a camera, as almost all of its faux-mission homes are private. But it is pure Miami. Start downtown at the Curtiss Parkway, which runs diagonally between Okeechobee Rd. and N.W. 36th Street and bisects the Miami Springs Golf Course. The adobe bungalows near the parkway are really stucco over wood and tar paper, and the roof support beams that protrude from them don't support anything—but the look is appealingly genuine.

Consider stopping downtown on the parkway at **Miami Springs Pharmacy** *(45 Curtiss Pkwy.),* housed in a handsome pueblo revival building. Inside is a small historical exhibit, along with a curious pharmacological archive. Just up the street is the **Fairhavens Retirement Home** *(201 Curtiss Pkwy.),* originally Curtiss's Country Club Hotel, another pueblo revival gem. There are a few cafés along here, convenient places to pause to consider whether you would be more in your element living in a home that makes you feel like an 18th-century Spanish colonial. ∎

An island-bound social mosaic with a composite personality distinct from those found in Miami across the bay

Miami Beach

Ocean Drive, South Beach—the place to see and be seen

Miami Beach

If you come to Miami Beach—a city east of Miami sprawled across a series of natural and man-made barrier islands—for a week or two, a stay in South Beach will probably deliver the most variety in the allotted time. If you come to stay a while longer, you will find exploring the communities claiming most of the 7 miles of shoreline south of the Dade–Broward county line rewarding as well. Each has its appeal—Surfside and Sunny Isles attract those more concerned with economy.

Miami Beach boasts a miles-long white-sand strand fronting the Atlantic Ocean.

NOT TO BE MISSED:

Five causeways connect Miami Beach with Miami, each landing you in a distinct neighborhood. In terms of views and en route attractions, the most interesting is the MacArthur Causeway, which vaults Biscayne Bay from Downtown Miami, touching down on Watson Island along the way, and deposits you at the bottom of South Beach.

South Beach

Located between 5th and 41st Streets, South Beach is the district with which Miami Beach is most popularly associated. Here you will find the majority of the island's 800 art deco buildings, most of its youth-and-beauty-oriented playgrounds, and its best known white-sand beaches.

South of South Beach

South of Fifth Street, things have gone through considerable redevelopment to include new and renovated buildings while retaining their hip, bohemian funkiness.

Northern Miami Beach

North of where the Julia Tuttle Causeway connects the island with Miami is a mélange of residential and commercial development. Trendy these neighborhoods are not, but they all face the same warm blue water and most are near lovely beaches. Not until you reach the older Surfside community do you find architecture as appealing and charming as in SoBe's Art Deco District. Visitors interested in doing some serious shopping will want to head to the mall at Bal Harbour.

Three Enclaves of Abundance

Look left (north) as you head toward Miami Beach on the MacArthur Causeway and you will see bridges leading to Palm, Hibiscus, and Star Islands, their ruler-straight shores bristling with sailboat masts and decorated with luxury manses. These are private communities that can, if they wish, limit access to residents and guests. The causeway touches land by the Miami Beach Marina (*300 Alton Rd., tel 305/673-6000*) a parklike public port with 400 berths that can handle vessels up to 250 feet in length.

Port of Miami

Dodge Island and Lummus Island, south of Miami Beach, make up the Port of Miami, the world's largest cruise port, where each year the gangways of floating pleasure domes stream with more than three million passengers. You can visit the port via a separate causeway (*N.E. Sixth St./Port Blvd.*) that leaves downtown's Biscayne Boulevard near the Bayside Marketplace. At night the ships are lit up like Las Vegas casinos. ■

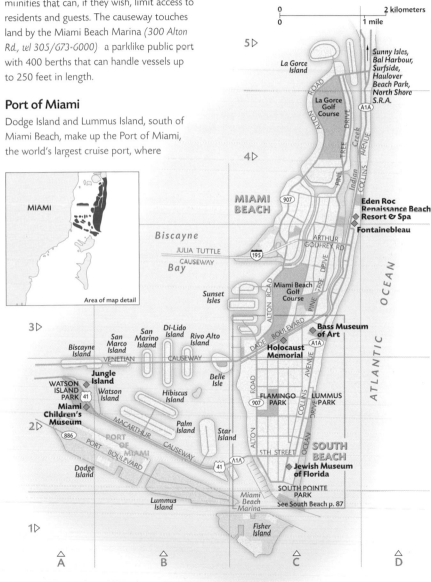

South Beach

Though Miami Beach is more than South Beach, the island's longtime image as the American Riviera today indisputably reflects most brightly from here, roughly a 40-block-long stretch beginning on 5th and running north to about 41st Street. Here are the cafés, refurbished streamline and moderne hotels and apartment houses, restaurants, shops, boutiques, museums, beaches, and photogenic habitués commanding the attention of travel magazines.

The Clevelander's rooftop offers stellar views of South Beach and the Miami skyline beyond.

South Beach
▲ See map p. 87
Visitor Information

www.visitsouthbeach online.com

Known to many as SoBe, it is a remarkable district, exciting to its residents, a sizable percentage of whom are gay. Here, too, is a significant cadre of artists, writers, musicians, and entertainers. It is a walkable, appealing community, blessed with one of the most inviting beaches in South Florida on its Atlantic side.

Ocean Drive

Ocean Drive is SoBe's most photographed street, a palmy beachfront lined with hotels painted in vibrant colors and trimmed with neon. Ocean Drive between 5th and 14th Streets often appears populated by pretty people for whom leisure is the order of the day. But behind this facade is a brisk economy spiked most notably by restaurateurs, hoteliers, retailers, and real estate developers.

On weekend nights, when some 30,000 people stream across the bay for the SoBe nightlife, it's almost impossible to drive. If you do, get your street parking early;

INSIDER TIP:

Both the cars and the people-watching are amazing on Ocean Drive, but beware: Parking your own car can be a nightmare. Luckily, most hotels and restaurants have valet parking.

—KAY KOBOR HANKINS
National Geographic designer

there is a small but convenient public parking lot with ten-hour meters at the corner of Tenth Street and Washington Avenue.

If you only have a short time in SoBe, visit Ocean Drive for a quick bite at one of its many sidewalk cafés or open-front restaurants, and be sure to cross the street to the Lummus Park beach and put your foot in the water, if only to experience the warmth of the Gulf Stream. It takes less than an hour to walk Ocean Drive's ten-block lineup of art deco confections, starting with the 1939 **Bentley Luxury Suites Hotel** at Fifth and Ocean.

Ocean Drive Cafés: To say that any Ocean Drive café guarantees a glimpse of SoBe archetypes would be glib, but an iced tea and sandwich outside the **Colony Hotel** *(736 Ocean Dr., tel 305/673-0088)* carries the likelihood of observing one of the willowy women and hollow-cheeked men from the fashion ads. The **News Café** *(800 Ocean Dr.; see p. 250)* has been described as a watering hole for the simply fabulous, so much so that its tables are often taken by tourists searching for famous faces. But the News is also an excellent eatery, one of SoBe's best. Between Eighth and Ninth is **Larios on the Beach** *(820 Ocean Dr.; see p. 249)*, a color-splashed Cuban restaurant owned by Miami singer Gloria Estefan. Another Cuban-style bistro, **Mango's Tropical Café**

EXPERIENCE: South Beach Boot Camp

You'll get the quintessential South Beach workout at Viktoria Telek's **South Beach Boot Camp** *(www.thesouthbeachbootcamp .com)*. The fitness model won Wilhelmina Models' 2009 hot body model search and has been featured in countless magazines and TV shows. Mornings and some early evenings, Telek leads longtime students and onetime visitors in boot-camp workouts at various locations along the beach. She concentrates on exercises to improve flexibility and balance as well as cardio and strength. Classes incorporate agility drills, sprinting races, core exercises, burpees, squats, and bicycle crunches.

Telek says that exercising on the beach is 60 percent more difficult than in a gym because participants are moving in the sand, not on a flat surface. And with beautiful scenery and fresh air, the reward is 100 percent better.

Check the website for up-to-date schedules and camp locations (class cost depends on location). If Telek isn't available, her partner at the South Beach Boot Camp, Keith Darby, also leads classes.

Beach volleyballers can find action at any number of Miami Beach locations, including Lummus Park.

(900 Ocean Dr.; see p. 249), at Ocean and Ninth, throbs at night with Caribbean music and overflows with singles seeking salsa dance partners.

SoBe's Club Scene

Come evening, South Beach's youth-oriented club scene commences. Doormen will only admit the prettiest and trendiest, and even if you are granted entry, what you often find within is a lot of empty attitude, self-conscious

posturing, deafening music requiring you to read lips, and haphazard (and pricey) bar service. That said, SoBe does have some places where the elegance is real, among them **Escopazzo** (1311 Washington Ave.; see p. 248).

If you must subject yourself to the club scene's cruel social Darwinism, do it a short walk away at **Mynt** (1921 Collins Ave., tel 305/532-0727), considered one of the more adult party-till-dawn clubs. Jazz and spirits are served with equal élan at **Jazid** (1342 Washington Ave., tel 305/673-9372), a friendly bar cherished by locals and tourists alike. With live music every night, this is one of the cooler, and more relaxed, places on South Beach for unwinding. For understated swank, the bar at the pretty streamline-style **Hotel Astor** (956 Washington Ave.; see p. 247) is hard to top in this part of town.

Miami Beach's Beaches

Before it was Miami Beach, it was Ocean Beach, where Miami-ans came first to picnic in the cooling trade winds and swim in the warm Gulf Stream current. The beaches that run some 16 miles from the Dade County line to the tip of Miami Beach gave birth to the notion of this as eastern America's Costa del Sol.

From 5th to 15th Streets, South Beach's wide Atlantic strand is a public recreation area called **Lummus Park,** an expanse of white sand running to a gentle surf and a bottom that slants

(continued on p. 90)

> ## Why South Florida's Seas Are So Blue
>
> In colder climes, where seawater with a lower temperature holds more dissolved oxygen and carbon dioxide, nutrients give rise to dense blooms of tiny plants (phytoplankton) that feed microscopic animals (zooplankton). This rich soup, the foundation of the ocean food chain, often makes chilly waters elsewhere appear murky. South Florida's warm currents hold far lower concentrations of dissolved gases, making them inhospitable to plankton. The absence of suspended matter leaves nothing to filter out the intense blue light that results when sunlight falls on a crystalline sea.

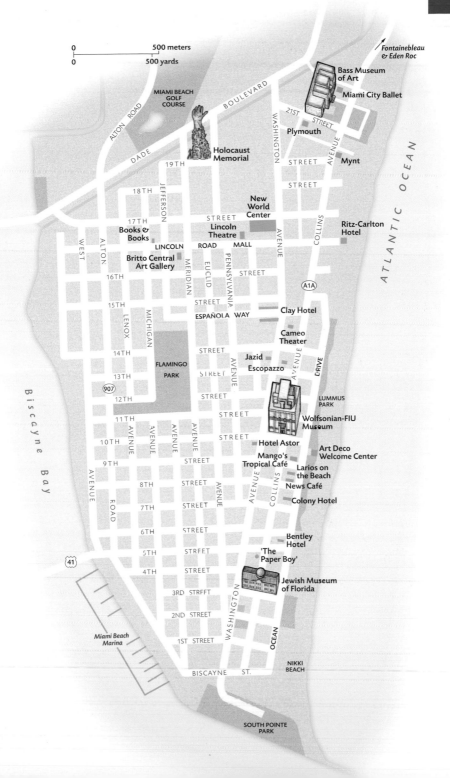

0   500 meters

0   500 yards

Fontainebleau
& Eden Roc

MIAMI BEACH
GOLF
COURSE

ALTON ROAD

DADE   BOULEVARD

21ST   STREET

WASHINGTON

AVENUE

Bass Museum
of Art

Miami City Ballet

Plymouth

Holocaust
Memorial

19TH

STREET

Mynt

18TH

STREET

17TH

JEFFERSON

New
World
Center

Ritz-Carlton
Hotel

Books &
Books

STREET

Lincoln
Theatre

LINCOLN   ROAD   MALL

COLLINS

AVENUE

WEST

ALTON

Britto Central
Art Gallery

16TH

MERIDIAN

EUCLID

PENNSYLVANIA

STREET

A1A

15TH

STREET

Clay Hotel

LENOX

MICHIGAN

ESPAÑOLA   WAY

Cameo
Theater

14TH

STREET

Jazid

AVENUE

DRIVE

Escopazzo

13TH

STREET

907

FLAMINGO
PARK

12TH

STREET

LUMMUS
PARK

11TH

STREET

Wolfsonian-FIU
Museum

10TH

AVENUE

AVENUE

AVENUE

AVENUE

STREET

Hotel Astor

Art Deco
Welcome Center

9TH

STREET

Mango's
Tropical Café

Larios on
the Beach

8TH

AVENUE

STREET

AVENUE

COLLINS

News Café

ROAD

7TH

STREET

Colony Hotel

6TH

STREET

5TH

STREET

Bentley
Hotel

41

4TH

STREET

'The
Paper Boy'

3RD   STREET

Jewish Museum
of Florida

2ND   STREET

WASHINGTON

1ST   STREET

OCEAN

Miami Beach
Marina

NIKKI
BEACH

BISCAYNE   ST.

Biscayne Bay

ATLANTIC   OCEAN

SOUTH POINTE
PARK

Art Deco District Walk

If it were not for the Miami Design Preservation League, a group committed to saving Greater Miami's architectural treasures, there would be no Art Deco District (which runs from 6th Street to 23rd Street), nor as many surviving examples.

Numerous art deco hotels, such as the Cavalier, line beachfront Ocean Drive, South Beach.

One way to see some of the district's some 800 outstanding expressions of art deco is to go on a 90-minute walking tour (*$$$$*) with a league volunteer. The tours begin at the Art Deco Welcome Center (*1001 Ocean Dr., tel 305/672-2014, www.mdpl.org, tours Tues.–Wed., Fri.–Sun. at 10:30 a.m., & Thurs. at 6:30 p.m.*). You can take the same tour on your own by renting an iPod (*$$$$*) at the center between 9:30 a.m. and 5 p.m., or by using your cell-phone (*$$$*). Alternatively, just create your own route, such as the one here.

Ocean Drive

A good place to begin is on Ocean Drive, between Sixth and Seventh Streets, and then head north. Among the handsomest

NOT TO BE MISSED:

Park Central Hotel • Miami Beach Main Post Office • Hotel Astor • The Hotel

buildings here is the **Park Central Hotel** ❶ (*630 Ocean Dr.*), completed in 1937. Its terrazzo floors and front steps, vast lobby, and etched glass details recall the luxurious backdrops of pre–World War II Hollywood musicals—no coincidence, as the vogue drew inspiration from films of that era.

Venture into the gorgeous lobby of the little **Colony Hotel** ❷ (*736 Ocean Dr.*), which

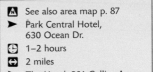

- See also area map p. 87
- ► Park Central Hotel, 630 Ocean Dr.
- ⏱ 1–2 hours
- ↔ 2 miles
- ► The Hotel, 801 Collins Ave.

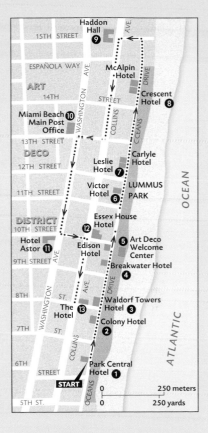

has a fireplace faced with green Vitrolite and a Ramon Chatov mural romanticizing South American rural life. Nor should you bypass the lovely terrazzo floor, molded ceiling treatments, and beautiful light fixtures in the lobby of the **Waldorf Towers Hotel ❸**, farther along Ocean Drive at No. 860.

In the next block at No. 940, the **Breakwater Hotel's ❹** 1939 facade mimics a Central American Maya temple. At night, neon lights on its concrete spire spell BREAKWATER in vivid blue. It shares a swimming pool with the adjoining Mediterranean Revival **Edison Hotel**, which opened in 1935. At this point you will have reached the **Art Deco Welcome Center ❺**, where you can pick up maps and get information. Walk around the center; the back side mimics the bridge of an ocean liner.

Cubism inspired the 1937 **Victor Hotel ❻** *(1144 Ocean Dr.)*. Purists appreciate the three-story **Leslie Hotel ❼** *(1244 Ocean Dr.)* for its classic simplicity.

The **Carlyle** *(1250 Ocean Dr.)* went up in 1941, its architect using the wide lot to stretch the deco style horizontally. Side by side in the 1400-block are two of the most exuberant expressions of it you will find on the Beach: the **Crescent Hotel ❽**, built in 1932, and the **McAlpin Hotel** next door, completed in 1940.

Collins & Washington Avenues

Continue to the junction with 15th Street and turn left. On the other side of Collins Avenue, one block up, is the three-story **Haddon Hall ❾** *(1500 Collins Ave.)*, the beach's finest streamline building.

Walk south on Collins and turn right onto 13th Street. Opposite, at No. 1300 on Washington Avenue, is the **Miami Beach Main Post Office ❿**, a wonderful and rare example of deco federal, which opened in 1939. Details inside the spacious circular rotunda include a beautiful historical mural. Turn left and continue down Washington Avenue. Another streamline beauty, the **Hotel Astor ⓫** *(956 Washington Ave.)*, is more restrained. Take Tenth Street back onto Collins Avenue. The nautical moderne design of the 1938 **Essex House ⓬** *(1001 Collins Ave.)* epitomizes art deco's intense infatuation with ocean travel on the great moderne ships of that age.

Conclude the walk a little farther south down Collins at the beautiful **The Hotel ⓭** *(801 Collins Ave.)*. With its metal spire and neon, this building is one of the finest expressions of art deco spirit on the island. It recently reopened as a small luxury inn.

South Pointe Park

⚠ See map p. 87

Española Way

⚠ See map p. 87

SOUTH BEACH LOCAL
The South Beach Local (*www.miamibeachfl.gov/ NEWCITY/sobe_local .asp*), operated by Miami–Dade Transit, is a bidirectional circular service to the entire South Beach area.

away slowly. Near Ocean Drive, Lummus has comfortable benches where you can watch pickup volleyball games, listen to the rustle of palm fronds above, or relax under a thatched hut. The park has a concrete walkway—popular with in-line skaters—running most of its length. There's little in the way of organized beach activity, but call park headquarters for information on events *(tel 305/673-7730)*.

INSIDER TIP:

Be sure to spend some time at Española Way. The open-air mall has a bohemian character, complete with European-style cafés, unique stores, and art galleries.

—SADIE P. QUARRIER
Photo editor, National Geographic *magazine*

South Pointe Park

Its name implies, South Pointe Park sits at the island's southern tip, at the bottom of Washington Avenue. Its 17 acres serve as a pleasant getaway place for families. Following a major renovation, the park reopened in 2009, complete with a striking new public art installation, "Obstinate Lighthouse," created by German artist Tobias Rehberger. In addition, a tot lot is popular with kids, and walking under fountain jets will cool everyone on hot days. Visitors enjoy spacious lawns, a wide

variety of subtropical trees and shrubs, and a native beach dune area, much of it with amazing vistas of the ocean. The park's pier is closed for construction in 2012. During the week, when Lummus Park's beach can be crowded, South Pointe's can be quieter. Families descend upon it on the weekends, however.

Walk west from the park to the Miami Beach Marina to see some of the most incredible yachts and megayachts you can imagine. You can also find fishing and diving charters here.

Española Way

Architect Robert Taylor called his 1925 Mediterranean Revival complex "a haven for artists and rogues." If so, they were genteel bohemians, for this fanciful Alhambra of gas lamp-lighted private alleys and courts, artists' studios, arched portals, and narrow streets is nothing if not elegant.

You will find the awnings and balconies of Taylor's "Historic Spanish Village" between Washington and Pennsylvania Avenues, sandwiched between 14th and 15th Streets. Remarkably, Taylor's intent still rules—the upper lofts are occupied by artists. Below, on the sidewalk level, are cafés, interesting shops and boutiques, and several fine art galleries.

The Miami Beach Preservation League (see p. 102) occasionally organizes 45-minute Saturday afternoon tours of the area, usually departing at 2 p.m. from the 1925 **Clay Hotel** (*1438 Washing-*

ton Ave., tel 305/534-2988; see p. 247). This is where Al Capone ran his infamous gambling ring and Desi Arnaz created the rumba craze. In recent years, Don Johnson, Sylvester Stallone, and Elton John have shot films and videos here. To explore this area, start with a look at the Clay's appealing lobby—found at 406 Española Way—then just roam.

When its curtain rose for the first time in 1938, the nearby **Cameo Theater** (1445 Washington Ave., tel 305/532-2667, www.cameomiami.com) screened foreign films. The building's curved facade, with sculptured moldings framing a wall of glass brick, is pure modernism. Lately it has been used as a dance club and rock music hall, attracting a young and determinedly hip crowd.

Lincoln Road Mall

Lincoln Road's history is a classic tale of Miami Beach's entrepreneurial beginnings: a dirt road through a mangrove swamp transformed by a visionary developer into a chic promenade that is now occupied by more than 300 restaurants, cafés, art galleries, specialty stores, clothing boutiques, and studio-galleries.

When Carl Fisher, who established himself as the creator of the Indianapolis Speedway, announced plans to create the "Fifth Avenue of the South," Miami Beach had no commercial district. Residents had to make the long drive across the old drawbridge to shop in Downtown Miami department stores. The site Fisher chose for his new shopping mecca had (continued on p. 94)

Lincoln Road Mall

🏕 See map p. 87

www.nws.org

Street performers regularly delight the crowds at the open-air Lincoln Road Mall.

Art Deco

The style takes its name from the 1925 Paris Exposition Internationale des Arts Décoratifs et Industriels Modernes, an exhibition of works embodying machine-age modernity. A stellar group of American designers, architects, and industrialists were soon applying modernism adornments to automobiles (like the Chrysler Airflow, which flopped), airplanes (like the DC-3, which flew), and even kitchen appliances.

The New York Central's sleek Manhattan-to-Chicago express train, christened the 20th-Century Limited, seemed the embodiment of the national faith in progress. Designers described their windswept creations as moderne, streamline, skyscraper, and "Jazz Age," a term coined by F. Scott Fitzgerald. Meanwhile "arts déco" remained a French term, used most often in reference to low-relief geometrical designs: parallel straight lines, zigzags, chevrons, and stylized floral motifs.

Ironically, it was the Depression that gave the art deco vogue its strongest push. Bank failures, bread lines, and factory closures had shaken Americans' faith in institutions. They wanted architecture, and public architecture in particular—office buildings, post offices, railroad stations—to be uplifting and encouraging. That was the challenge given to architect Howard Cheney, commissioned to build Miami Beach's new post office at 1300 Washington Avenue in the late 1930s. He succeeded brilliantly.

But what accounted for art deco's extraordinary popularity in Miami Beach? Some say its air of ease appealed to hard-working, winter-weary vacationers. Others suppose that the style's classic foundations appealed to former Europeans who accounted for many of the area's visitors and residents, while its thoroughly American look reminded them that they were far from the horrors of European fascism.

Art deco has an assertive handsomeness that many associate with verve and confidence.

Terrazzo

Made of stone chips set in mortar and polished, terrazzo was used by most of the architects who worked here in art deco styles to create patterned floors and stairways. (Elsewhere, the effect is sometimes emulated using linoleum inlays.) Architectural historians believe Miami Beach's Art Deco District holds the world's richest collection of this decorative art.

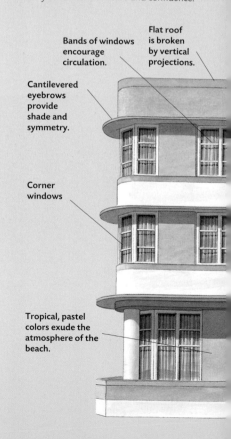

Flat roof is broken by vertical projections.

Bands of windows encourage circulation.

Cantilevered eyebrows provide shade and symmetry.

Corner windows

Tropical, pastel colors exude the atmosphere of the beach.

The theatricality of even the smallest hotels, like the "seagoing" Essex *(1001 Collins Ave.)* and the "Maya" Breakwater *(940 Ocean Dr.),* each topped with a spire advertising itself in neon, exudes an appealing, amusing air of youthful jauntiness. In 1940, as Franklin Roosevelt's social engineering seemed to be turning things around, architect Anton Skislewicz adopted the heroic pylons of the future-worshipping temples of the decade's world's fairs for his posh Plymouth resort hotel *(336 21st St.).* Did it matter that you were not a star if you could live in an apartment tower like Robert Collins's Helen Mar *(2421 Lake Pancoast Dr.)* overlooking Lake Pancoast—as chic as anything in Holly-

wood—on an ocean far bluer and warmer than the chill Pacific that sweeps California's coast?

For all its make-believe, art deco was nonetheless practical. Given South Florida's wood-rotting dampness and paint-peeling sunlight, its use of concrete, smooth-faced stone, and metal as exterior architectural coverings enabled art deco buildings to better withstand subtropical weather. Its elements—accents created with colored terra-cotta, rose mirrors, stainless steel, plate glass, Bakelite, Vitrolite, glazes, aluminum, and tubular steel—were durable as well. Miami's builders had a rich palette from which to choose, and they used it to build a thousand priceless expressions of the style.

Art Deco Style

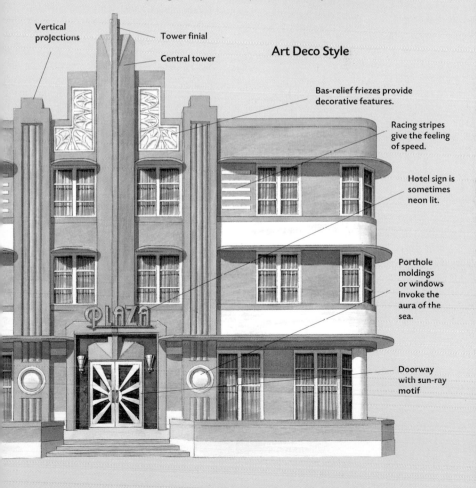

Vertical projections
Tower finial
Central tower
Bas-relief friezes provide decorative features.
Racing stripes give the feeling of speed.
Hotel sign is sometimes neon lit.
Porthole moldings or windows invoke the aura of the sea.
Doorway with sun-ray motif

Romero Britto

Romero Britto's colorful, vibrant pop art and neo-cubism works reflect multicultural Miami. The city's most famous visual artist moved here from Brazil in 1988 and the following year was selected, along with Andy Warhol and others, to reimagine Absolut Vodka bottles. Since then, Britto's paintings and sculptures have been exhibited around the world, including in the Louvre. Locally, his works appear in public places such as the Miami Children's Museum (see p. 102) and on the facade of a high-rise, visible from I-95, as well as galleries and homes.

**Britto Central
Art Gallery**

🅰 See map p. 87
✉ 818 Lincoln Rd.
☎ 305/531-8821
www.britto.com

**New World
Center**

🅰 See map p. 87
✉ 500 17th St.
☎ 305/673-3331
**www.newworld
center.com**

the disadvantage of being below sea level. Undaunted, he had it built up with sand dredged from Biscayne Bay, widened and paved the road, and named it for his hero, Abraham Lincoln. He replaced the coconut palms (which sometimes dropped fruit on the unsuspecting) with royal palms. He sold space to prestigious tenants like Saks Fifth Avenue, Bonwit Teller, Packard, and Chrysler, and Lincoln Road soon acquired a reputation for being posh.

It still is, on the whole, its bazaar reaching from Alton Road to the Atlantic shoreline. (The pedestrian mall stretches between Washington and Lenox Avenues.) Leave your car at the 17th Street parking lot and stroll. If you see a crowd gathered in front of the **Regal South Beach 18** (1100 Lincoln Rd., tel 305/674-6766), a giant glass-walled theater, then it's movie time. The striking **Lincoln Theatre** (541 Lincoln Rd.), opened in 1936 by

Wometco as a movie theater, is now a multipurpose performance venue. Between events the building is usually locked, but its facade is pleasing to behold all the same.

For a more cerebral adventure, visit **Books & Books** (933 Lincoln Rd., tel 305/532-3222). This very popular bookstore hosts talks by authors, has book signings nearly every evening, and also houses an inviting café well worth a visit, the Russian Bear. Sip on your favorite beverage while reading works by authors from Miami and around the world.

To embrace the visual arts, visit **Britto Central Art Gallery.** The joyous work of Romero Britto (see sidebar this page), Brazil's contemporary pop artist, has been shown everywhere from the White House to Absolut Vodka bottles.

A small antiques fair sets up on Saturdays, and a farmers' fruit and vegetable market opens on Sunday mornings.

New World Center

Opened in 2011, the New World Center is the dazzling venue for the New World Symphony, America's Orchestral Academy. Architect Frank Gehry's only Florida building seats 756 patrons in its concert hall and has several performance and rehearsal studios.

Regarding its debut, the *Miami Herald* wrote, "Through an expansive, 80-foot-tall window made of the clearest glass available, Gehry's signature torqued forms, erratically stacked up six stories high, were bathed in white LED lights and, seen from the outside, resembled giant, Picasso-esque dancers cavorting on a stage."

Outside the building, every night from sundown to midnight, video is projected onto its 7,000-square-foot front wall. Sometimes it shows a concert that's taking place inside, sometimes it shows a film, and sometimes it shows video art. Projections of New World Symphony concerts have attracted 2,000 aficionados to the adjacent **SoundScape Park,** with many sitting on blankets or lawn chairs and having picnics with wine.

Docent-led, half-hour tours *(reservations required, $)* of the New World Center are offered on Tuesdays and Thursdays at 4 p.m. and on Fridays and Saturdays at noon.

The flagship of the center is the New World Symphony *(www .nws.org),* which premiered in 1987. With more than 60 performances annually, NWS brings to Miami many renowned classical soloists, composers, and conductors.

Founded by artistic director Michael Tilson Thomas, who also conducts, composes, and plays the piano, NWS has performed in New York's Carnegie Hall, London's Barbican Centre, and Argentina's Teatro Colon. The symphony has worked with acclaimed conductors Leonard Bernstein, Sir Georg Solti, and Marek Janowski as well as violinists Anne-Sophie Mutter and Gil Shaham and the multidimensional musicians Yo-Yo Ma and Gloria Estefan.

Wolfsonian–FIU Museum

Many people find this unusual museum inexpressibly fascinating. Officially, the Wolfsonian examines the "decorative and propaganda arts" and "material culture," which is about as revealing as saying that *War and Peace* is a book about Russia. The museum occupies an imposing seven-story, Spanish-Moorish-style former storage company building, and holds more than 70,000 objects, predominantly

Dudley Vaill Talcott's 1929 aluminum "Wrestler," Wolfsonian–FIU Museum

Wolfsonian–FIU Museum

🅐 See map p. 87
✉ Washington Ave. & 10th St.
☎ 305/531-1001
🕐 Closed a.m. & Wed.
💲 $$

www.wolfsonian.org

Bass Museum
of Art

🅰 83 C3
✉ 2121 Park Ave.
☎ 305/673-7530
🕐 Closed Mon.–
Tues.
💲 $$

www.bass
museum.org

from North America and
Europe, that "reflect the cul-
tural, political, and technological
changes that swept across the
world in the century preceding
the Second World War."

Mitchell Wolfson, Jr., heir
to the Wometco Theater chain
fortune, spent years amassing
this trove of furniture, paintings,
sculptures, architectural models,
posters, books, glass, ceramics,
metal works, and ephemera—
a fever chart of the modern
psyche, tracing its swings between
mankind's beauty and beast
natures. The exhibits are startling
and eclectic: streamline Jazz Age
kitchen appliances; a flattering
bronze bust of Mussolini; a pinball
machine exhorting American kids
to kill Axis warlords; and a hand-
tooled Braille version of Hitler's
Mein Kampf.

INSIDER TIP:

The Bass Museum of Art features the only mummy and Egyptian sarcophagus in the state of Florida.

—SILVIA KARMAN CUBIÑA
Executive director & chief curator,
Bass Museum of Art

The 52,000-square-foot
building was built in 1927 to store
the possessions of Miami Beach's
patrician set during the low
season. Inside, all is now modern,
with humidity and temperature
carefully controlled to preserve
thousands of rare volumes and
fragile documents.

Bass Museum of Art

Like the Wolfsonian's unusual
building (see p. 95), the Maya-
themed structure housing the
European art collection of the
Bass family (the museum's bene-
factors) was originally devoted
to another use, in this case to
serve as the Miami Beach Library
and Art Center. It is built of key-
stone—the same rough, mottled
gray rock, created by eons of
coral-building, that underlies
much of South Florida.

The Bass is the only repository
of fine art on the island, and
its holdings include some **old
masters** and an interesting array
of **ecclesiastical artifacts** said
to be the finest of its kind in
southeast Florida. Don't expect
to see internationally renowned
paintings. However, you will find
interesting works by Peter Paul
Rubens, Albrecht Dürer, and Henri
Toulouse-Lautrec, among other
important artists. Particularly
unusual and rare are the pair of
huge **Flemish tapestries** dating
from the 1500s.

This thoughtfully curated
institution makes smart use of
its limited but attractive spaces,
mounting changing exhibitions
supplemented by screenings of
related films and documentaries
in its auditorium. The Bass sits on
a plot of land donated to Miami
Beach long ago by city father John
Collins (honoree of Collins Ave-
nue). Collins' architect grandson
Russell Pancoast designed the
building, completed in 1930.

Take a close look at the trio of
deeply cut **keystone bas-reliefs**
above the museum's portals, all by

Gustav Bohland, one of a locally prominent group of architects whose works often reflected the fantasy vogues of Florida's prosperous early-century boom years. The center relief is most interesting, depicting a stylized pelican against a beautifully rendered art deco background of palm, mangrove forest, and ocean. Look closely, too, at the exterior wall of the building, and in the keystone and you will see fossils of ancient sea creatures.

Jewish Museum of Florida

The Jewish Museum of Florida is a remarkable archive devoted to the multifaceted story of Florida's Jewish population, whose saga traces back some 250 years. The museum occupies two reincarnated art deco buildings, both placed on the National Register of Historic Places in 1980.

The main museum, dating from 1936, was originally an Orthodox synagogue for Miami Beach's first Jewish congregation, Beth Jacob, and was rededicated to its present station in 1995. (Its slanted floor, which improved acoustics and enabled rabbis to be better heard, remains.) Eighty stained-glass windows bathe its interior in sanguine light. The second restored synagogue, built in 1928–1929, was the original home of Congregation Beth Jacob. The former sanctuary now houses a second exhibit venue where public programs are held.

The museum's permanent **"MOSAIC: Jewish Life in Florida"** exhibit is the centerpiece of its cultural documentary. Intriguing revelations include the little-known saga of Jewish people in Cuba, a life that came apart when Castro-style communism came to power there. You don't have to be Jewish or understand Jewish traditions to be charmed by the museum's personal approach, which includes family photographs (for example, baby "Felix Glickstein on a stuffed alligator in Jacksonville, 1916" and "Miss Florida, Mena Williams, in Tallahassee, 1885"); heirlooms such as a set of Passover china from the mid-19th century; poignant documents like

the Cuban passport of Elisa Gerkes, who immigrated from Poland to Havana in 1917 as a child; and Florida zaniness like the seashell-covered dress Fannie Moss made for a Purim party in 1916.

Other remembrances might make you sad. Old photographs of Miami Beach's "Gentiles Only" hotel signs are especially ironic, given that Miami Beach later became the largest and most vibrant Jewish community in the American Southeast. Be sure to watch the three historical videos.

Jewish Museum of Florida
- 83 C2
- 301 & 311 Washington Ave.
- 305/672-5044
- Closed Mon. & Jewish holidays
- $$

www.jewishmuseum.com

Become a Part of History

The Jewish Museum of Florida continually collects material of the Jewish experience in Florida to pass on to future generations. From this, the museum produces exhibitions that change three times a year. Florida Jewish residents who would like to have their family heirlooms, artifacts, and/or photographs documented and preserved at the museum should contact the registrar (tel 305/672-5044 ext. 3167).

Holocaust Memorial

Holocaust Memorial

🅰 83 C3

✉ 1933–45 Meridian Ave., bet. 19th St. & Dade Blvd.

☎ 305/538-1663

www.holocaust mmb.org

Miami Beach, which has one of America's largest enclaves of Holocaust survivors, has a memorial to the six million Jews who perished in Europe during the Nazis' reign of terror. Dedicated in 1990 in a ceremony that featured Nobel laureate Elie Wiesel, the memorial is laden with symbolism and bears the triple burden of memorializing victims, solacing survivors, and ensuring that future generations do not forget what happened.

Located near the junction of Dade Boulevard and Meridian Avenue, it's constructed mostly of rose-hued Jerusalem stone and surrounded by a wide reflecting pool. On close inspection, details conceived by the memorial's architect and sculptor, Kenneth Treister, assert themselves to create an interpretive monument. A trio of panels forming part of a semicircular black granite wall portray an overview of events from Hitler's ascent to power in 1933 to his suicide amid the ruin of Berlin a dozen years later.

By tracing these events you are drawn to an enclosed, shrinelike space leading into a confining tunnel with walls bearing the names of death camps. Its ceiling presses lower as you advance. The intent, said Treister, is to symbolize the victims' sense of a diminished self. From this grim enclosure you emerge into open air and a circular plaza where a great **bronze forearm** reaches 42 feet toward the sky. Look closely and you see that its forearm is wrapped in a frieze of nearly 100 tormented people clustered in family groups. Examine the hand to find on it a tattooed number. Venture farther and you come to the memorial wall of victims' names. These names are added as they are submitted by those who remember and honor them. ∎

At the Holocaust Memorial, bronze sculptural works lie scattered across a circular plaza.

Miami's Jewish Heritage

Miami has the second largest Jewish community in America after New York. Jews came to Florida for reasons similar to those drawing others: clement weather and a chance to establish themselves in a young, still forming economy. A few settled in 19th-century Key West, finding opportunities in the city's booming maritime salvage trade; others found refuge in Cuba from European pogroms, later establishing a close-knit community in Miami.

Among the first to arrive were merchants from the Northeast, who saw Henry Flagler's and his rivals' railroad building on the Florida Gulf Coast as a sign of an economy poised to expand. By 1912 Miami had a sufficiently large Jewish enclave to establish the city's first synagogue, Beth David (originally B'nai Zion).

The migration from the Northeast that established Miami Beach's reputation as a Jewish retirement community peaked in the years between the World Wars. The giddy upward spiral of real estate prices attracted many, while a growing economy created jobs for the educated and opportunities for the learned. Underlying everything else was Miami's aura as a "tropical" city with a healthy climate.

Bitter winter weather elsewhere in the East guaranteed Miami's tourist trade. Jews from the vast New York–New Jersey metropolis and from Chicago's urban sprawl established a tradition of winter sojourns, sparking Miami Beach's building boom in small residential hotels. In 1927 the Reform Temple Israel, one of the most handsome in the country, opened here, followed in 1929 by Congregation Beth Jacob, Miami Beach's first synagogue, now home to the Jewish Museum of Florida (see p. 97).

Along with the flowering, however, came anti-Semitism: There were restrictive covenants forbidding Jewish folk from renting or buying homes in certain areas (struck down by the Supreme Court in the 1950s) and many restaurant signs read "No Dogs, No Blacks, No Jews." Upper-crust social enclaves such as the Nautilus Club made it known that Jews need not apply. But Jewish families still came by the thousands, checking into Miami Beach's art deco hotels.

Marble bimah, Jewish Museum of Florida

Miami's conversion into a military training center during World War II brought thousands of troops from all around the country. Soldiers (including many who were not Jewish) found themselves invited into Jewish homes on holy days, and the memories of this unexpected community brought thousands back after the war to settle here and raise their families.

Meanwhile, Miami Beach's popularity as a winter resort continued to grow, and in the 1950s Jewish families began to venture away to neighborhoods in Miami and up the coast. In a little-known historical footnote, after Fidel Castro's ascent to power, some 10,000 members of Cuba's Jewish community left their island, most settling in Miami and Miami Beach.

At the start of the 21st century, Miami's Jewish community now shares Greater Miami with Cubans and other Caribbean immigrants. Generations pass, yet still beneath the sun hats of the Jewish elderly, there is a deep awareness of having escaped a past many did not, of an improbable odyssey to a safe place in the sun, and a determination to remember and give thanks.

Resorts & Towers

Standing out from the rest of the 1950s and 1960s high-rise hotels that line Collins Avenue north of 23rd Street in central Miami Beach are the eye-catching Fontainebleau and Eden Roc. These resort-era icons created and define a style of American architecture that resists description in the standard lexicon of most critics. Vying for attention with these longtime stars is the glitzy new Ritz-Carlton Hotel, a mile or so to the south.

The Eden Roc's lobby reflects architect Morris Lapidus's unique design style.

Fontainebleau

🏔 83 C3

✉ 4441 Collins Ave.

☎ 305/538-2000 or 800/548-8886

www.fontaine bleau.com

Fontainebleau

This hotel's curves and candy-swirl rooms have been photographed by some of America's most visually acerbic documentarians. Writers have struggled to explain what it represents. (A decadent culture in decline? A time in America whose passing ought to be mourned? The Cheops of Kitsch?) Built in 1954 and recently renovated and expanded, the Fountainbleau is still going strong. Pricey, well run, and well maintained, this grande dame of hotels still impresses people as an icon of a confident, unapologetic postwar America. Others say the twin-towered, 17-story, 22-acre behemoth with 1,504 guest rooms and suites is just a big hotel prone to decorative excess. It is probably all of these—splashy, splendid, and

INSIDER TIP:

Fontainebleau and Eden Roc are several miles north of the SoBe nightlife, but their amazing (and pricey) bars and clubs are definitely worth a trip one evening.

—MATT PROPERT
National Geographic photographer

utterly unapologetic, the creation of developer Ben Novak and architect Morris Lapidus, who began his career designing department store interiors. Despite much critical bashing he has been dubbed the Architect of the American Dream.

As you approach the Fontainebleau, you pass "middle" Miami Beach's golf courses and upscale manses lining the Indian Creek waterway across Collins Avenue, along which yachts and colorful sailboats dock. If you cannot find street parking, use the hotel's garage and wander for a while, starting in the lobby with Lapidus's signature, oddly shaped decorative elements he called "woggles." The visual interest lies in these areas, where the vogue in retro American culture is attracting a younger crowd to a hotel traditionally associated with older vacationers. The faux-tropical lagoon is featured in the opening scene of the 1964 James Bond movie *Goldfinger*, in which Sean Connery surveys the fun and says, "Now, this is the life."

Eden Roc Renaissance Beach Resort & Spa

Another Morris Lapidus creation, a contemporary and rival of the adjoining Fontainebleau, the 18-story Eden Roc has perennially had to suffer the notion that it is somehow less popular, less successful, and less everything than its flamboyant Collins Avenue neighbor. The Roc's swoopy curves will forever testify to its mid-century vintage; however, its bright color scheme, a result of a multimillion-dollar makeover aimed at attracting a new generation of loyals, gives it an appeal that goes far beyond mere flamboyant. At the Fontainebleau, Lapidus's cutout ceiling holes and squiggly columns grab your attention; inside the Eden Roc it is the Caribbean palette you notice immediately upon entering the hotel's ballroom-size lobby. Throughout the 535-room resort you will encounter exuberant splashes, streaks, and explosions of color.

Ritz-Carlton, South Beach

The venerable Ritz-Carlton chain now boasts three hotels in Miami, though none of them are as stylish as the one at 1 Lincoln Road in South Beach. This impressive 375-room resort debuted after massive renovations to the DiLido, a hotel created by Lapidus. But instead of de rigueur art deco, it was designed in the art moderne style with clean lines and minimal decoration. The Ritz-Carlton features a black terrazzo floor, a "bubble wall" in the lobby, and aluminum railings along staircases. ∎

Eden Roc Renaissance Beach Resort & Spa
🅐 83 C4
✉ 4525 Collins Ave.
☎ 305/531-0000
www.edenroc miami.com

Ritz-Carlton, South Beach
🅐 See map p. 87
✉ 1 Lincoln Rd.
☎ 786/276-4000
www.ritzcarlton.com

More Places to Visit in Miami Beach

Bal Harbour

A 250-acre enclave of affluence, Bal Harbour is largely reserved for its residents. Sample the lifestyles here by browsing the Bal Harbour Shops *(9700 Collins Ave.),* a gleaming, upscale mall built on the initially unpromising site of a World War II army barracks, and dominated today by international fashion and jewelry, including Hermes, Prada, Jimmy Choo, and Tiffany and Co. In addition to all the designer labels typically associated with wealth, you can enjoy the myriad restaurants.

www.balharbourshops.com ⚑ 83 D5
☎ 305/866-0311

Haulover Beach Park

It costs nothing to enjoy the secluded soft sand, warm water, and downcoast views of South Miami Beach at Haulover Beach Park, just north of Bal Harbour. The vegetation hides apartment buildings inland, creating a sense of escape. You can rent kayaks to paddle up the nearby Oleta River.

Since 1991, nude sunbathing has been permitted at the north end of the park.

EXPERIENCE: Architectural Tours

The **Miami Design Preservation League** offers special excursions to unique neighborhoods such as Surfside. There are bus tours focusing on interior detailing, and subgenres of art deco, including tropical deco, a whimsical nod to the gorgeous streamline ocean liners like the long-gone *Bremen.* Some tours take you inside apartment buildings and private homes; others visit the district's hidden world of lushly planted private tropical gardens. For special tour descriptions, schedules, and costs, go online at *www.mdpl.org.*

(People behave quite decorously, although it sometimes attracts indiscreet gawkers.) ⚑ 83 D5 ✉ 10800 Collins Ave. ☎ 305/947-3525

North Shore State Recreation Area

Located near Surfside between 79th and 87th Streets, the North Shore State Recreation Area is a bucolic, 40-acre preserve of dunes and native sea grape. Boardwalks lead to changing rooms, picnic tables, barbecue pits, and bike paths. Lifeguards watch over those who swim.

⚑ 83 D5 ☎ 305/993-2032

Surfside & Sunny Isles

In the old-fashioned neighborhood of Surfside is the **Harding Townsite Historic District,** home to the late Yiddish scribe Isaac Bashevis Singer, who learned of his 1978 Nobel Prize for literature over breakfast at the now shuttered Sheldon's Drugstore.

A look of the past also lingers pleasantly in Sunny Isles Beach, whose vintage beachfront hotels are favored by older, longtime regulars, especially those from Miami's Russian community (see sidebar p. 74).

⚑ 83 D5

Watson Island

On Watson Island, look for **Jungle Island** *(1111 Parrot Jungle Trail, tel 305/400-7000, www.jungleisland.com, $$$$$).* The park—part of which is an aviary, filled with feathered expatriates from the world's jungles—is home to an array of mammals, primates, reptiles, and fish. It also offers daily shows featuring its denizens. Opposite Jungle Island lies the **Miami Children's Museum** *(980 MacArthur Causeway, tel 305/373-5437, www.miamichildrensmuseum.org, $$$).* Among other things, the facility features 12 galleries, classrooms, and a 200-seat auditorium.

⚑ 83 A2

Shell-strewn beaches, lush parks, and resort communities located only a few minutes from downtown Miami

Key Biscayne & Virginia Key

Hobie Cat sails and flags, Hobie Beach

Key Biscayne *&* Virginia Key

The view of Miami's skyline from the Rickenbacker Causeway is one of the best possible, although you probably won't enjoy it too much until you are off the bridge and safe on Virginia Key, where a left turn off the pavement brings you a view of the city across the water. Better yet are the Keys' long reach into Biscayne Bay, which in spite of the development along its shores remains a remarkably fertile cradle of wildlife. Venturing seaward via the causeway will cost you $1.50 (return trip included).

The palm-dotted beach at Crandon Park, Key Biscayne, is consistently rated one of America's best.

The 5.5-mile span is named for its original builder, America's leading World War I flying ace, Eddie Rickenbacker, who returned a national hero with 26 victories. He brought his aviation expertise to Miami, founded Florida Airways Corporation in 1926, and soon after launched Eastern Airlines, which for some 60 years thereafter was one of America's major carriers. He charged a toll as well, and then, as now, most considered it a bargain price for access to Greater Miami's best beaches and premier oceanside parks.

Virginia Key

The road leading north from the causeway boulevard onto Virginia Key, however, is uninviting. Few signs indicate where you are, creating the impression that you are trespassing on government or private property. When you reach Virginia Key, you will notice lengthy Hobie Beach, named for the manufacturer of the Hobie Cat— the speedy small catamaran. The beach is popular with windsurfers and stand-up paddleboarders. You can picnic here under a little palm, but this shoreline is mostly artificial and its broken coral "sand" is gritty.

In 1992, Hurricane Andrew hit Virginia Key's Atlantic-facing southeast shore especially hard, but restoration work has brought a revival. The key's southern end is home to the historic Virginia Key Beach Park, established in 1945 and once the only beach in Miami open to African Americans. Closed since the 1980s, it reopened in early 2008 after extensive renovations.

Key Biscayne

Continue south to visit the public beaches and parklands of Key Biscayne. First you'll see the complex of recreational facilities and sheltered beaches within Crandon Park—once a huge coconut plantation—which also boasts a major tennis center and stadium. Next comes Key Biscayne proper, a residential resort community where President Richard Nixon once took his leisure. Finally, at the island's rustic southernmost tip you'll enter the dune-laden shores and low thickets of 415-acre Bill Baggs Cape Florida State Park, the most remote Greater Miami retreat reachable by land. ■

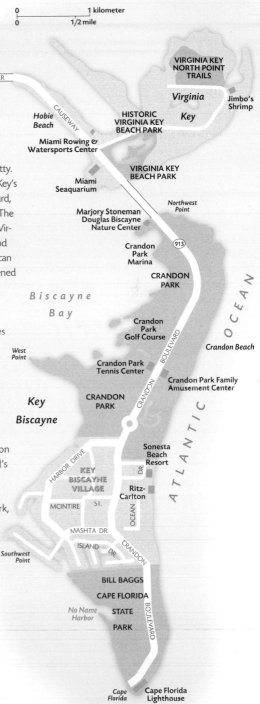

Biscayne Bay

The first Europeans to visit these isles were Spaniards commanded by Juan Ponce de León, whose ships replenished their drinking water nearby in 1513. By the 1700s, the resident Tequesta Indians had been wiped out by Old World diseases. Seagoing bandits encamped here until routed by the U.S. Navy in the 1820s. Turtle hunters and sponge fisherman worked the bay the rest of the century, while farmers had some success growing pineapples, Key limes, tomatoes, and grapefruit amid native mahogany that was logged off by the early 1900s.

A disastrous hurricane ended agriculture in 1906, leaving the offshore hummocks to serve as getaways for Miami's yachting set and, during Prohibition, hideaways for smugglers of Cuban rum. Following World War II, as development spread to the Keys, some voiced concern that the bay's coral reefs, its sea creatures and birds, and the shoreline vegetation essential to their survival were threatened. Things got so bad that a bayside garbage dump grew to 150 feet, earning it the dubious distinction of being the highest point in Dade County. Few realized that the bay was an ecosystem whose grandeur belied a fragile constitution. Few noticed the thinning of its 175 bird species, particularly cormorants and pelicans. One of those who did was Marjory Stoneman Douglas.

She devoted her life as a journalist and writer to campaigning to preserve the Everglades. She ran up her battle flag in 1947 by publishing *The Everglades: River of Grass*, a book warning of damage done by development and ill-conceived flood control projects. It rallied conservationists. When she died in 1998, aged 108, newspapers canonized her the patron saint of the Florida Everglades.

Crandon Park

Douglas expressed concern for the northern Biscayne Bay, too. It was, in her words, "one of the most important collections of natural habitats in the country." That is why the **Marjory**

Participants study a seashell on the Seagrass Adventure at the Marjory Stoneman Douglas Biscayne Nature Center.

EXPERIENCE: Paddle an Outrigger Canoe

If you're fitness-minded and looking for a fresh exercise adventure, look no further than the **Kana Lui Miami Outrigger Canoe Club** (www.kanaluimiami.com), a Virginia Key nonprofit that welcomes visitors to paddle with them for free. It is ideal. You'll not only get an intense upper-body workout but also enjoy being sprayed by cool ocean water while catching glances of downtown Miami and nature. Many times paddlers have seen sharks, dolphins, and manatees, but for sure you'll see various birds and fish.

Along the way, you'll commune with a motley group of locals of both sexes:

doctors and cooks, retirees and youths—all enjoying a water sport introduced from Hawaii. The club's regular paddlers lead it in races around Florida.

Kana Lui practices two nights a week and on Saturday mornings, for about two hours a session (you don't paddle the whole time); the website lists scheduled times. To join them for a session, wear clothes and footwear that can get wet and show up on the patch of land near the **Miami Rowing and Watersports Center** (3601 Rickenbacker Causeway), where Kana Lui is based. All ages are welcome—even toddlers, provided they can swim.

Stoneman Douglas Biscayne Nature Center at Crandon Park bears her name. It briefs visitors on the bay's natural world. One of its popular offerings is the Seagrass Adventure ($$$), a naturalist-guided walk along Key Biscayne's Atlantic shore. Participants drag nets through shallow beds of sea grass capturing a Noah's ark manifest of sea creatures: shrimp, crabs, sea cucumbers, even sea horses, which are examined and returned to the water unharmed.

Next door is **Crandon Park Marina** (tel 305/361-1281), a port for fishing boats and scuba outfitters. Down the road is 18-hole, par-72 **Crandon Golf Key Biscayne** (6700 Crandon Blvd., tel 305/361-9129, www.crandongolf.net, $$$$$ green fee). Seven saltwater lakes, many sand traps, mangrove thickets, a dogleg par-5 over-water hole,

and another flanked by water create sufficient difficulty to rate it among Florida's top public courses and make it a stop on the Senior PGA Tour. Top-seeded professionals also come to the 27-court **Crandon Park Tennis Center's** 7,500-seat stadium.

Crandon's main attraction is a 2-mile-long beach (tel 305/361-5421) consistently rated among America's top ten. The sand is soft, the water calm, the improvements many (winding promenade, picnic areas, and ample parking). The beach is what's called a lagoon-style or low-surf-impact beach, with a shoreline sloping from wading depth to about 12 feet, depending on the tide. Thirteen lifeguard stations watch over you. You can take a turn on a restored 1949 carousel at the **Crandon Family Amusement Center**. There's an old-fashioned roller rink here too, along with other vintage rides. ∎

Crandon Park
- Map p. 105
- Key Biscayne

Marjory Stoneman Douglas Biscayne Nature Center
- Map p. 105
- 6769 Crandon Blvd., Key Biscayne
- 305/361-6767
- Parking $
- www.biscaynenaturecenter.org

Bill Baggs Cape Florida State Park

No one knows how many ships lie in the shallows off the Cape of Florida, the name Ponce de León gave to the southern reach of Key Biscayne. Low, sandy, and serene, it gives no hint of the offshore perils responsible for hundreds of maritime casualties: reefs and sandbars, swift currents, shifting winds, sudden squalls, and hurricanes. In 1825, a lighthouse was put up. And though mariners argued that the faintness of its oil lamp made it likely they'd run aground trying to find it, the light signaled the beginning of South Florida's transition from a contested and dangerous frontier.

The Cape Florida Lighthouse, a lifesaving beacon since 1825, has survived war, fire, and hurricanes.

The lighthouse moves in and out of view above the trees as you approach the park, named for a *Miami Herald* newspaperman who led the campaign to have the cape designated a state preserve. Its entrance is all the more appealing for being such an abrupt departure from Key Biscayne's condo culture to what appears as a barely tamed if gentle wilderness. State policy is to manage Florida's public preserves so that they appear, to the greatest practical extent possible, as they did to the first Europeans who saw them. Today, nicely weathered wooden boardwalks insinuate themselves through vegetation to beaches stretching over a mile, and a nature walk that winds through the tall scrub.

What to See & Do

A pedestrian/bicycle **nature trail** loops through the bucolic thickets between the parking lots and the bayside seawall that protects the low-lying spit from storm surges. Starting at the park's northernmost parking area, it winds west and follows the seawall south to end near a parking area and fishing pier a short distance from the lighthouse. It's a pleasant stroll, requiring less than 30 minutes to complete the circuit.

The **lighthouse**—a white-washed, 95-foot brick tower—still warns sailors away from the watery graveyard offshore, but it did go dark for a few years. By 1836, Key Biscayne had attracted many settlers. That summer, during the Second Seminole War—an uprising against settlers' encroachments and forced relocation to Western reservations—the Seminoles struck like commandos, arriving by canoe and besieging the lighthouse, which they attempted to torch, killing one of its two caretakers. The beacon was only relighted in 1842. It was shut down again by Confederates during the Civil War until 1866. Guided tours—limited to the first ten people (over age 8) to show—are offered twice daily (*10 a.m. & 1 p.m.*), Thursday through Monday; arrive 30 minutes early to climb to the top of the beacon.

The **beach** ends by the old brick pillar. To the east, beyond a low surf of slappy waves, lies Africa; to the south, the mostly uninhabited mangrove islands of Biscayne National Park appear as low shapes on the horizon. Like Crandon Park's shore 2 miles north (see p. 107), this 1.25-mile strand has a nearly permanent place among America's top-rated beaches in tourist polls. Some people snorkel offshore under the gaze of lifeguards, scuba divers surface and submerge farther out,

INSIDER TIP:

At the Lighthouse Café, get the majuas. Small whole fish lightly dredged in spicy flour and deep fried, served with lime and Tabasco—fabulous! They aren't on the menu—you have to ask.

—JOHN DUFRESNE
Author & Florida International University professor

and families gather for cookouts in the shade of 18 covered picnic pavilions. If you'd rather not rough it, try the park's Lighthouse Café, a casual eatery with outdoor tables overlooking the ocean. The concession next door rents bikes, in-line skates, paddleboats, kayaks, and sailboards, as well as beach chairs and umbrellas.

If you arrive at the park under sail, you can drop anchor in **No Name Harbor,** where overnight mooring (*$$$$*) is available, and pay a visit to the lighthouse. ∎

Bill Baggs Cape Florida State Park
- Map p. 105
- 1200 S. Crandon Blvd.
- 305/361-5811
- $$

www.floridastateparks.org/capeflorida

Hobie Beach to Key Biscayne

Although Hobie Beach is neither secluded nor particularly pretty, its convenience makes it a popular family destination and draws hundreds to its picnic tables. One result is that the stretch of land between the Rickenbacker Causeway and Key Biscayne's residential midsection is a bazaar of rental conveyances. You'll find concessionaires eager to rent you a bicycle, a windsurfer or stand-up paddleboard, a Jet Ski, and, up the road at the Key Biscayne Marina, even a sailboat large enough to sleep an entourage of friends.

The sheltered yet open waters of Biscayne Bay make for delightful sailing when the wind is up.

Hobie Beach
⛰ Map p. 105

Steady breezes make Hobie Beach, on the Biscayne Bay side of Virginia Key, an excellent place to windsurf. No one says this wonderful pastime is easy to learn or easy to pursue, but the nice part is that it isn't dangerous, and even if you fall over (which you will, often) you always have something buoyant to grab on to. If you have a neoprene wet suit or vest, bring it.

The sea bottom here is a maritime cemetery, and its warm shallow waters make wreck diving comfortable and safe. On Key Biscayne, wreck dives are a main entrée on the day-trip menu of Divers Paradise (*4000 Crandon Blvd., tel 305/361-3483, www.keydivers.com*), scuba outfitters doing business out of the Crandon Park Marina (see p. 107).

Biscayne Bay, whose barrier islands block Atlantic surges, is ideal for would-be mariners. Take a sailing lesson: During a one-hour introductory sail you'll be at the tiller immediately. A great school, for both able-bodied and disabled participants, is Shake-A-Leg Miami *(2620 South Bayshore Dr., tel 305/858-5550, www.shakealegmiami.org)*, which operates out of Coconut Grove just across Biscayne Bay. It teaches basic skills and fundamentals, including boat dynamics, boat safety, tacking and jibing, and reading the weather and the environment. Individual instruction is available with reservations and is tailored to the needs and schedules of participants.

Miami Seaquarium

When the resident orcas—black and white carnivores also known as killer whales—blast up from the Seaquarium's huge saltwater pools at the behest of young trainers, arc through the air with a ponderous grace, and belly flop back into their blue world, you realize immediately that they are awesome, powerful, and extremely intelligent. They are the stars, along with a supporting cast of performing sea lions and porpoises, and a group of manatees, of Miami Seaquarium, a long-standing attraction. The 38-acre complex includes some interesting marine life exhibits, including a coral reef habitat. During Miami's hot and muggy low season, consider taking in an evening show.

Virginia Key Beach Park

Miami is one of the most diverse U.S. cities, so it's hard to believe racial segregation was once enforced here. Virginia Key Beach opened in 1945 as the city's only beach "for the exclusive use of Negroes," where they could swim, sunbathe, barbecue, and play games. By the early 1960s blacks were allowed at any beach in Miami and in the 1980s the so-called "Colored Beach" closed.

For decades, few residents and tourists speeding over the Rickenbacker Causeway to Key Biscayne realized that Virginia Key was a cultural treasure trove. In 2002, it was added to the National Register of Historic Places.

The beach reopened in 2008. In addition to relaxing under the sun, people of all races can stroll the boardwalk to one of the country's oldest surviving coastal mangrove communities. On weekends and holidays, parkgoers can ride the vintage carousel and a replica of the park's mini-train.

Miami Seaquarium

Map p. 105

4400 Rickenbacker Causeway, Virginia Key

305/361-5705,

$$$

www.miami
seaquarium.com

Virginia Key Beach Park

Map p. 105

4020 Virginia Beach Dr., Virginia Key

305/960-4600

$ (weekends & holidays)

www.virginiakey
beachpark.net

Scenes for many movies and television series have been filmed at Jimbo's Shrimp.

Jimbo's Shrimp

 Map p. 105

✉ Duck Lake Rd.,
Virginia Key

☎ 305/361-7026

www.jimbosplace.com

Jimbo's Shrimp

No one puts in a longer day than the fishermen who mine Florida waters for *Crago vulgaris,* the edible variety of the backward-swimming marine decapods called shrimp. Shrimpers are to South Florida what truffle hunters are to France; among the most distinguished in Miami's shrimper society is James Luznar—aka Jimbo—for more than half a century the proprietor of Jimbo's Shrimp, hidden on an overgrown mangrove channel on Virginia Key.

Begun as a trawler base for off-loading catches, Jimbo's evolved into a beer joint with a bocce ball court and a salmon smokehouse, where fillets are smoked to perfection for restaurants and anyone who finds their way here. Though it may appear to be a squatter's camp, as you'll see, this is a picturesque backwater. Buy a piece of salmon, along with a beer to cut its oily aftertaste, sit down outside at the picnic table, and enjoy the conversation with Jim and his weathered cronies. If Jimbo challenges you to a game of bocce, don't play for high stakes, for he rarely loses. ∎

Mountain Biking on Virginia Key

The **Virginia Key North Point Trails** *(4201 Rickenbacker Causeway, www .virginiakeybicycleclub.com, $$)* mountain bike park occupies Virginia Key Park land at the northern tip of Virginia Key. Opened in 2011, it has quickly become a popular new site for exercising outdoors in Greater Miami.

The 7-mile trail system was designed for novice, intermediate, and hard-core riders. On many of the ten trails, dense foliage makes pedalers feel like they're in a different realm, although occasional openings present views of the urban jungle across Biscayne Bay. The foliage also provides important shading from the sun's intense heat and short-term relief from rain showers. Mountain bikers also relish the trails' twists and hills, which are rare for an otherwise flat city.

Even if you do not ride the trails, while driving from Miami to Virginia Key's Miami Seaquarium you'll likely see cyclists and runners. They trudge up the Rickenbacker Causeway, the city's highest point, for much-needed "hill work."

Miami's first suburb, created in 1873 by pioneers attracted by the offer of free farmland along Biscayne Bay

Coconut Grove & Beyond

Stairwell, Vizcaya Museum & Gardens

Coconut Grove & Beyond

In 1873, pioneers attracted by the offer of free farmland settled along Biscayne Bay and applied for a post office charter under the name of Cocoanut Grove, creating Miami's first suburb. Rural somnolence characterized life here until the arrival of Henry Flagler's trains in Miami, which brought winter tourists in numbers. Typically, many vacationers came back to live. Their homes were often built by a community of Bahamian craftsmen who brought shipbuilding and carpentry skills, along with their families, from the British islands.

An English couple, Charles and Isabella Peacock, opened Cocoanut Grove's first hotel, the Bay View House, in 1884. By the mid-1890s Cocoanut Grove had a yacht club, setting a tone of affluent leisure that still marks the community, while at the same time acquiring a curious cosmopolitan cross section of people: Northern industrialists, expatriate European nobles, displaced Southerners seeking to reestablish themselves after the Civil War, and a community of Bahamian fishermen, who, along with their home-building countrymen, established a Little Bahama district they named Kebo.

Cocoanut Grove lost its "a" in the new century, but retained the small village character that set it apart, then and now, from the mercantile style of central Miami. That distinction is perhaps the main reason why residents of the Grove—as the locals call it—will say they live in Coconut Grove rather than Miami, even though the Grove was incorporated into

Greater Miami in 1923. The Grove's boundaries are indistinct, but its visual trademarks include large, handsome old coral rock homes set back from Brickell Avenue on sweeping lawns; lush overgrowth that gives residential side streets an air of landscaped seclusion; and luxury condominiums in the shape of Maya temples overlooking forests of sailboat masts at Dinner Key Marina, where the last Pan Am "clipper" flying boats took to the air for South America.

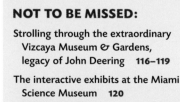

The most scenic route of entry from Downtown Miami is via either Brickell or South Miami Avenues south from downtown, past the entrance to the Rickenbacker Causeway, where the two streets merge to form South Bayshore. The route takes you along a curving, palm-lined boulevard with sudden flashes of blue—views across sweeping park lawns to Biscayne Bay. The high-rises to the inland side of Bayshore comprise some of Miami's most sought-after accommodations: architecturally distinguished condominium homes whose quality of design set standards for luxury cooperative homeowning across America.

Touring the Grove

If you tour Coconut Grove by car you will inevitably find your way to its busy central shopping district, dominated by a three-level, courtyard-style complex of shops, cafés, boutiques, and bistros known as the CocoWalk. The spectrum of quality is broad, from kitsch to collectible, with haute couture

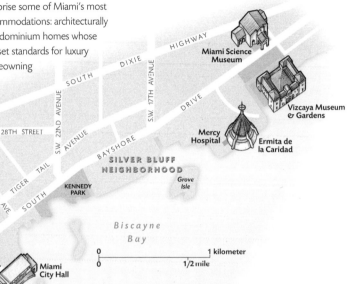

the rule in the Grove's other shopping center, the Mayfair in the Grove. CocoWalk restaurants reflect Greater Miami's diversity, their menus offering Caribbean, Cuban, and Central and South American fare, as well as mainstream French and Italian cuisine.

At the end of the day, it's the Grove's mixture of leisure and garden-variety languor that is most appealing. Among the moneyed Northerners who were attracted by this spirit to build mansions along Brickell Avenue at the turn of the last century, none were more moneyed and lavish and entranced with South Florida living than industrialist James Deering. His Vizcaya estate and gardens are the ultimate expression of the desire for an exotic tropical escape that has drawn millions to Florida. ∎

Vizcaya Museum & Gardens

Once a solitary man's private retreat, Vizcaya opens its gates to around 185,000 people every year. In 1994 it hosted receptions for the 34 heads of state attending the Summit of the Americas, rivaling in opulence the national palaces of all. Yet it remains a personal place, a fantasy unlike any other, save perhaps William Randolph Hearst's Enchanted Hill at San Simeon in California.

Vizcaya Museum & Gardens
- 🗺 Map p. 115
- ✉ 3251 S. Miami Ave.
- ☎ 305/250-9133
- 🕐 Closed Tues.
- 💲 $$$

www.vizcaya museum.org

James Deering was a retired vice president of the International Harvester Company, whose tractors and farm machinery rattled across American farmlands in tens of thousands. He was also an heir to the company, which was founded by his father. A bachelor immersed in a consuming fascination with the European Renaissance, James had enough wealth to do what he pleased. He purchased 180 acres on the water in north Coconut Grove, and commissioned three classically trained architects to build a Renaissance Italian villa and formal garden such as he'd seen on his European odysseys, along with a functioning northern Italian-style village to house his employees. He wanted the villa to appear as if it had been here since the 16th century, occupied by successive generations of an Italian noble family. For its name he chose a Basque word describing the site, which gently inclined to overlook Biscayne Bay from a low rise: Vizcaya ("an elevated place").

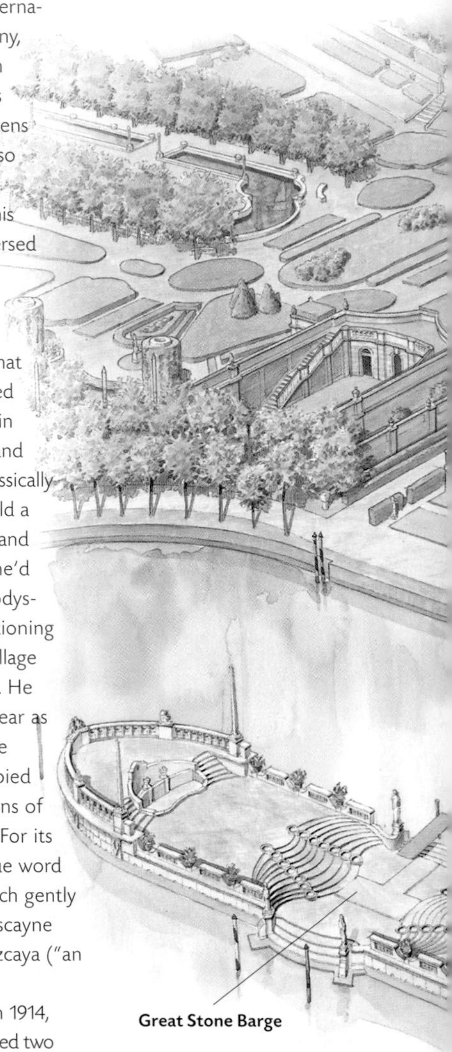

Construction began in 1914, and when it was completed two

Great Stone Barge

years later, in time for Deering to celebrate Christmas there, his guests were astonished at what an army of 1,000 workers—10 percent of Miami's population then—had built. Deering led them through a three-story palace of 34 rooms filled with treasures ranging from the 15th century through the 19th—furniture, tapestries, rugs, wall panels, ceilings, mantels, door cases, wrought iron, sculptures, and paintings. The villa's sturdy reinforced concrete skeleton was hidden behind painted stucco and limestone. Outside, cut from mangrove and hardwood jungle, was a terraced 10-acre garden mixing the styles of 16th- and 17th-century Italian hillside estates with those

Courtyard

Entrance

South Terrace

Dining Room

Music Room

East Hall

Sitting Room

Living Room

Vizcaya Museum & Gardens

of 17th-century France, a serene place of dripping fountains, with a reflecting pool and statuary walks that would not be fully completed until 1921. Offshore, flanked by two piers (one a yacht landing, the other a teahouse), was an ornately carved island, called the Great Stone Barge, recalling the coronation gondolas of Venetian princes. Maintaining all this was a staff of domestic workers living in second-floor chambers and in the Italian village, which included a farm with livestock. A concealed private telephone system permitted the mogul and his majordomos to orchestrate his elaborate world of nearly real make-believe.

Deering's health, however, was poor, often leaving him so weary that he rarely attended the suppers served to guests on Vizcaya's gold-trimmed china. His beloved barony was barely completed when he died in 1925, leaving a few staff members to look after it for his heirs. A violent hurricane hit Miami the following year, devastating the city and badly damaging the villa and its gardens. Over time the deteriorating estate became too much for Deering's inheritors, who sold off all but 28 acres. In 1952 they gave it to Dade County in exchange for one million dollars in revenue bonds, and made the county a gift of the villa's art and furnishings. Succeeding decades brought extensive restoration work, including a glass enclosure to seal off the villa's open court so that the house and its contents could be preserved by a climate and humidity control system. Hurricanes Katrina and Wilma in 2005 devastated Vizcaya, though its recovery has been remarkable.

Ermita de la Caridad

Just south of the estate entrance, near Mercy Hospital, you'll find one of the city's more affecting monuments to the "loss" of Cuba—a point of view that even after more than 50 years keeps Miami's displaced Cubans ready to return to the island at a moment's notice to demand the return of confiscated property.

They were the force behind this 90-foot-high conical shrine, called Ermita de la Caridad (Hermitage of Charity; *map p. 113, 3609 S. Miami Ave., tel 305/854-2404*). It is intended to resemble a beacon and is designed so that those who attend daily Mass here face Cuba. A mural above the shrine's circular base depicts Cuba's ever turbulent history. The shrine occupies a pretty, serene piece of Deering's former hideaway, and it looks out on a typically beguiling stretch of Biscayne Bay—making it a lovely spot to take a meditative break.

Exploring Vizcaya

The best way to explore this great house and its gardens, a national historic landmark, is in the company of a guide *(tours offered four times daily),* who can tell you all about the place, imparting not only the information but also the spirit that created it all in a brisk 45-minute tour. If you prefer to wander on your own, get a copy of the "Museum and Gardens Guide & Map," which has floor plans, a suggested tour route, and detailed descriptions. Highlights you should not miss:

The **Entrance Hall,** whose wallpaper panels were printed

The lavishly decorated Music Room, where many concerts for guests were held

from wood blocks and hand-colored in Paris in 1814.

The **Reception Room's** tinted plaster ceiling, from a Venetian palace.

The **Living Room's** 16th-century fireplace, 2,000-year-old Roman marble tripod, and an extremely rare 15th-century Spanish carpet, one of only a few known to exist.

In the **East Hall,** a 15th-century Italian coffered ceiling of terra-cotta heraldic tiles.

Painted wall and ceiling panels in the **Music Room,** with decorations from the Milanese palace of a noble Italian family, the Borromeos, whose son Carlo, a priest, is a Catholic saint.

Two 16th-century tapestries in the **Dining Room,** once belonging to poets Robert and Elizabeth Barrett Browning, that depict the life of Hermes, messenger of the Roman gods. The marble table in the room is Roman, from the first century A.D.

In the **Tea Room,** gates of bronze and wrought iron opening into the courtyard, another treasure that was originally part of a Venetian palace.

The **Butler's Pantry,** considered state of the art in 1916, where Vizcaya's formal china and crystal are displayed.

The **Manin Room,** which is decorated in the style of 19th-century Austria.

The **Pantaloon Room,** reflecting the cheerful bucolic styles of 18th-century Venice.

The **Vizcaya Café,** a modern amenity with little of the villa's opulence, is nevertheless a pleasant place to rest after climbing stairways and walking in gardens. The gift shop sells Italian crafts including ceramics and jewelry. On occasion the garden is open for moonlight tours, from 6 p.m. ■

Miami Science Museum

Miami parents seeking to introduce their children to the world of the new take them to the Miami Science Museum, a double bill of natural history and cosmic mystery situated near the Vizcaya estate, just south of the Rickenbacker Causeway entrance.

A bald eagle at the Falcon Batchelor Bird of Prey Center

Miami Science Museum

 Map p. 115

✉ 3280 S. Miami Ave.

☎ 305/646-4200

$ $$$

www.miamisci.org

National traveling exhibits start with the basics—gravity, light, sound—and work up from low- to high-tech. The orientation is toward the young; adults without kids in tow might find it shallow. But there's still much of interest for everyone here.

One of the museum's permanent exhibits is "Smithsonian Expeditions: Exploring Latin America and the Caribbean," in which children discover rare treasures just like Indiana Jones. Children also gravitate toward a second permanent exhibit, "Newton's Notions: Force, Motion & You."

The **Miami Planetarium** features daily classic star shows in its 65-foot-high dome, where you can recline in the dark and watch the constellations move and the universe evolve. On the first Friday of the month the museum puts on a laser light show set to the tunes of Pink Floyd, the Beatles, Bob Marley, and other musicians. Come Friday night, weather permitting, the museum hosts free telescopic viewing. (Call first to find out what the celestial target is, as it changes regularly.)

To its credit, the museum also focuses attention on South Florida's natural world, keeping a menagerie of creatures on display at its small wildlife center. In addition, the **Falcon Batchelor Bird of Prey Center** houses and rehabilitates injured eagles, ospreys, hawks, owls, and falcons that have been rescued from the wild.

Note: The museum is slated to move in early 2015 to a new downtown Miami location currently under construction, Museum Park. ∎

Energy Tracker

Throughout Miami Science Museum you'll find hands-on, interconnected exhibits showcasing energy. One of the most popular is "Energy Dance Floor." When kids and adults alike bounce around on it, the floor captures and then converts their energy to electricity that powers colorful lighting pulsing around them. The exhibit includes a second dance floor whose thermal camera shows dancers' energy escaping their bodies as heat.

Around Coconut Grove

Ask directions to the heart of the Grove, and a knowledgeable guide will direct you to South Bayshore Drive's roundabout union with Main Highway at Grand Avenue. This central district is a dense concentration of restaurants, shops, and small businesses that's easy to explore on foot. Fans of CocoWalk bazaar at Virginia Street and Grand Avenue claim this multilevel carnival of food, drink, and fashion is the Grove's true center. So do those who depend upon the continued success of the nearby Mayfair in the Grove mall.

Away from the Grove's retail hub, however, you may find it more practical to explore by car.

Architectural Highlights

Visit the **Silver Bluff Neighborhood** along South Bayshore Drive, where the blocks numbered from 1600 through 2100 hold architecturally distinctive residences designed in the decade following World War I. Look for the limestone outcropping—a spur of the Atlantic coastal ridge once trod by the creatures whose bones lie within the Deering Estate (see p. 138). A short distance south, at 2484 South Bayshore, is a handsome Mediterranean Revival manse built in 1923, now owned by the Coral Reef Yacht Club.

Search out the cottages built during the 19th-century flowering of Coconut Grove's Bahamian community, which survive along **Charles Avenue** (bet. S.W. 37th Ave. & Main Hwy.). They are of a long, narrow design, with rooms opening off a side hall running from front to back.

Make your way to one of the Grove's most splendid architectural antiques, the stone mission-style **Plymouth Congregational Church** near Main Highway

(see p. 138).

EXPERIENCE: Run or Walk a 5K or the Miami Marathon

If you want to keep your competitive foot forward while on vacation, there's no better place to find a 5K run/walk than Miami–Dade County. In recent years, charity run/walks and endurance races have multiplied in the county. Because winter is the region's dry and cool season, most occur from November to April, with nearly every weekend featuring a run/walk. If you're looking for something a little longer, plan your vacation around the annual ING Miami Marathon and Half Marathon It takes place in January. In 2011, 17,000 people ran the marathon, which coursed through Coconut Grove, downtown Miami, and Miami Beach. Visit www.active.com (and search for Miami) or www.runmiami.com for more information and schedules of races.

(3400 Devon Rd., tel 305/444-6521, www.plymouthmiami.com). It is the handiwork of a Spanish mason, finished in 1917 when the California-inspired vogue was sweeping the country. Note the church door, hard-carved from walnut planks laid upon oak, taken from a 17th-century monastery in the Pyrenees. Its 11-acre grounds include a rectory, completed in 1926, and Dade County's first public schoolhouse, a one-roomer

CocoWalk
- Map p. 115
- Virginia St. & Grand Ave.

www.cocowalk.com

Mayfair in the Grove
- Map p. 115
- Mary St. & Grand Ave.

Barnacle Historic State Park

⬛ Map p. 115

✉ 3485 Main Hwy.

☎ 305/442-6866

🕐 Closed Tues.–Thurs.

$ $

www.floridastate
parks.org/
thebarnacle

built in 1887 with wood salvaged from shipwrecks. It was moved here in 1970 from its original site near the Peacock Inn (which did not survive).

It's easy to miss, but you should try to visit the **Barnacle Historic State Park,** a 5-acre patch of native Florida hardwood surrounding the beautifully crafted 1891 home of pioneer and master boatbuilder Ralph Middleton Munroe. Many of Miami's residential architects consider it a shrine to thoughtful design. Munroe, whose grandfather manufactured America's first lead pencils, anchored the house against hurricanes by sinking a termite-proofed, pine log foundation deep into the earth, and gave it extra strength by using stout beams salvaged from shipwrecks and bolted to the foundation. Tours of the house *(at 10 a.m., 11:30 a.m., 1 p.m., & 2:30 p.m., $)*

reveal that the two-story house was originally a bungalow, until Munroe jacked it up in 1908 and added a level beneath it. Note the unusual roof structure, whose skylights are opened by ropes and pulleys to boost circulation and vent warm air; it reminded the Biscayne Bay Yacht Club founder of a barnacle attached to a hull.

Diagonally across the street from the Barnacle is another notable attraction. The Spanish-flavored building started out in 1927 as a movie theater, but in the 1950s thespian-minded folk converted it to the **Coconut Grove Playhouse** *(3500 Main Hwy.).* They demonstrated its high standards in 1956 by mounting the first U.S. performance of Samuel Beckett's *Waiting for Godot.* The struggling theater closed in April 2006 due to sizable debts. While revitalization is being debated, its fate is uncertain. ∎

Despite CocoWalk's wealth of shops and restaurants, Coconut Grove retains a small-town ambience.

Miami City Hall

Miami City Hall is housed in the old Pan American marine terminal on Dinner Key, a vestige of one of the most romantic eras in American air travel, the time of the great flying boats. Built in the art deco style, the building characterizes the romance and luxury that Pan American Airways promised the passengers aboard its "clippers."

Pan Am's founder, Juan Trippe, determined to build a global airline second to none in service, luxury, and panache, commissioned the New York architectural firm of Delano & Aldrich, designers of New York's elegant La Guardia Marine Air Terminal, to create another art deco masterpiece at Dinner Key. The champagne corks popped on May 27, 1934, and reporters rushed to declare it the "most beautiful marine air transport base in the world," and it was.

Step Back in Time

Though today you turn off South Bayshore Drive and follow Pan American Drive to the terminal (which has served as Miami City Hall since 1954), Dinner Key, as its name suggests, was once an island. In 1917, Navy engineers filled in the channel separating it from the shore to create a seaplane base.

Park at the bottom of the circular drive and walk across the lawn to the historical marker and its account of Dinner Key's past. Look across the channel at the hangars, now a boatyard, that housed the clippers and admire the terminal building's horizontal lines. The row of globes that once framed Pan American World Airways now flank Miami City Hall.

Enter City Hall's lobby, once an airy waiting room, to see a floor mosaic of the globe. In 2001–2003, the building underwent an extensive renovation that returned the old terminal back to aviation's pioneering days of the 1920s and 1930s. At the far end of the room hangs the original Pan Am clock.

INSIDER TIP:

The restored lobby is amazing. You can now see how it looked in 1934, with murals of birds, early seaplanes, and Leonardo da Vinci's flying ship. Also look up to see the muraled ceiling.

—PAUL GEORGE
*Professor of history,
Miami-Dade College*

Behind the building, palm trees rustle beside the shimmering blue water in the channel opening out to the Caribbean, where the first clippers journeyed from Key West to Havana, flying without radios but with carrier pigeons ready to fly away for help in case of a ditching. As you think about that, this place takes on a peculiar and wholly pleasant timelessness. ∎

Miami City Hall
- Map p. 115
- 3500 Pan American Dr.
- 305/250-5300
- Closed Sat.–Sun.

Main Highway to Old Cutler Road

The drive south from Vizcaya is memorable for its subtropical sights: residential neighborhoods sunk in vines and overflowing with bougainvillea; mangrove channels reaching inland like crooked fingers, hiding little marinas and waterside houses; wonderfully exuberant arboretums such as the Fairchild Tropical Botanic Garden; and beautifully designed bayside public parks such as Matheson Hammock, where you can picnic by Biscayne Bay in the shade of a palm tree.

The Biltmore's spire, modeled after Seville's Giralda, reflects its builder's lifelong fascination with Spanish antiquity.

Main Highway to Old Cutler Road
⚑ Map p. 115

Although it's hard to get lost if you stay close to the bay shore, taking along a road map will alert you to turnoffs and let you better plan your exploration. From Vizcaya, take South Bayshore Drive south to central Coconut Grove, where it enters a kind of roundabout of streets and turns into Main Highway.

Near Coconut Grove's southern boundary, beside a lagoon at 4013 Douglas Road, is a home built in the 1870s to emulate an Indonesian retreat. Known as the **Kampong,** the inspiration of the brother of early Coconut Grove hotelier Charles Peacock, it eventually passed into the hands of David Fairchild, founder of the Fairchild Tropical Botanic Garden, who landscaped the home with exotic flora. Today, the Kampong functions as a tropical plant research site. Although it is private, guided tours are offered on Wednesdays and Saturdays *(tel 305/445-8076).*

Continue down Ingraham Highway until it merges with Le Jeune Road, along the way passing by lovely secluded residential neighborhoods. Turn off onto any street and you'll find houses that epitomize an ideal image of South Florida living, many of them hidden behind overgrown walls.

Ingraham becomes Old Cutler Road, which leads on to **Matheson Hammock Park** *(map 135 D4; see p. 137)* and the **Fairchild Tropical Botanic Garden** *(map 135 D4; see p. 136).* Just south, Old Cutler comes to a T-junction at Red Road (also Fla. 959).

This is a good place to begin your return journey. Turn right (north) onto Red Road, and let it take you back 5 miles into the heart of Coral Gables, where the spire of the **Biltmore Hotel** *(map p. 127; see p. 129)* rises above the City Beautiful. ∎

A former citrus grove turned utopian subdivision of Mediterranean Revival houses, the 1921 brainchild of George E. Merrick

Coral Gables

Detail from an Edouard Duval-Carrié
triptych, Lowe Art Museum

Coral Gables

Miami's land boom was running at full throttle in the 1920s, and in five years George Merrick's Coral Gables claimed 10,000 acres. He opened the luxurious Biltmore Hotel, its great Spanish-Moorish tower and buildings rising grandly above Anastasia Avenue like a king's palace. A towered building with a 40-foot arch was put up at the city's Douglas Road entrance, making it clear to visitors that they were entering a special place.

Merrick called his creation the City Beautiful, and it was: with broad streets connecting broad plazas, public amenities such as the gorgeous Venetian Pool on De Soto Boulevard, and a fantasy of waterfalls and grottoes. Those who bought homes here became zealous apostles, keeping their lawns manicured, trees trimmed, and sidewalks swept clean, while urging friends to join them. It was a vision of utopia, it was real, and it lasted, surviving the collapse of the Florida land boom right up to the present day.

Merrick would be proud. Coral Gables' houses are still every bit as desirable, sought after by buyers who make up the affluent core of the city's 46,500 residents. Its corporate residents include over 140 of the biggest and most important businesses and financial institutions in South Florida. The 260-acre University of Miami's Coral Gables campus counts some 15,500 students and a faculty of 1,500, and has an unusually rich repository of fine art and antiquities at its Lowe Art Museum.

NOT TO BE MISSED:

Wandering around the historic
Biltmore Hotel **129**

A swim in the Venetian Pool, South
Florida's prettiest public pool **130**

Window-shopping along the Miracle
Mile **131**

The priceless masterpieces
on display in the Lowe Art
Museum **132**

Exploring Coral Gables

Coral Gables' 12 square miles are bounded on the east by Douglas Road (S.W. 37th Ave.) and on the west by Red Road (S.W. 57th Ave.). Its northern boundary line is the Tamiami Trail (S.W. 8th St.), and its southern frontier traces Sunset Avenue (S.W. 72nd St.) and Old Cutler Road, putting Coral Gables' southeast corner close to Biscayne Bay and its shoreline tropical gardens.

Coral Gables' streets are legendary for being confusing. You will probably get lost here, so your only hope is to use a map. The Chamber of Commerce (224 Catalonia Ave., tel 305/446-1657, closed Sat.–Sun.) stocks an array of brochures, including the city's official map. Another excellent source of where-to-go, what-to-see information and advice is the staff at the city's Department of Historic Preservation (405 Biltmore Way, tel 305/460-5216), who occupy a small office in City Hall during weekday business hours. Ask about architectural brochures and booklets that may be in stock.

Mediterranean Revival architecture dominates Coral Gables, but other exotics bloomed here, too. Sloped tile roofs distinguish the Chinese Village on Riviera Drive at Menendez Avenue. The rural residences of 17th-century Dutch South African colonials are re-created at Maya Street and Le Jeune Road. Antique French urbanity is revived on Hardee Avenue at Maggiore Street, and the tastes of Normandy dress up Le Jeune Road at Vizcaya Avenue. Italian village life is the theme on Altara Avenue at Monserrate Street, and on Santa Maria Street, houses in the Colonial Village celebrate Miami's Yankee heritage. ■

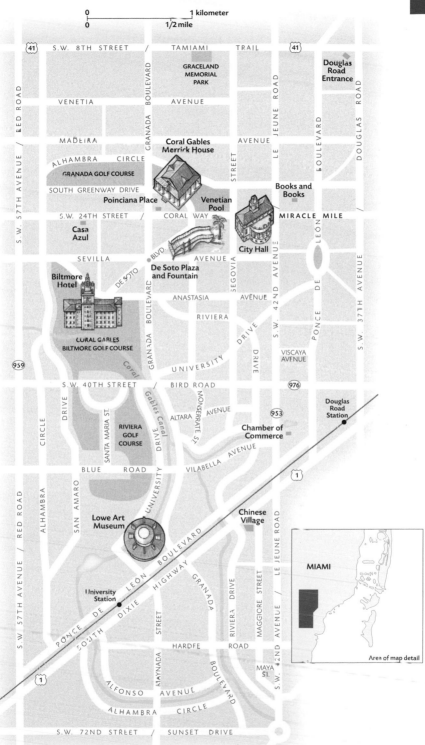

0   1 kilometer
0   1/2 mile

41   S.W. 8TH STREET /   TAMIAMI   TRAIL   41

GRACELAND
MEMORIAL
PARK

Douglas
Road
Entrance

VENETIA   AVENUE

RED ROAD

GRANADA   BOULEVARD

LE JEUNE ROAD

BOULEVARD

DOUGLAS ROAD

MADEIRA

Coral Gables
Merrick House

AVENUE

LE JEUNE STREET

S.W. 57TH AVENUE /

ALHAMBRA   CIRCLE

GRANADA GOLF COURSE

SOUTH GREENWAY DRIVE

Poinciana Place

Venetian
Pool

Books and
Books

S.W. 24TH STREET /   CORAL WAY

MIRACLE MILE

Casa
Azul

SEVILLA

BLVD.

DE SOTO

City Hall

AVENUE

PONCE DE LEON

S.W. 37TH AVENUE

Biltmore
Hotel

De Soto Plaza
and Fountain

ANASTASIA   AVENUE

RIVIERA

SEGOVIA

S.W. 42ND AVENUE

CORAL GABLES
BILTMORE GOLF COURSE

UNIVERSITY   DRIVE

DRIVE

VISCAYA
AVENUE

Coral

GRANADA BOULEVARD

Gables Canal

959

CIRCLE

DRIVE

SANTA MARIA ST.

RIVIERA
GOLF
COURSE

S.W. 40TH STREET /   BIRD ROAD

MONSERRATE ST.

ALTARA   AVENUE

976

953

Douglas
Road
Station

Chamber of
Commerce

BLUE   ROAD

VILABELLA   AVENUE

1

RED ROAD

ALHAMBRA

SAN AMARO

UNIVERSITY

Lowe Art
Museum

Chinese
Village

LE JEUNE ROAD

MIAMI

S.W. 57TH AVENUE /   RED ROAD

University
Station

PONCE DE LEON   SOUTH DIXIE HIGHWAY

BOULEVARD

GRANADA

STREET

RIVIERA DRIVE

MAGGIORE STREET

S.W. 42ND AVENUE

Area of map detail

MAYNADA

HARDEE   ROAD

MAYA
ST.

1

ALFONSO   AVENUE

BOULEVARD

ALHAMBRA   CIRCLE

S.W. 72ND STREET /   SUNSET DRIVE

Coral Gables Merrick House

The 19th century was coming to an end, and Solomon Merrick, a New England Congregational minister turned Florida homesteader—and father of George Merrick, the visionary behind Coral Gables—wanted his family to have a proper residence. Their avocado and citrus orchards were flourishing, and there was money to do it right.

From this once rural family home of coral rock came the name for George Merrick's dream city.

Coral Gables Merrick House

- Map p. 127
- 907 Coral Way, bet. Toledo St. & Granada Blvd.
- 305/460-5361
- Open Wed. & Sun. 1 p.m.– 4 p.m.; or by appt.
- $

Solomon's wife, Althea, sketched the house's design: a slanted tiled roof with prominent gables topping columns and walls of termite-resistant Dade County pine and keystone, the coral rock underlying this part of the county. She circled the building with a veranda and added classical details to entrances and windows. When the house was completed in 1906, they called it Coral Gables. It was the start of one of America's first planned communities.

Today the house the Merricks built is a community shrine, used for meetings, lectures, and receptions. The building, not its few furnishings, is the reason to visit. Some of the Merricks' original fruit trees still grow in the garden. You can wander about on your own, or join a guided tour (*offered on the hour*). ■

INSIDER TIP:

George Merrick's boyhood home—a handsome coral rock structure—will give you a feel for life in South Florida in the early 20th century.

—THOMAS SWICK
Travel writer

Biltmore Hotel

Since his childhood, George Merrick intended to be a writer, living an artist's life among the Iberian castles he had seen in picture books. He got his Spanish castle in 1926 when he opened the Biltmore. He rejected perfectly good U.S.-made "Spanish" roof tiles, importing thousands from Spain because they were authentic, and he paid the same wonderfully stubborn attention to details throughout, determined that his hotel would rival anything in Europe.

When you enter its vast lobby you sense the intensity of his ambition—a 8,500-square-foot room, with ceilings 45 feet high and massive stone columns. The detail is also in keeping: tropical songbirds in an ornate cage, bellhops quietly moving luggage, telephones muted.

Merrick's castle soon faltered, however, as a result of a brutal hurricane, the collapse of Florida's land boom, the 1929 market crash, and the Depression. In 1941, the Army moved in, turning suites where Bing Crosby, Judy Garland, and the Duke and Duchess of Windsor had stayed into wards for the wounded. The Biltmore remained a military hospital until the 1960s, barely escaping demolition. Eventually added to the National Register of Historic Places, it was reopened in 1992 after a multimillion-dollar renovation. Two years later it hosted the presidents and prime ministers attending the Summit of the Americas, acquitting itself impeccably and announcing that life truly can begin at 70.

Biltmore Decadence

You don't have to be a guest to experience some of its finer points. Enjoy Sunday brunch in the central Fontana restaurant,

a sumptuous affair with roving flamenco guitarists and fountains doing what fountains do best. Marvel at the 22,000-square-foot pool; better yet, drop by the ground-level fitness center to check the menu of nonguest packages, which include access to the water. Play a round on the 18-hole, par-71, championship golf course. And relax in the hotel's many lounges, redolent with luxury and ambience.

At night the Biltmore's 18-story tower is softly illuminated, rising above Coral Gables' neighborhoods like a benevolent feudal castle. Looking at it, you wonder who builds such places. The answer is, no one anymore. ∎

Biltmore Hotel
 Map p. 127
✉ 1200 Anastasia Ave.
☎ 305/445-1926 or 800/915-1926
www.biltmore hotel.com

Merrick's Ambition

Called home from college to manage the family's 3,000-acre tract of citrus and pineland following his father's death, George Merrick married Eunice Peacock. They created a salon of artists and dreamed of creating a city that would have the sophistication and beauty of the European places that fired their imaginations.

Venetian Pool

There are swimming pools, and then there are swimming pools. This is one of the latter, the prettiest public splash-o-rama in South Florida. The pool began as an ugly duckling: a hole in the ground left by stonemasons quarrying limestone for Coral Gables' construction.

An abandoned quarry in central Coral Gables became Greater Miami's most fanciful swimming pool.

Venetian Pool

- Map p. 127
- 2701 De Soto Blvd.
- 305/460-5306
- Closed Dec.– Jan.
- $$–$$$

www.thevenetian
pool.com

NOTE: No children under age three allowed.

Artist and designer Denman Fink and architect Phineas Paist, who built much of the city, had a choice: Either fill it up or find a use for it. The creative pair concocted a Venetian fantasy of diving platforms, waterfalls, cave grottoes, street lamps faithfully modeled on those in the fabled City of Canals, an observation tower, and an island connected to the pool deck by a graceful arch-bridge. It opened in 1924, and everything is still lovely, including the pool's tilework and the vine-draped Italianate loggia.

During the 1920s, the Venetian Pool was used as a showcase for beauty pageants and fancy parties. There's a nice selection of vintage photos here to prove it. Until 1986, the unfiltered pool was drained nightly, then refilled with 820,000 gallons of fresh artesian well water. These days, the water is recycled through a natural filtration system.

Though you will hear it said about nearly every swimming pool in Greater Miami, the incomparable water ballerina Esther Williams really *did* perform here, as did Hollywood's archetypal Tarzan, Johnny Weissmuller (a champion swimmer and high diver). A swim here will be unlike any other you've ever had. ■

Coral Way

Lined with trees and flower beds for much of its length through Coral Gables, Coral Way served in George Merrick's day as the city's chief thoroughfare. Today, it still remains the main road through the downtown business district, where the stretch between 37th and 42nd Avenues is known as the Miracle Mile.

Miracle Mile

Some say the real miracle along this retail and restaurant stretch of Coral Way is that it has survived so long. The arrival of national chains has some worried that the one-of-a-kind Coral Gable originals that make many of these storefronts unique are on their way out.

Architectural Highlights

Coral Gables' architecture is indeed pleasing to the eye—the fundamental beauty of the City Beautiful. There are splendid examples along Coral Way, including **De Soto Plaza and Fountain,** where Sevilla Avenue and De Soto and Granada Boulevards come together. Merrick designed 14 of these water plazas, and this one is among the most handsome.

Casa Azul, a private home at 1254 Coral Way *(bet. Madrid St. & Columbus Blvd.),* owes its name to a roof of azure glazed tiles. The architect, H. George Fink, was so esteemed in Spain for his well-publicized use of Spanish designs in Coral Gables that King Alfonso XIII summoned him to an audience and made him Don Jorge.

Poinciana Place *(937 Coral Way, bet. Toledo St. & Granada Blvd.)* was George and Eunice Merrick's first home, put up

before Merrick commenced building his city. This is the kind of house the area's citrus-growing elite lived in before Coral Gables turned everyone into pretend Mediterraneans.

The **Merrick House** *(832 S. Greenway Dr. at Castile Ave.),* not to be confused with Merrick's boyhood home (see p. 128), is now a private museum. Merrick decided he needed a bigger house to impress prospective home buyers. His cousin Don H. George designed a rock and stucco Alhambra for him, sprawling over a city block, secluded behind a wall with a distinctive covered gate. ∎

Coral Way

⬛ Map p. 127

Coral Gables City Hall

George Merrick wanted a civic headquarters worthy of his vision of what the City Beautiful would become, and he was willing to invest $200,000—a lavish sum in 1928—to achieve it. Viewed from any angle, the semicircular City Hall *(405 Biltmore Way, tel 305/446-6800, closed Sat.–Sun.),* with its triple-tiered, Spanish-Renaissance clock and bell tower, and imposing array of columns, is impressive—so much so that it is on the National Register of Historic Places. The gray blocks in its walls are of oolitic limestone, quarried locally from ancient coral reefs marooned above sea level eons ago. From breaking ground to ribbon-cutting, the building took four months to complete, a remarkable achievement.

Lowe Art Museum

Tucked away on the campus of the University of Miami is South Florida's first art museum, known chiefly for its collections of Renaissance, baroque, American, Native American, pre-Columbian, and Asian art, any one of which would do a museum proud. You could spend a day here and not see everything on show.

Sandy Skoglund's room-size "Breathing Glass" installation delights visitors.

Lowe Art Museum

🅰 Map p. 127

✉ 1301 Stanford Dr., University of Miami Campus, off US 1 / S. Dixie Hwy.

☎ 305/284-3535

🕐 Closed Mon. & Sun. a.m.

💲 $$

www.lowe museum.org

There is jade from ancient Japan, Ecuadorian and Colombian antiquities, and cloth woven in the American Southwest by Navajo, Pueblo, and Rio Grande people before Europeans arrived. You might not be able to recall what it was about the abstracts by Frank Stella, or what the girl in the Lichtenstein painting said—there's just too much to take in—but the gauzy rainbows of Bierstadt, the sanguine Yankee palette of Rembrandt Peale, Tintoretto's gently smiling Renaissance faces gazing from out of time, John Sloan's gritty early 20th-century working men, Claude Monet's blues, and Paul Gauguin's deep earth tones you will not forget.

Lying under glass are the Lowe's Egyptian antiquities—those almond-eyed gods clutching their staffs and snakes, half-smiling as if amused by the cosmic joke of once ruling an ancient kingdom and then ending up in Coral Gables, Florida.

Buy an exhibition catalog from the superb bookstore to take away the memories of Picassos you have only seen in art books, and African masks, textiles, and beadwork so rare they cannot be sold, but only loaned to other museums. ∎

A land of century-old farming plains, called South Dade by Miamians, with both natural and historical appeal

South Miami

Floridians love flamingos, though plastic ones far outnumber live ones.

South Miami

Despite spreading residential and commercial development—mini-malls especially popped up overnight like mushrooms in a yard—much of South Dade remains what Miami once was: rural Southern "pick-up" country where everything from avocados to zinnias thrives in the fertile, fragrant soil, and the pace is slower, particularly in the miles of agricultural flatland running west to the great Everglades wilderness.

Most people drive through on their way to the Everglades, Biscayne National Park, or the Keys, letting the flat fields and fruit stands flash by, their windows rolled up, the air conditioner on high. That's a shame, because one of the things people say about this rural interlude between urban Miami and the cluttered Upper Keys is that it smells so nice—of blossoms, standing fresh water, even the pleasantly clean oily smell of a wooden barrel of nails in an old hardware store.

Inevitably, this has been noticed by urbanites seeking a change. Farmhouses left to rot a generation ago are being jacked up and set back down on new foundations under new roofs, turned into weekend rural getaways.

Agriculture—strawberries, turnips, citrus, onions, tomatoes, squash, herbs, avocados, and a score of other mainstays—sets the tone of South Dade. Orchids thrive in its irrepressible fertility, the result of nutrient-rich topsoil, abundant water, and a hothouse sun. Specialty organic farms supply Greater Miami's restaurants and gourmet kitchens.

Exploring South Miami

You can speed down from the Greater Miami area on US 1, the South Dixie Highway, but unless you're on a tight schedule you should take the slower, more scenic path along the Atlantic shore: South Bayshore Drive to Main Highway, through Coconut Grove, continuing south on Ingraham Highway, and then picking up Old Cutler Road, famous for its lush ficus canopy and exclusive gated communities. The advantage is aesthetic: The route is prettier, more relaxing, and reveals more of South Florida's subtropical nature and the way it affects how people live and work. It also takes you to one of Greater Miami's finest and prettiest oceanside public greens, Matheson Hammock Park, and the Fairchild Tropical Botanic Garden, a splendid preserve where the prima donnas of the world's most exotic flora are fussed over, groomed, and dressed up for daily performances.

Marking the southern fringe of hurricane-battered South Dade, the city of Homestead suffers as the butt of jokes, maligned for homeliness and a lack of sophistication (fine dining and nightlife are not among its strengths). As its name implies, its first settlers were mostly

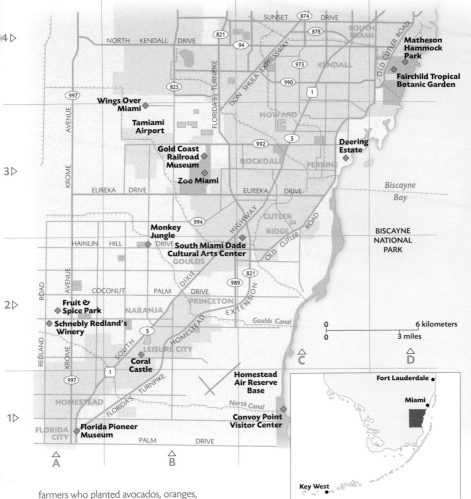

farmers who planted avocados, oranges, lemons, and limes. Railroad workers employed by Henry Flagler made Homestead their South Florida base, and filled up its cottage community, buying their food in farmers markets and living a rural village life. Florida City fares little better, its humble avenues built paycheck by paycheck and not through grand schemes like George Merrick's Coral Gables.

In 1992, Hurricane Andrew delivered a catastrophic blow to both cities, leaving them strewn with the wreckage of shattered houses and stripping natural foliage down to a white-boned nakedness. Recovery has been slow, but most of the damage is nearly erased.

With a good map in hand, it's worthwhile setting out to explore this wide-open rural grid of streets and avenues, some with numbers, some with names, many sharing both. You'll discover an out-of-the-way corner of the Real Florida stretching east–west from Biscayne Bay to the Everglades within which lie such gems as the Fruit & Spice Park, where you'll learn all about South Florida's agriculture, and Zoo Miami, the United States' only tropical zoo. ■

Fairchild Tropical Botanic Garden

South Florida is the only region in the continental United States where tropical and subtropical plants can survive the year. For that reason, southeast of Coral Gables on Biscayne Bay you'll find the largest American tropical botanical garden outside of Hawaii, an exquisite 83-acre greenery in its seventh decade as one of the world's leading centers for botanical research.

Orchids and a wealth of other vibrantly colored flowers bloom along the botanic garden's winding nature trails.

Fairchild Tropical Botanic Garden

🅰 135 D4
✉ 10901 Old Cutler Rd.
☎ 305/667-1651
💲 $$$$$

www.fairchild garden.org

You can ponder life beside 11 lakes and lily pools in this palmy oasis of orchids, ferns, and flowering trees. It also lets you explore South Florida's ancient environments, such as a pristine mangrove preserve and a hardwood hammock, the Florida of the Tequesta people. Children are entranced by the vine-draped, tunnel-like limestone pergola, and hidden passages through rain forest canopies shading all in green-tinted light.

The design of the garden creates magic. It opened in 1938 and is named in honor of Dr. David Fairchild, a globe-trotting botanist and writer whose adventures in far-off places earned him a reputation as a plant explorer, the Indiana Jones of orchids. His memoir, *The World Was My Garden,* is to some botanists what *The Compleat Angler* is to flycasters.

A United Nations of ferns, plants, and orchids grows round the lakes here: Australia's fire tree, Brazil's birthwort, South Africa's Pride of the Cape, the passionflower of Nicaragua and

INSIDER TIP:

Don't be deterred by the heat or Fairchild's lush extent of displays; there are ample benches with views worth savoring plus tram tours.

—CHRISTINA WOOD
Freelance writer

Venezuela, Vietnam's herald's trumpet, and Burma and Thailand's shower of orchids. The variety is overwhelming, a strong argument for joining a guided walking tour along the garden's many theme paths. Narrated tram tours, included in the price of admission, run hourly. ∎

Matheson Hammock Park

The driveway into Dade County's oldest park suggests you have arrived at some billionaire's secluded Biscayne Bay hideaway, with its well-tended lawns and spiffy marina. It is, in fact, the legacy of Commodore W. J. Matheson, a manufacturer of dyes and chemicals, once the owner of Key Biscayne, whose will bequeathed the first 100 of the park's 520 acres to the county in 1930.

Around 400,000 visitors a year make Matheson's gift one of Greater Miami's most popular outdoor recreation spots, not surprising given its design—a man-made swimming lagoon (Atoll Pool) refreshed by the tides, a handsome coral rock restaurant building, picnic pavilions and cooking grills, and a Biscayne Bay panorama. Nature trails wind through the park's mangrove swamp, a piece of primeval Florida that accounts for much of the acreage.

A lovely **wading beach** with sandbar shallows, making it especially safe for children and non-swimmers, can be found next to parking lot 5; to reach it, take the turnoff to the marina and yacht club and continue past the boat ramp south along the shore. This area is also a popular destination for guided naturalist tours focusing on shallow-water sea life. The north fork of the entrance road passes the marina and dead-ends beside the **swimming lagoon,** where you'll find a lifeguard on duty, a snack bar, and restrooms. An asphalt walk circles the lagoon's sandy beach and park benches face Biscayne Bay.

A park map shows both walking paths and bicycle trails. ∎

**Matheson
Hammock Park**
🅰 135 D4
✉ 9610 Old Cutler Rd.
☎ 305/665-5475
💲 $

www.miamidade
.gov/parks/parks/
matheson_beach

Matheson Hammock Park boasts an impressive view of downtown Miami's high-rises.

Deering Estate

In 1913, Charles Deering bought 420 acres on Biscayne Bay, south of Coconut Grove (then called Cutler). While brother James enjoyed the opulent Vizcaya (see pp. 114–117), Charles set about developing his own winter retreat. The property includes two of Cutler's oldest structures—a homestead and a cottage-style inn, rare examples of South Florida's early frame vernacular architecture.

One of the Stone House's main rooms

INSIDER TIP:

On the wooden path that winds through the mangroves, you will spot spiders that look like they're on steroids! You may also meet some mosquitoes, so pack the bug repellent.

—CHRISTINE CRUZ
News anchor, WSVN-7

Deering Estate
🅰 135 C3
✉ 16701 S.W. 72nd Ave.
☎ 305/235-1668
💲 $$$. Addl. fees for some tours
www.deering estate.org

A collector like his brother, Charles built a Mediterranean Revival home of coral rock; filled it with paintings, tapestries, antiques, rare books, and wine; and christened it **Stone House.** A man-made boat basin allowed him to sail his yacht nearly to the front door. In the 1980s the property was sold to the state of Florida and Miami-Dade County.

The park displays not only historic homes but also a fossil pit of animal bones and teeth from mammoths, dog-size horses, tapirs, jaguars, sloths, and bison dating from 50,000 years ago. Of greater interest perhaps are the remains of Paleo-Indians, believed to have arrived here about 10,000 years ago. Tequesta traces found at the site date from the time of Christ.

When you grow weary of moneyed manors, take a stroll on one of the many nature trails. Be sure to explore the 150-acre stand of pine rockland forest, one of the last of these primordial ecosystems growing in the continental United States. This unusual glade is surrounded by rare native orchids, bromeliads, ferns, live oaks, gumbo limbos, and pigeon plums, as well as about 35 other tree species. The estate also includes 130 acres of bayside mangrove and salt marsh—a boardwalk winds through the shoreline mangroves—and the offshore mangrove island of **Chicken Key,** which you can visit on a canoe tour (reservations required). ■

Gold Coast Railroad Museum

Where did all the great locomotives and plush sleeping cars of railroading's golden era go? Gone to scrapyards mostly. But fate has saved a few. You will find 30 of them at this retired World War II naval air station, including a 1949 Silver Crescent dome car and the most history-laden piece of rolling stock that ever traveled the nation's steel roads: the magnificent *Ferdinand Magellan*, a 1928 Pullman sleeping car redesigned in 1942 for President Franklin D. Roosevelt.

FDR was content to travel by regular Pullman, but the war was on and his security detail feared Nazi assassins, so the *Magellan* was purchased and fitted with armor plate and 3-inch-thick bullet-resistant glass. Its dining cum conference room was enlarged and an observation lounge added, along with escape hatches and features permitting Roosevelt, semi-disabled by polio, to move about more easily. The car's weight increased from 160,000 pounds to 285,000. It was the heaviest American passenger railcar ever used, and it is the only one designated a national historic landmark.

Roosevelt and Winston Churchill huddled over its solid mahogany conference table in the war's darkest days. The President traveled some 50,000 miles aboard the *Magellan*, at a preferred speed of 35 miles an hour, including his final journey to Warm Springs, Georgia, on the last full day of his life. Harry Truman, who used the Pullman for his trademark whistle-stop campaigns, logged 28,000 miles, setting the throttle at 80 miles an hour. Dwight Eisenhower also made use of it while in office. Future Presidents opted for air travel, but during his 1984 presidential campaign, Ronald Reagan borrowed Truman's bully pulpit for speeches between Dayton and Toledo, Ohio. A train ride is included in the price of admission. ∎

Gold Coast Railroad Museum

🅰 135 B3

✉ 12450 S.W. 152nd St.

☎ 305/253-0063 or 888/608-7246

💲 $$

www.gcrm.org

EXPERIENCE: Tour a South Florida Winery

The tranquil farmlands near Homestead offer a unique sight: a winery that relies on orchards rather than vineyards. **Schnebly Redland's Winery** (30205 S.W. 217th Ave., Homestead, tel 305/242-1224, http://schneblywinery.com), 20 miles southwest of the Gold Coast Railroad Museum, began in 2003 when Peter and Denisse Schnebly, who own a tropical-fruit farm, experimented with making wine. Eventually they were producing table, sparkling, and dessert wines made from mango, guava, lychee, passion fruit, and carambola.

On Saturdays and Sundays, Schnebly offers half-hour tours ($$) of the winery, allowing you to see and learn about each step of the winemaking process. The winery's large, opulent tasting room and lush courtyard, open daily, offer wonderful settings for sampling wine. Occasionally evenings are filled with live Latin and top-40 music.

At the end of 2011, Schnebly expanded into brewing beer, utilizing many of the tropical fruits that go into its wines. Beers are available for sale and sampling.

Zoo Miami

Zoo Miami is not one of those old-fashioned bleak concrete animal prisons that make you want to set the inmates loose. Its 290 acres of jungle, grassland, and forest make up what is considered one of America's finest wild animal parks, and its only subtropical one, home to more than 500 species of rare and exotic creatures that roam free.

A Himalayan black bear, a threatened species seen at the zoo

Zoo Miami

🅰 135 B3

✉ 12400 S.W. 152nd St.

☎ 305/251-0400

💲 $$$$

www.zoomiami.org

There are no cages, no bars; you walk among animals seldom seen except on TV, on well-marked protected footpaths, or ride above the herds in air-conditioned monorail trolleys. Rare white Bengal tigers recline regally on the "ruins" of a 13th-century Cambodian temple modeled on Angkor Wat, and silverback gorillas peer out from a tropical jungle, while reticulated giraffes, along with zebras, gazelles, and ostriches roam a Serengeti-like African plain.

In another habitat, the black rhinoceros and the African elephant, whose wild populations have been decimated by poaching, scuff the sunburned veldt as barrel-bodied warthogs run back and forth on spindly legs.

There is a wildlife carousel and also a petting zoo for kids. Not for petting are a pair of Komodo dragons, 10-foot-long, 300-pound carnivorous lizards from Indonesia. In the Asian River Life exhibit you walk in the mist of tropical waterfalls, surrounded by otters, clouded leopards, water monitors, and primitive muntjac deer. Half a world apart in terms of habitat, kangaroos, wallabies, and koalas inhabit the zoo's Australian Outback. Times are posted for animal feedings, which tend to reveal intriguing if less charming aspects of the creatures' personalities. ■

EXPERIENCE: Be a Zookeeper for a Day

If you've ever wanted to feed an elephant, here's your chance. On Saturdays and Sundays at Zoo Miami, you can become a "zookeeper for a day." From 7 a.m. to 4 p.m., you'll work alongside a real-life zookeeper, helping to feed the animals and maintain the exhibits while learning about other aspects of the job. The program, open to adults only (age 18 and up), costs $147 and includes lunch and a T-shirt. Reservations (tel 305/251-0400 ext 84940) are required.

More Places to Visit in South Miami

Wings Over Miami features an array of vintage aircraft, including this North American AT-6G Texan.

Coral Castle

Call him obsessed or neurotic or whatever you please, but no one calls Ed Leedskalnin a 97-pound weakling. A slender Latvian immigrant who stood 5 feet tall, Leedskalnin spent 28 years, beginning in 1923, building his bizarre Coral Castle (once called Rock Gate Park). He often worked at night so no one could see how he moved the massive blocks of oolite, including a 9-ton gate, that make up and furnish his strange home. Three of his original 10 acres are open to the public. It's said he built it as a monument to a lost Latvian love, a 16-year-old girl named Agnes Scuffs who broke their engagement and, reputedly, Ed's heart as well.

That's not quite the whole story, and this place isn't quite a castle either. It's missing a roof, and is more of a courtyard filled with coral chairs, a banquet table in the shape of Florida, odd sculptures, a sundial, and a rock "telescope" fixed on the North Star. Coral Castle may have failed to win back Ed's girl, but it did establish him as the undisputed king of Florida kitsch.

www.coralcastle.com 🅰 135 B2 ✉ 28655 S. Dixie Hwy./US 1, Homestead ☎ 305/248-6345 💲 $$

Florida Pioneer Museum

This small but informative museum of local pioneer and Indian artifacts is an example of South Dade's frame vernacular architecture— shady veranda, clapboard siding, peaked roof, attic, and dormer windows—built in 1904 to house a Florida East Coast Railroad station agent, and moved to this site in 1964. This was the nation's last railroad frontier. The old caboose outside is believed to be one of only a few wooden models still in existence. Opening hours can be irregular. It is wise to call ahead to confirm times. *www.pioneerfloridamuseum.org* 🅰 135 A1 ✉ 826 Krome Ave. ☎ 305/246-9531 🕐 Closed Sun.–Mon. 💲 $

Fruit & Spice Park

South Florida's agricultural fecundity has, from the early 1800s, inspired agronomists to experiment, often wildly, and sometimes

South Miami Dade Cultural Center

In another sign of the region's burgeoning arts environment, in 2011 the South Miami Dade Cultural Arts Center *(10950 S.W. 211 St., tel 786/573-5300, www.smdcac.org),* a gleaming facility envisioned as two clapping hands, premiered. This Cutler Bay $51 million multipurpose center was designed by Arquitectonica, a firm responsible for many of Miami's striking buildings.

The cultural center's offerings include classical, jazz, and blues music concerts; classical ballet and contemporary dance shows; and theater productions. Ticket and event information can be found on the center's website.

with edible results. About 35 miles south of Miami, near Homestead, is a layman-friendly outpost of serious planting and experimentation that is probably the last word on this business—the unusual Fruit & Spice Park, a county park established in 1944 to showcase what South Florida was capable of producing. The 32-acre garden cultivates around 500 varieties of exotic and subtropical fruit, nut, and spice trees, along with many varieties of herbs. And it works with other plant centers around the world to develop new and better strains. (The carambola, or star fruit, was developed here.) There's even an area devoted to poisonous plants.

Activities and programs include classes and tours of nearby fruit- and vegetable-growing regions, and lectures on gardening and botany. The gourmet-style gift shop sells preserves, chutneys, jellies, marinades, spices, seeds, and other exotic ingredients often hard to find, along with regionally oriented cookbooks and culinary guides, and treatises on plant propagation. There's history here, too, in rustic, vintage, coral rock buildings, including a schoolhouse built in 1912, which in the

Redlands qualifies it as a pioneer relic.

Unless you really know your fruits and spices, you'll probably enjoy yourself more on a guided tour *(11 a.m., 1:30 p.m, & 3 p.m.)*—there's so much to see here. You're not supposed to pick from the trees, but anything on the ground is yours to take.
www.fruitandspicepark.org 🅰 135 A2
✉ 24801 S.W. 187th Ave./Redland Rd. at S.W. 256th St. ☎ 305/247-5727 💲 $$

Monkey Jungle

You can see just as many monkeys at nearby Zoo Miami (see p. 140)—but you will not get as close to them there as you can here. In this 30-acre garden of botanically correct Amazonian jungle, you, not the primates, are caged. They run free (or think they do), swinging from limb to limb and screeching wildly. The simian family is extended here, from baboons, orangutans, and macaques to small, lesser known species, whose eyes seem to register constant surprise. If you have young children along, odds are they will enjoy this place.
www.monkeyjungle.com 🅰 135 B2
✉ W of US 1 at 14805 S.W. 216th St./ Hainlin Mill Dr. near S.W. 147th St.
☎ 305/235-1611 💲 $$$$$

Wings Over Miami

Among aviation buffs, Miami enjoys mythical status for attending the birth of Pan American World Airways, one reason champion aerobatics pilot Kermit Weeks founded an air museum at the old Kendall-Tamiami Airport in southwest Miami. Now called Wings Over Miami, it has assembled an impressive fleet of vintage aircraft, many in flying condition, including some of the burly warbirds that turned the tide in World War II.
www.wingsovermiami.com 🅰 135 B3
✉ 14710 S.W. 128th St. Take the Florida Turnpike to S.W. 120th St., go W to S.W. 127th Ave. ☎ 305/233-5197 🕐 Closed Sun. a.m. & Mon.–Tues. 💲 $$

A land of scenic wonders, from Biscayne Bay's islands and reefs to the Everglades' sloughs and Big Cypress's knobby-kneed trees

Excursions From Miami

An anhinga, a common waterbird of the Everglade sloughs

Excursions From Miami

Immense areas of incomparable beauty and sheer otherworldliness lay beyond Greater Miami, none more so than in Biscayne and Everglades National Parks. The former is an underwater wonderland of brightly colored corals and fish, the latter a "river of grass" unlike anything else in the world. There's also the Miccosukee Indian Reservation, Big Cypress National Preserve, and the sun and surf found at fun-loving Fort Lauderdale.

Recently hatched alligators, Everglades

To say that Everglades National Park encompasses 1.5 million acres, or even that its shimmering wetlands, in reality a river sometimes only inches deep but always miles wide, are not duplicated anywhere on Earth, does not prepare you for its peculiar wilderness. This is the only place in the world where alligators and crocodiles exist side

by side amid a chorus of birds (more than 300 nesting and migratory species), myriad fish, and a painter's palette of butterflies, manatees, and Florida panthers, to cite only a few examples of the wildlife.

If you have a day to spare, you can drive into its outer regions and walk on nature trails and boardwalks, shake hands with the denizens of this primordial soup, and take home indelible impressions of the world as it was before humankind. Despite what some believe is irreparable damage done to the Everglades by agriculture, development, and flood-preventing ditches and dikes that diminished the flow of source water into these magnificently placid wetlands, their protected areas still look pristine and are, for many, a captivating remnant of the vanishing Great American Wild.

Less evident, but no less vital, is the hidden wilderness beneath the waves of sheltered Biscayne Bay, in particular the 180,000 acres enclosed by the boundaries of Biscayne National Park (only 5 percent of which is land). It encloses a vital portion of the only living reef within the continental United States, protecting not only that underwater world but all the ecosystems, from upper Biscayne Bay to the Keys, that depend upon the health of this reef.

The Miccosukee depended upon these wilds for their survival, living among the Everglades in traditional thatched-roof wooden dwellings called chickees. For this branch of the Creek Indians, who lived in southern Alabama and Georgia in the 1700s, the balance most difficult to achieve was not ecological but political— finding an accommodation with the Seminole, their Muskogee-speaking Creek cousins.

NOT TO BE MISSED:

Tensions between them compelled the Miccosukee to move south, an odyssey beginning in the late 18th century and ending in the Everglades. There the tribe of 5,000 found themselves forced to address an even more aggressive people: Spanish and Anglo-American settlers, who demanded their allegiance even as they pushed the Miccosukee from their domains. After the Seminole uprisings, disease, deportation, and despair diminished their number until the Miccosukee rolls counted only 100 members. They fled deep into the Everglades, keeping their culture alive through devotion to traditional ritual and religion and sustaining themselves by hunting and fishing.

Here they lived in relative peace until the early years of the 20th century, when the appetite of Florida's land boom elbowed them from the dinner table on which they depended.

Roads cut into the wetlands brought motorists who gawked at these strange people in their brightly colored garments and wondered how anyone could live this way. Keep this in mind when you drive west on the Tamiami Trail into the Everglades and the Miccosukee Indian Reservation, some 300,000 acres, mostly underwater, running across two counties toward Naples. Today the tribal roll numbers about 650. It's a determined band of people, utterly American in their striving for community and a dependable way of life that holds the promise of a future of renewal and growth for the Everglades as well as for themselves.

And when you've had your fill of South Florida's Everglades and other watery delights, you can soak up some culture and relax on the beach in Fort Lauderdale, approximately 25 miles north of Miami. ■

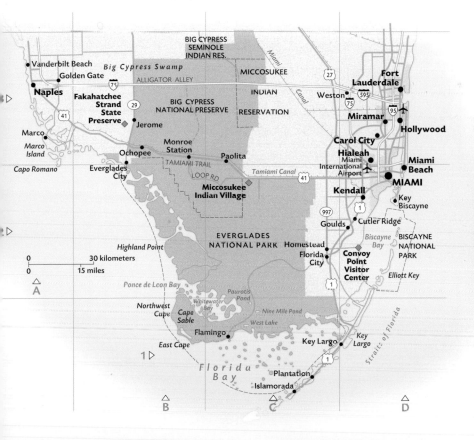

Biscayne National Park

Biscayne is one of the most accessible national parks and also among the most remote. Unless you have a boat, the 95 percent of the park that is underwater, and the 40 or so small barrier islands that compose its allotment of land, are beyond reach. You must either comb its beaches and mangrove fringes, or let a concessionaire's boat take you out across the water to the park's secret splendor: the rainbow-colored coral reefs beneath the waves.

Biscayne National Park

🏔 145 D2

✉ 9700 S.W. 328th St., Homestead

☎ 305/230-7275

www.nps.gov/bisc

Getting to Biscayne from Miami is easy. The most direct driving route is via S. Dixie Highway (US 1), a drive of about an hour from downtown. Take it south for 25 miles, past Cutler Ridge to Goulds (some 15 miles north of Homestead), and then look for a park sign. Turn left here onto S.W. 137th Avenue (Tallahassee St.) and proceed to S.W. 328th Street (N. Canal Dr.).

Turn left and continue to the end of the road 6 miles ahead. The entrance to Biscayne's Convoy Point, the hub for most park activities and home to the **Dante Fascell Visitor Center,** is on the left. If you go via the Florida Turnpike, follow the Homestead extension south to Campbell Drive exit. Turn right from the ramp and continue east to the next intersection (Kingman Rd.). Turn right and continue to S.W. 328th Street and follow as described above.

Reef Cruise

The most popular excursion at Biscayne is the Reef Cruise, a three-hour voyage from the visitor center aboard a glass-bottom boat *(www.biscayneunderwater .com, $$$$$)*. Save for a sun hat, sunglasses, and sunscreen—all mandatory items—you need no equipment. (Do bring a camera and binoculars, however.) The trip begins with a park ranger's briefing on the things you will see and their significance. The boat has a viewing chamber running lengthwise, comprised of thick-paned glass ports opening downward. The water's natural tint is green, diminishing slightly the colors of the fish, coral, and other life-forms that pass

Glass-bottom boats offer visitors a dry way to marvel at the mostly submerged acreage of Biscayne National Park.

by below, but the clear water makes for fascinating views. Unless you have snorkeled or dived in tropical waters, this will introduce you to a wholly new world, most of it less than 10 feet deep.

INSIDER TIP:

Hike Elliott Key's Spite Highway, a 6-mile tract bulldozed down the key's length in 1968, now reclaimed by vegetation, to explore a tropical hardwood hammock.

—JANE SUNDERLAND
National Geographic contributor

Look up and you'll see pelicans skimming the water, their ungainly waddles on land replaced by graceful flight. Look back down to the sandy plain of waving sea grass blowing in the warm current, stalked by spiny lobsters and crabs. Flashes of color identify some of the 500 species of fish that live in these calm waters, protected by barrier islands from Atlantic surges. Herons and cormorants skim and soar, cocking their heads to peer through surface glare in search of fish.

One trip highlight is the close look at the offshore barrier islands, the northernmost Florida Keys, fringed with mangroves, their interiors dense with tropical hardwood forest dating from prehistory. Beyond, as far out as 7 miles, are the reefs, where some

Family Fun Fest

Children of all ages will enjoy Biscayne National Park's Family Fun Fest, which takes place at the Dante Fascell Visitor Center on the afternoon of the second Sunday of every month, December through April. At each event, a different aspect of the park is featured, such as marine plants, animals, or shipwrecks. Wildly creative, with unique hands-on activities and games interpreting themes such as "Hairy Otter and the Magical Ocean" and "Biscayne Wrecktacular," the fest has won awards for education and public outreach.

50 shipwrecks—rusting skeletons lying amid massive brain coral and great mounds of star coral, fish, and sea fans—testify to the peril in these gorgeous shallows.

Other Activities

If your itinerary doesn't permit a half-day on the water, you'll take away an experience that in its way is just as memorable by spending an hour walking the mangrove-tangled shoreline of **Convoy Point,** which is also a lovely place to picnic. Although they are elusive, bald eagles and peregrines do frequent this area, as do manatees, to feed and find cover beneath the dense overhead canopy.

At the visitor center, check the schedule of events and ask about guided nature tours, including boat trips to **Elliott Key.** Inquire about canoe tours and rentals, as well as snorkeling and scuba diving excursions; you can also make reservations *(tel 305/230-1100).* ∎

Everglades National Park

Everglades National Park protects the largest remaining subtropical wilderness in the continental United States and is the third largest national park outside Alaska. It is designated a World Heritage site, an international biosphere reserve, and a wetland of international significance. Until you venture in and have a look for yourself at the saw-grass marsh—the "river of grass"—you cannot imagine how different it is from anything you've ever encountered.

A maze of mangrove islands and waterways is found along the park's Gulf Coast shoreline.

Everglades National Park

🅰 145 B2–C2 & B1–C1

✉ 40001 Fla. 9336, Homestead

☎ 305/242-7700

💲 $$ per car for Shark Valley entrance; no fee at other entrances

www.nps.gov/ever

Plan to spend a long day in the park, whether you visit the Shark Valley region west of Miami or venture southwest to visit to the park's southern half and its Florida Bay shore. Either way, you must wear a sun hat and sunglasses, and plaster on insect repellent. In the Everglades, mosquitoes are a crucial part of the food chain, and without repellent you will become part of it, too. Park weather is mild and pleasant from December through April, but summers are hot and humid, with temperatures and humidity

in the 90s and occasional afternoon thunderstorms. Wear loose-fitting, long-sleeved shirts and pants, and bring drinking water and snacks, since these are not widely available. Information on mosquito levels in summer is available (tel 305/242-7700).

Shark Valley

Shark Valley allows visitors to venture into the essence of the Everglades. The entrance and visitor center (tel 305/221-8776) lie 25 miles west of Miami via S.W. Eighth Street (US 41/ Tamiami Trail) on the park's

INSIDER TIP:

You can really get a feel for the Everglades ecosystem by visiting Shark Valley, the park's closest location to Miami—plus there are lots and lots of alligators here.

—MATT PROPERT
National Geographic photographer

northern border. Beyond the gates is the heart of the great river, whose flow runs imperceptibly from Lake Okeechobee to the Gulf of Mexico, a distance of only 100 miles. The river is so broad that the volume spilled into Florida Bay is enormous.

Park your car and board the concessionaire-operated open-sided tram for a two-hour narrated tour *(tel 305/221-8455, www.sharkvalleytramtours.com, $$$$)* along a 15-mile loop road, one of the best ways to view park wildlife,

including alligators. At the road's midpoint stands a 65-foot-tall observation tower that offers panoramic views. You can also rent bicycles from the tram operator (children 16 and under must wear helmets, purchasable at the tram office) and tour the road yourself (a two- to three-hour circuit), but if you do, bring water and ask a ranger for tips on social etiquette for meeting the alligators. You'll also encounter wading birds and turtles and, across the waters, tree islands called tropical hardwood hammocks and small shrubby ones known as bayheads.

You can also stroll the 0.3-mile **Bobcat Boardwalk** and 1-mile **Otter Cave Hammock Trail,** both near the visitor center, for photogenic views of these little turfs, whose elevation above the water makes them mini-Noah's arks of resident wildlife.

The Lower Everglades

From Miami, take the Florida Turnpike (Fla. 821) south to the Florida City exit. Turn right at the

---

EXPERIENCE: Paddle the Wilderness Waterway

The 99-mile mangrove-studded Wilderness Waterway between Everglades City, on the Gulf Coast, and the community of Flamingo, at the southern tip of Everglades National Park, winds through one of the largest uninhabited expanses in the East. Immerse yourself in it by paddling the waterway's length in a canoe or kayak (it'll take about eight days) and overnighting in Miccosukee-style chickees—raised and roofed wooden platforms. The best time to make this journey is mid-December to

mid-April. You can arrange drop-off and pick-up services with an outfitter. Trip costs include a park permit *($$)*, nightly camping fees *($)*, boat rental, and shuttle service (the last two vary by outfitter; shop around).

Guides, maps, and a list of outfitters are available from the national park. The **Florida National Parks and Monuments Association** *(tel 305/247-1216, www.ever gladesassociation.org)* offers charts of the route, marked by numbered pilings.

first traffic light onto Palm Drive and follow the signs to the Ernest F. Coe Visitor Center *(tel 305/242-7700)* at the park boundary. Check postings for ranger-guided walks at the Royal Palm Visitor Center, 4 miles west, and also for that day's cruises from Flamingo Visitor Center on Florida Bay, 38 miles southwest of the entrance via a scenic and interesting park road featuring a world of water and wildlife.

Stop at the **Royal Palm Visitor Center** for a stroll along the 0.8-mile round-trip **Anhinga Nature Trail** and the half-as-long **Gumbo Limbo Trail.** The Anhinga—named for the long-necked, black bird often seen here—is a boardwalk that visits a freshwater slough; wildlife is plentiful. Gumbo Limbo skirts a saw-grass marsh, hardwood hammocks, and thickets of the red-barked gumbo limbo tree (look for bark peeling like

skin after a sunburn). Try to join one of the ranger-led walks on these trails.

Stop again to walk the half-mile round-trip **Pineland Trail,** 7 miles down the road, through remnants of the pine forest that once covered most of southeastern Florida. To admire the largest mahogany tree in the United States, stop another 13 miles down the road at **Mahogany Hammock.** Beyond that, you'll find inviting picnic spots at **Paurotis Pond, Nine Mile Pond,** and **West Lake.**

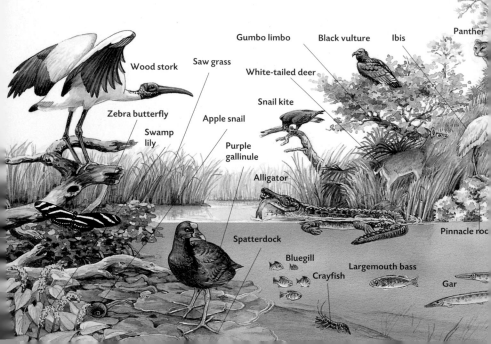

Bald eagle

Slash pine

Panther

Gumbo limbo

Black vulture

Ibis

Wood stork

Saw grass

White-tailed deer

Zebra butterfly

Snail kite

Swamp lily

Apple snail

Purple gallinule

Alligator

Pinnacle roc

Spatterdock

Bluegill

Largemouth bass

Crayfish

Gar

At **Flamingo,** sign up for a two-hour backcountry boat tour (*www.evergladesnationalpark boattoursflamingo.com,* $$$$$) at the marina ticket office near the visitor center. It takes you into the deep wild, places impossible to reach by land, places impossible to anticipate. ∎

Royal palm

Strangler fig

Roseate spoonbill

Wildlife of the Everglades

Brown pelican

Air plant

Barred owl

Mangrove

Great white heron

Crocodile

Snap fern

Coon oysters

Mangrove snapper

Pink shrimp

Turtle grass

Manatee

Loggerhead turtle

Tamiami Trail Driving Tour

The name Tamiami Trail—US 41—was coined in 1928 to signify its endpoints, Miami and Tampa, but it is the 106-mile Miami–Naples stretch for which it is best known. The opening of the trail across the Everglades took little note of the road's ecological and social consequences. It impeded the great river's southward flow, and forced change upon the Miccosukee Indians, who clung to that point to traditional ways.

That said, the Tamiami serves up a remarkable sampler of wild Florida. Its eastern miles skirt the northern boundary of Everglades National Park (see pp. 148–151), affording an opportunity to stop at the **Shark Valley Visitor Center ❶** and walk for a while, and perhaps take the tram tour along the 15-mile loop road that plunges south into soggy saw-grass marshes and hardwood hammocks, where alligators lie in the sun.

A few miles west, the Miccosukee tribe maintains the **Miccosukee Indian Village ❷**, a bridge between old ways and new lifestyles that engage the larger world. Handicraft outlets present a public face, while issues of tribal autonomy and welfare are debated elsewhere by lawyers, state officials, and tribal representatives. Meanwhile, tourists stop at mile marker 25 at the **Miccosukee Restaurant** (tel 305/223-8380, www.miccosukee.com) for home-cooked catfish and frog legs served breaded and deep-fried, with a side dish of pumpkin bread.

Continue west to **Big Cypress National Preserve ❸** (Ochopee, tel 239/695-1201, www.nps.gov/bicy), nearly three-quarters-of-a-million acres of marshland, prairies wet and dry, stands of hardwood, mangrove, pine, and, of course, cypress, the "big" referring not to size but number. Despite logging, cypresses grace about a third of the preserve. A different kind of wild exists here, explained by the

NOT TO BE MISSED:

Shark Valley Visitor Center • Miccosukee Indian Village • Big Cypress National Preserve • Fakahatchee Strand State Preserve

Oasis Visitor Center's 15-minute film. The **Tree Snail Hammock Nature Trail** introduces you to creatures that live here, including the rare, elusive Florida panther. During winter, rangers lead walks along the path. The 26-mile loop road

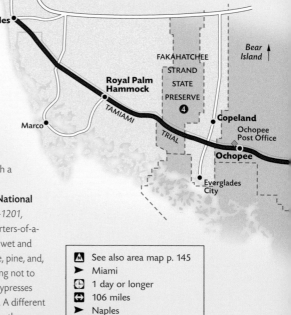

```
                              Naples ●
                                        FAKAHATCHEE          Bear ↑
                                         STRAND              Island ↓
                          Royal Palm      STATE
                          Hammock        PRESERVE
                              TAMIAMI       ❹
                      Marco ●                        ● Copeland
                                          TRIAL        Ochopee
                                                       Post Office
                                                    ● Ochopee
                                          ● Everglades
                                            City
```

🅐	See also area map p. 145
►	Miami
🕐	1 day or longer
↔	106 miles
►	Naples

EXPERIENCE: Full-moon Cycling in the Everglades

For a haunting experience, cycle through the Everglades with only the moon to light your way. Everglades National Park is open around the clock, and when there's a full moon, lots of cyclists show up at Shark Valley to ride through the moonlight-bathed landscape.

From the Shark Valley Visitor Center, set off down the 15-mile Tram Road loop. Pedal slowly to see the various critters lurking at road's edge. Roughly 7 miles into the ride, stop at the Observation Tower and climb to the top to get a panoramic view of the park. You'll likely see many alligators congregating in the "gator hole" nearby while all around pockets of hardwood hammock dot the Shark River

Slough. Throughout the Everglades ride, listen to the nighttime chorus of frogs, birds, insects, and more.

Come prepared. It's a good idea to have a light on your bicycle in case the skies become cloudy. Bring plenty of drinking water, as none will be available, and wear a helmet. Mosquito repellent is also a good idea.

Bike rentals are only available at Shark Valley for day use, so bring your own or rent one from a Miami shop, such as **Mack Cycle and Fitness** (5995 Sunset Dr., tel 305/661-8363, www.mackcycleandfitness .com) and **Elite Cycling and Fitness** (13108 S. Dixie Hwy., tel 786/242-3733, www.elite cycling.net); prices start at $50 a day.

---

and two other auto routes are scenic but best suited to high-clearance, four-wheel-drive vehicles. If you've brought a bicycle with you, ask about rides in the Bear Island area. Picnic tables make this a pleasant place for a driving break.

A side trip 3 miles north on Fla. 29, beyond tiny Ochopee, leads to the

Fakahatchee Strand State Preserve ❹ *(Copeland, tel 239/695-4593, www.friendsof fakahatchee.org).* Its elevated walkway angles through an unusually pretty stand of bald cypress, a community of royal palm, and colorful bursts of wild orchid. The group of royals is said to be North America's largest, the **Ochopee post office** America's smallest. Ask the rangers on duty about the scenic drive.

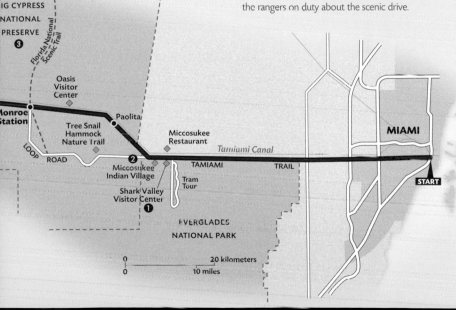

Fort Lauderdale

During spring break, thousands of college students come from afar to crowd Fort Lauderdale bars and Fort Lauderdale Beach, and act out the verb "to party"—restrained somewhat by strict public and private policies—but during the rest of the year, this city defines a kind of living wonderfully free of, say, San Francisco's self-consciousness about being San Francisco, or New York's self-importance, yet achieves a level of comfort and beauty rare among American cities.

Sun and surf draw visitors by the thousands to Fort Lauderdale.

Fort Lauderdale
🅰 145 D3

Museum of Art Fort Lauderdale
✉ 1 E. Las Olas Blvd.
☎ 954/525-5500
🕐 Closed Mon.
💲 $$

www.moafl.org

Like Miami, Fort Lauderdale has a history of wild booster-ism, with more than 300 miles of canals, channels, and rivers, most dating from the 1920s land boom, served by water taxis with colorful guides. An all-day pass permits unlimited boardings (www.watertaxi.com).

From Miami, take I-95 north to the Broward Boulevard exit, turn toward the Atlantic and follow Broward to one-way N.W. First Avenue. To cruise the city, go right onto N.W. First and go south until it takes you left onto Las Olas Boulevard.

The well-respected **Museum of Art Fort Lauderdale** stands on the corner. For scholars and art lovers who find a unique appeal in older works produced during what was once consid-ered the avant-garde movement in Copenhagen, Brussels, and Amsterdam, this collection is a treasury. It occupies an Edward Larrabee Barnes building that architectural critics adore, which was expanded in 2001. Its permanent collection is noted for 20th-century American and European masters: Alexander Calder, Salvador Dalí, Henry Moore, Pablo Picasso, Andy Warhol, and Frank Stella, among others.

The New River runs through Fort Lauderdale's central district, flanked by a glittery arts and entertainment district, where you can applaud touring Broadway plays by the river at the glassy Broward Center for the Performing Arts. If you come here on business, this is a pleasant district in which to book a hotel, not least because of its after-hours clubs featuring music—mostly jazz, blues, rock, and reggae, in that order. There are cafés ideal for a casual dinner on a warm evening.

After dinner, take a stroll along the **Riverwalk,** a mile-long promenade on the river's north bank, which crosses over and continues for another half-mile on the south side. What's particularly nice about this ramble are the tropical landscaping, interpretive displays that tell you about Fort Lauderdale, and the river overlooks.

Also of Interest

At Las Olas and S.E. Sixth Avenue is the city's oldest standing structure, built in 1901, **Stranahan House** (tel 954/524-4736, www.stranahanhouse.org), which retains its original furnishings.

Handsome Spanish colonial arcades house designer boutiques, jewelers, and several fine art galleries on Las Olas, between 6th and 11th Avenues. The Isles, at the end of Las Olas, is acknowledged as Fort Lauderdale's preeminent address, where finger islands are lined with luxurious manses.

The **Fort Lauderdale History Center** (219 S.W. 2nd Ave., tel 954/463-4431, www.oldfort lauderdale.org, closed Mon.,) relates the melodramatic history of this nevertheless relaxed region.

INSIDER TIP:

Some 40 African green monkeys live wild between Fort Lauderdale's airport and the Intracoastal Waterway. You can see them from Taylor Road.

—CHRISTOPHER BOYKIN
Project coordinator, Florida Dept. of Environmental Protection

The **Broward County Main Library** (100 S. Andrews Ave., tel 954/357-7444, www.broward .org/library) is a beautifully designed Marcel Breuer building.

Fort Lauderdale Beach is reached by following Las Olas to its dead end, where you can take Atlantic Boulevard along the water in either direction and stop according to your tastes. This is a world of beach umbrellas claimed by people with fat paperback novels and slim cell phones, particularly between Las Olas and Sunrise Boulevards.

Bonnet House Museum & Gardens (900 N. Birch Rd.,

Broward Center for the Performing Arts
✉ 201 S.W. 5th Ave.
☎ 954/462-0222
www.broward center.org

Hugh Taylor Birch State Recreation Area

✉ 3109 E. Sunrise Blvd.

☎ 954/564-4521

💲 $

www.floridastate parks.org/hugh taylorbirch

tel 954/563-5393, www.bonnet house.org, closed Mon., $$$$), once the 35-acre winter residence of an artist couple, Frederic and Evelyn Bartlett, is in the beach area. Their aesthetic estate still exhibits the same youthful zest for art, beauty, and romance that inspired George Merrick and his bride to create Coral Gables.

The **International Swimming Hall of Fame Museum** (1 Hall of Fame Dr., tel 954/462-6536, www .ishof.org, $$) is perhaps the only grand South Florida swim-ming hole that doesn't claim to have been graced by Johnny Weissmuller and Esther Williams. The museum, which includes an aquatic complex with two 50-meter pools, celebrates the

achievements of the two actors, and has a theater that screens their films. The specialty archive is chockablock with trophies won by athletes honored here.

The **Hugh Taylor Birch State Recreation Area** is reputedly the finest natural place away from Fort Lauderdale's shoreline: 180 acres of tropical landscaping etched by a meandering nature trail that is really more of a poet's walk. Let others spike volleyballs, lob horse-shoes, paddle canoes, pedal bikes, take Segway tours (M. Cruz Rentals, tel 954/235-5082), or press their noses to glass in the pioneer-oriented **Birch House Museum.** Take your walk, spread out a pic-nic, and read Marjory Stoneman Douglas's River of Grass. ■

EXPERIENCE: A Day Out at Billie Swamp Safari

The Seminole, the longest residents of Florida's interior, retain an innate knowledge of the Everglades, which today they share with visitors while stressing the importance of protecting said environ-ment. **Billie Swamp Safari** (30000 Gator Tail Trail, Clewiston, tel 863/983-6101, www .billieswamp.com), named after a historic tribal member, offers a Safari Swamp Day Package ($$$$$) that includes an airboat ride and a swamp buggy ecotour on the Big Cypress Seminole Indian Reservation, which is isolated by Everglades and swamps from other communities.

Most popular are the airboats that glide passengers over giant saw grass and into cypress domes, where you will see lots of alligators and possibly turtles and snakes. The 20-minute airboat ride offers family adventure for young and old alike. Your captain will occasionally stop the boat to talk about wildlife and history.

On the 45-minute swamp buggy ecotour, you'll travel in a tall, open vehicle over bumpy, age-old trails through the bush and splash through water while tra-versing swampy areas (you probably won't get wet). As you wend through wetlands, cypress heads, and hardwood hammocks, your guide will identify native plants and animals, as well as some imported exotics. Midway through the journey, you'll stop at a preserved Indian camp.

Back at Billie Swamp Safari, visitors can catch a couple different animal shows (one features alligators) and feast on alligator tail nuggets and frog legs in the restaurant (there's also cheeseburgers and hot dogs if you're not into eating reptiles).

If time permits as you drive back to the highway, stop in at the tribe's **Ah-Tah-Thi-Ki Museum** (www.ahtahthiki.com), which means "a place to learn." Behind it is a 1-mile boardwalk above the swamp.

A low-lying archipelago of jungle coral isles arcing southwest from the mainland—one of America's most naturally exotic places

Upper Keys

Old-fashioned diving suit, Florida Keys History of Diving Museum, Upper Matecumbe Key

Upper Keys

The scenic, 126-mile Overseas Highway links more than 40 inhabited isles, crossing 42 bridges and skimming blue tropical waters—the Gulf of Mexico on one side, the Atlantic on the other. It vaults over coral reefs, saltwater mangrove forests, sea-grass meadows, and flowering jungle hammocks sprawling between idiosyncratic tourist towns, and terminates in raffish Key West, continental America's southernmost city. Starting in Florida City, green mile markers (MM) provide a countdown from MM 126 to MM 0 at Key West.

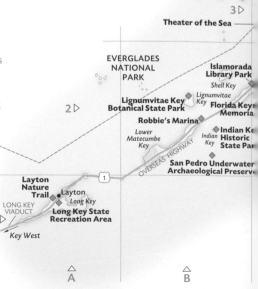

Even as the light begins to fade, fishermen still actively angle the fish-plentiful waters of the Keys.

History of the Keys

The Keys were once the domain of the Calusa—sometimes spelled Caloosa—an indigenous tribe. Europeans first laid eyes on their world on Sunday, May 15, 1513. The Europeans were led by Christopher Columbus's ambitious Spanish lieutenant Juan Ponce de León, who was searching for the fabled Fountain of Youth. The expedition's chronicler, Antonio de Herrera, later wrote that "To all this line of islands and rock islets they gave the name of Los Martires (The Martyrs)." To the Span-iards the islands seemed, as they rose into view, to resemble the prostrate forms of suffering

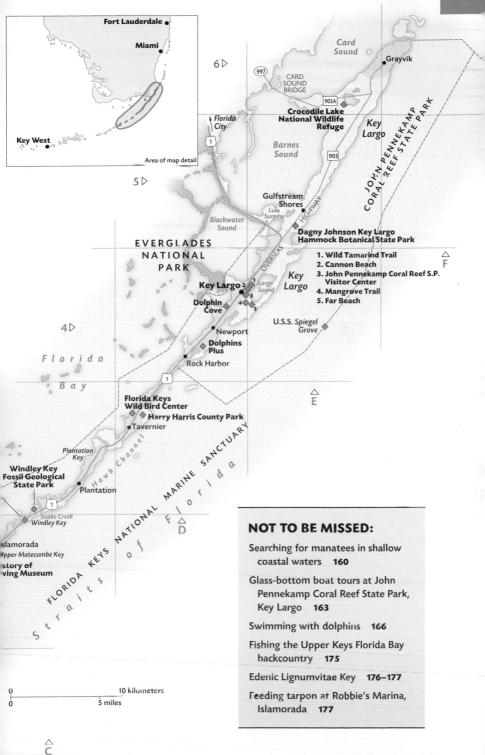

Fort Lauderdale
Miami
Key West
Area of map detail

6
Card Sound
Grayvik
997
CARD SOUND BRIDGE
905A
Crocodile Lake National Wildlife Refuge
Florida City
1
Barnes Sound
905
Key Largo

JOHN PENNEKAMP CORAL REEF STATE PARK

5
Gulfstream Shores
Lule Surprise
Blackwater Sound
Dagny Johnson Key Largo Hammock Botanical State Park

EVERGLADES NATIONAL PARK

OVERSEAS HIGHWAY

Key Largo

F

1. Wild Tamarind Trail
2. Cannon Beach
3. John Pennekamp Coral Reef S.P. Visitor Center
4. Mangrove Trail
5. Far Beach

Key Largo 2 1
Largo Sound
3
4
5

Dolphin Cove

4

Florida
Bay

U.S.S. Spiegel Grove

Newport

Dolphins Plus

Rock Harbor

1

E

Florida Keys Wild Bird Center
Harry Harris County Park
Tavernier

Plantation Key

Windley Key Fossil Geological State Park

Plantation

Hawk Channel

1

FLORIDA KEYS NATIONAL MARINE SANCTUARY

Snake Creek
Windley Key

D

slamorada
pper Matecumbe Key
story of
ving Museum

Straits of Florida

0   10 kilometers
0   5 miles

NOT TO BE MISSED:

Searching for manatees in shallow coastal waters **160**

Glass-bottom boat tours at John Pennekamp Coral Reef State Park, Key Largo **163**

Swimming with dolphins **166**

Fishing the Upper Keys Florida Bay backcountry **175**

Edenic Lignumvitae Key **176–177**

Feeding tarpon at Robbie's Marina, Islamorada **177**

C

men. "The name remained fitting," wrote de Herrera, "because of the many that have been lost there since."

The conquistadores' interest in the islands waned in the absence of gold, and three centuries passed before the first Anglo-American settlement was staked out at what is today Key West. Another half century went by before homesteading settlers arrived in the Upper Keys. They built houses of the driftwood and flotsam heaped on the beaches by a never ending succession of ships that gutted themselves on the submerged reefs. Before the advent of lighthouses, maritime mishaps were so frequent off the islands that many "wreckers" became wealthy from the salvage trade, an occupation discredited by a few unscrupulous entrepreneurs who set up false lighthouse beacons to lure unfortunate mariners off course.

Most of the Upper Keys' newcomers were farmfolk who, for a time, coaxed harvests of lemons, limes, melons, tomatoes, and pineapple from the meager topsoil and shipped them north by sea. They cheered when Henry Flagler's railroad reached Key West in 1912, believing a link to mainland markets ensured prosperity. But they were soon edged out by cheaper produce shipped to Key West from Central and South America. Successive battering by hurricanes administered a coup de grace to the Keys' agricultural hopes.

The 20th century brought chronic hard times, during which many islanders eked out livings in the fishing trade. Dreams of a strong locally generated economy died hard in the Depression, when islanders, assisted by federal programs, commenced the development of the island's tourist industry.

A Unique Landscape

What has not died, however, is the isles' promise of an escape to peace and recreation. The Upper Keys themselves begin unobtrusively enough when US 1

EXPERIENCE: Search for Wild Manatees

One of Florida's most intriguing denizens is the manatee. If you spot one in the wild, count yourself lucky. Officially called West Indian manatees and nicknamed sea cows, the half-ton herbivores gently graze in saltwater and fresh water alike. Despite their bulkiness, the bewhiskered mammals move gracefully through the water with the aid of two front flippers and a large paddlelike tail. Average adults can reach up to 10 feet long and live up to 60 years.

As the manatees are endangered nomads, it's hard to track them down. But they do gather periodically at certain locations, particularly in warm waters during the winter, such as near Turkey Point Nuclear Plant in Homestead. In Miami, manatees suddenly appear at marinas, and just as suddenly disappear. In Coral Gables, you might see them in canals on the campus of the University of Miami.

Search for them in shallow coastal areas and up rivers and canals. Watch for growing, shadowy blobs as they surface to breathe every five minutes or so. But if the water is murky, look for sudden ripples and noses that from a distance might appear to be coconuts.

Joining a manatee tour will up your chances of spotting one of these sea creatures in the wild. In Key Largo, **Captain Sterling's Everglades Eco-Tours** (tel 888/224-6044, http://floridakeys .homestead.com, $$$$$, reservations required) runs three manatee tours a day, departing from Sundowners at MM 104, from early December to early March. Although offering a variety of trips, the manatee tours aboard Captain Sterling's deck boat, which seats a maximum of six people, go to what he calls his "secret manatee spots."

A small cottage in Tavernier, a laid-back, colorful town at the lower tip of Key Largo

crosses over the placid channel between Barnes Sound and Blackwater Sound via the 223-foot-long Jewfish Creek Bridge at MM 106, officially becoming the Overseas Highway. The crossing takes only a few seconds by car, but it delivers you into a region unlike any other in North America.

In the Upper Keys, the trick is to make a point of pulling off the highway to explore. You'll find anchorages crowded with charter fishing boats rigged for marlin and blue dolphin, scuba diving outfitters eager to show you the reefs—home to more than 600 species of fish—and concessionaires keen to rent any kind of water conveyance you desire. Anglers come in search of the elusive bonefish and permit, and the feisty tarpon and jack cravalles, the quest for which is regarded by aficionados as being close to meditation. Hidden in foliage beyond roadside kitsch are resorts, many of them funky, a few surpassingly luxurious. People come to sojourn, beachcomb, or wander paths through junglelike thickets of pigeon plum, poisonwood, Jamaica dogwood, satin leaf, and palm. Their curiosity is rewarded by glimpses of such beautiful creatures as the

How the Keys Came to Be

In primordial times, coral reefs grew atop limestone ridges in these shallow seas. Between 120 to 100 thousand years ago, polar ice caps enlarged and the oceans receded, dropping sea levels by 20 to 30 feet and exposing the top of the reef, which died and became a barren archipelago of fossilized coral or limestone rock. Over the millennia, waves, tides, and storms deposited seaweed, driftwood, and other organic debris, which decayed to form soil. Seeds drifted ashore or were brought in the stomachs of migrating birds. Those that sprouted eventually created the Keys' distinctive junglelike tropical hammocks, virtual samplers of the West Indies' flora from which they derive.

great white heron (rarely seen elsewhere), mangrove cuckoos, roseate spoonbills, and white-crowned pigeons. Diverse possibilities define the Keys, beginning with the longest, hence its Spanish name Cayo Largo (Long Key). ∎

Key Largo

It's easy to overlook what's offered by this 30-mile-long island, as the dive shops, motels, billboards, and short-order outlets facing the roadway can spark an impulse to drive on—or retreat to Miami. But this is friendlier, more interesting country than you might suspect, for the local inhabitants depend upon the goodwill of travelers, and make up with cordiality and humor what their often humble establishments might lack in big city–style sophistication.

The colorful fish and corals of John Pennekamp Coral Reef State Park make it a premier scuba diving locale.

If you arrive via US 1 from the direction of the Everglades, you might miss North Key Largo's expanse of virgin hardwood hammock and mangrove. Coming from Miami, it's simple to veer east and take Card Sound Road (Fla. 905) south from Florida City. (If you missed North Key Largo southbound, take Fla. 905 north.) The Card Sound Bridge charges a toll ($), whereas US 1 is free, but the fee is worth the opportunity to experience the Keys as the wilderness they were before settlement began—not to mention the two-time winner of *Miami New Times*'s Best Tollbooth. Card Sound Road and US 1 join at Lake Surprise, at which point, if southbound, you are now truly in the Keys.

Take time to find a side road to the Atlantic side of the island for your first view of the only living coral reef found off the continental United States. Eons ago this natural barrier formed the Keys. Scarred by collisions with ships, broken by boat anchors and the dynamite of commercial coral collectors, it is now ailing from effluents dumped into the sea. It faces an uncertain future but continues to protect the islands it created from the grinding action of ocean waves—that's why so few beaches here have fine sand.

John Pennekamp Coral Reef State Park

Many guidebooks call this mostly underwater preserve the premier natural attraction in the Keys. The 54,000-acre park is 25 miles long, extends 3 miles out into the Atlantic, and, combined with the adjoining Key Largo section of the **Florida Keys National Marine Sanctuary,** protects a 178-square-nautical-mile sweep of coastal water and 2,350 acres of tropical hammock and mangrove forest. Its centerpiece is an undersea coral reef garden of ethereal beauty.

Underwater Attractions:

You can't see much of the preserve from shore, however; you must venture seaward. Weather permitting, the park offers daily glass-bottom boat tours (tel 305/451 6300, $$$–$$$$), snorkeling tours (tel 305/451-6300, $$$$–$$$$$), and scuba tours (tel 305/451-6322, $$$$$); call for times. Boat tours depart from the park marina adjoining the visitor center and last about 2.5 hours, with mask-and-fin expeditions about 90 minutes.

The pellucid world beneath the sea is spectacularly abundant—a magical garden decorated by gracefully waving sponges, sea fans, whips and plumes, barnacles, 27 species of anemonelike Gorgonians, spiny sea urchins,

and 55 varieties of coral. It is patrolled by crabs, snails, lobsters, shrimp, worms, mollusks, sea stars, sea cucumbers, sand dollars, and more than 500 species of vividly colored fish.

There's snorkeling at **Cannon Beach** (behind the visitor center) and at the **Far Beach area,** a rocky reef-sheltered lagoon at the terminus of the entrance road from MM 102.5, where tropical fish congregate. (You can rent equipment at the main concession building.) The cannon, anchor, and ballast stones of the Spanish galleon shipwreck scattered on the pale bottom in shallow water about 130 feet offshore are re-creations, put there by park officials. Spanish galleons often came to grief in storms along this coast, though, and more than one bather has walked out of the water considerably wealthier than when he or she waded in.

Other Activities: If you prefer to remain on dry land, you can

Key Largo
 159 D4

Visitor Information
✉ Key Largo Chamber of Commerce, 106000 Overseas Hwy.
☎ 305/451-1414 or 800/822-1088

John Pennekamp Coral Reef State Park
◮ 159 E4–E5
✉ Park entrance at MM 102.5
☎ 305/451-1202 (information & camping); 305/451-6300 (sea kayak & canoe rentals)
💲 $ per car, $ per person; addl. fees for camping, boat slips, & mooring
www.pennekamp park.com

The End of Eden?

Environmentally, Florida Bay and the Everglades are Siamese twins; if one dies, the other is doomed. Farming and development have drastically reduced the Everglades' area and vitality, agricultural pollution has sickened it, and water diversion to protect adjacent homes and farms from natural flooding has dried up wetlands. The results include once crystalline Florida Bay water clouded by algal blooms, its sea-grass "prairies" killed and turned to mud, and sponge die-offs robbing young shrimp, fish, and lobsters of food. Despite new laws intended to protect the Everglades, its prognosis is uncertain.

still have an eyeball-to-eyeball encounter with some of the reef's resident creatures at the visitor center's 30,000-gallon **saltwater aquarium,** a living Technicolor kaleidoscope of fish darting among tentacled anemones, graceful coral, and sponges. Several touch tanks

hardwood hammock. Hammock is a Southern variation of the word "hummock" and refers to a thickly wooded tract of fertile land that's usually elevated. Save for the foot-paths, this is prehistoric Florida—a dense knotted jungle of gumbo limbo, West Indian mahogany, strangler fig, and thatch palm.

Egrets frequent the mangrove forests in John Pennekamp state park.

let you reach safely underwater to feel the peculiar textures of these fanciful-looking creatures. Take the time to view at least one of the films shown here continuously, for the more you learn, the more wonderfully mysterious the reef becomes.

Don't leave without strolling two short and easy trails through a living encyclopedia of local flora. A looping footpath that begins and ends near the visitor center parking lot, the **Wild Tamarind Trail,** circles through a

Winding away from the Far Beach area, the **Mangrove Trail** follows an elevated boardwalk that pro-vides a close-up look at saltwater forests of red, black, and white mangroves. These trees, perched upon bowed spider-leg trunks, create a virtually impenetrable barrier between sea and shore that are havens for young fish.

Another way to explore this enchanting preserve is by canoe, along a serpentine, 2.5-mile waterway of placid tidal creeks through mangrove forests. The main concessionaire rents canoes and sea kayaks. The trail ends at the Far Beach area, an inviting swimming spot with showers to wash off the salt when you're finished for the day.

The preserve has 47 campsites with showers, water, and power, half of which can be reserved for a moderate fee.

Crocodile Lake National Wildlife Refuge

Had you been one of the uncounted thousands of Spanish fortune seekers shipwrecked along this coast, and managed to escape being crushed between your ship's hull and the reef that tore it open, your joy at survival might have waned as you swam toward Key Largo's mangrove-tangled shore. For lurking in these pale green shallows were not only the Calusa, a tribe of tall men and women known to enslave castaways, but swarms of crocodiles whose main interest was feeding. The reptiles are still here—as many as 100 winter at the Crocodile Lake National Wildlife Refuge, which lies on the island's dreamily serene backcountry coast. While not open to the public, it is worth taking a look from Card Sound Road (Fla. 905).

In the 1950s this tract in upper Key Largo was slated to be the site of a new city "an imitation Mediterranean coastal village." The Nature Conservancy and the federal government bought the land from its bankrupt would-be developers. For now the fragile swampy expanse—which protects one of the largest tracts of tropical hardwood hammock—is undeveloped. There are plans to install an observation platform and a boardwalk through the wetland, and a butterfly meadow was recently developed along Fla. 905, across from the refuge entrance, approximately 2 miles north of the intersection of Fla. 905 and US 1 (Overseas Highway).

INSIDER TIP:

For those visitors to John Pennekamp who can't or won't get into the water, the park's saltwater aquarium is definitely worth a visit, as the real joys of this place are below the surface.

—MATT PROPERT
National Geographic photographer

The 6,700-acre refuge's crocodile community is believed to be North America's most populous. Using binoculars, you can observe the exceedingly shy lizards sunning themselves on the banks farthest from the observation road. A threatened species, the American crocodile can be 7 to 15 feet long, weigh 150 to 450 pounds, and live some 60 to 70 years. Resist the impulse to wander down to the water; it is illegal to trespass, puts you in rattlesnake territory, and also destroys the ground-level nests of migratory terns that roost here.

Crocodile Lake National Wildlife Refuge

 159 E6

✉ Entrance on Card Sound Rd., 2 miles N of intersection of Card Sound Rd. & Overseas Hwy., at MM 106

☎ 305/451-4223

www.fws.gov/ nationalkeydeer/ crocodilelake

Dagny Johnson Key Largo Hammock Botanical State Park

⚑ 159 E5

☎ 305/451-1202

💲 $

www.floridastate parks.org/keylargo hammock

Dagny Johnson Key Largo Hammock Botanical State Park

Time was when the Upper Keys were for the most part a vast bristle of West Indian tropical hardwood fringed by mangrove. Where much of this perfect chaos once rustled softly in the trade winds, you can now park your RV, order up Key lime pie or a beer, buy bait, charter a fishing boat, or book a motel room.

Inside the Dagny Johnson Key Largo Hammock Botanical State Park, more than 2,000 acres of this ancient scrub endure. The tract, just north of US 1 on Fla. 905 in north Key Largo on the ocean (Atlantic) side of the highway, is the largest remaining stand of hardwood hammock and mangrove wetlands in the Keys—the jungled shoreline that Juan Ponce de León saw as he charted the islands in the early 16th century (see p. 158).

You can easily and enjoyably explore the preserve on your own, guided by the information brochure given out at the park entrance. Points of interest are keyed to numbered boulders along a paved nature trail, which is wheelchair-negotiable. As you stroll, read about many of the 84 species of protected plants and animals found here, a large number of them rare or endangered. You can even sample some of the

EXPERIENCE: Swimming With Dolphins

Nothing can compare with the wonder of swimming with dolphins. They'll buddy up to you, letting you rub their slick, rubbery skin, and likely squeak to show their willingness to play. You might even begin to wonder if they're trying to smile through their long, unbending beaks. Once your dolphin streaks forward, it'll swim along the surface, maybe going around obstacles, then dive deep. Seconds later it'll shoot up into the air and seem to walk on its tail for a few exhilarating seconds.

There are five main locations for swimming with Atlantic bottlenose dolphins in the Keys. Programs vary, but most locations offer a "structured" swim: a 30- to 45-minute educational lesson on dolphins and swim protocols followed by a 20- to 30-minute swim with the dolphins under the supervision of trainers. Some locations offer "natural" swims (no contact with the dolphins unless they initiate it) and shallow-water encounters.

Young children (under 7) typically cannot swim with dolphins but some locations offer dockside encounters too. Structured swims run about $185, natural swims about $135.

Dolphin Connection (61 Hawks Cay Blvd., Duck Key, tel 888/251-3674, www .hawkscay.com) At Hawk's Cay Resort. Supervised dolphin-contact programs, including swims in a saltwater lagoon.

Dolphin Cove (101900 Overseas Hwy., Key Largo, tel 877/365-2683, www.dolphins cove.com) See p. 167 for details.

Dolphins Plus (31 Corrine Pl., Key Largo, tel 305/451-1993, www.dolphinsplus.com) See p. 167 for details.

Dolphin Research Center (58901 Overseas Hwy., Marathon, tel 305/289-0002, www.dolphins.org) See p. 184 for details.

Theater of the Sea (84721 Overseas Hwy., Islamorada, tel 305/664-2431, www .theaterofthesea.com) See p. 171 for details.

Parasailing gives visitors a unique aerial view of Key Largo and its long, undulating shoreline.

native fruits. An additional 6 miles of backcountry trails (free permit required, obtained at John Pennekamp Coral Reef State Park; see p. 163) allow further exploration.

Here, as at Crocodile Lake National Wildlife Refuge (see p. 165), government agencies are buying up adjoining tracts to block encroachment and expand the trail system. This is a battleground of environmentalists and developers: Coming out of a thicket, you're likely to confront the shells of uncompleted and abandoned buildings.

Dolphin Cove & Dolphins Plus

Want to get close and personal with Flipper? Key Largo is the place to learn about dolphins, which are among the most intelligent and playful mammals on the planet. At Dolphin Cove and nearby sister facility, Dolphins Plus, you can swim with these engaging creatures and spot them on nature tours.

Dolphin Cove: Dolphin Cove, set on a 5-acre natural lagoon, has a wide range of interesting programs. Most visitors come here for the Shallow Water Dolphin Encounter, an in-water program that includes direct involvement with frisky Atlantic bottlenose dolphins. The adventure starts with a 30-minute ride aboard an Everglades deck boat through the beautiful Keys backcountry, with experts on hand to lecture about all aspects of the creatures, from their anatomy to the behavior and social structure of dolphins in the wild—they live and travel together in groups called pods—and how they communicate with humans.

Dolphin Cove
- ✉ MM 101.9
- ☎ 305/451-4060 or 877/365-2683
- 💲 $$$$$ for swims, $$ to watch
- **www.dolphins cove.com**

Dolphins Plus
- ✉ 31 Corrine Pl. (just S of MM 100)
- ☎ 305/451-1993 or 866/860-7946
- 💲 $$$$$ for swims
- **www.dolphins plus.com**

Birds of the Keys

The 19th-century ornithologist and artist John James Audubon was astonished by the variety of birds in the Keys. Millions of migratory birds such as terns flutter down to roost in spring and fall, joining a permanent population of wading birds including the heron and egret. The Keys also abound with bald eagles, ospreys, barred owls, brown pelicans, and pileated woodpeckers. None, however, surpass the ability of the swallow-tailed kite to perform an aerial ballet on the gentlest of breezes.

To protect this wealth of bird life, never leave fishing hooks and line in the wild. If your lure snags in a tree, do everything possible to retrieve it. Never discard hooked bait or fishing line by tossing it into the water. If you hook a bird, don't let it fly away without cutting away any attached line, as it dooms the creature to entanglement and death by starvation. If a bird has swallowed a hook or is badly entangled, bring it to the Florida Keys Wild Bird Center or call for a pickup (tel 305/852-4486). When cleaning fish, don't toss unwanted parts into the water, as birds can choke on them if they are larger than their usual prey.

Harry Harris County Park
- 159 D3
- MM 93.5, via Burton Dr.
- 305/852-7161

Florida Keys Wild Bird Center
- 159 D3
- 93600 Overseas Hwy., Tavernier
- 305/852-4486
- Donation

www.fkwbc.org

Environmental issues and the threats to dolphins play a key part in this educational journey, and there is careful instruction on how to interact responsibly with dolphins when you eventually meet them in the water.

You can learn more about dolphins in workshops, and there are opportunities to explore the area on a guided kayak tour, and even go scuba diving.

Dolphins Plus: Dolphins Plus is on a canal adjacent to the ocean. Visitors enter the water with mask, fins, and snorkel for a session that involves no direct contact but simulates swimming with dolphins in the wild.

Tavernier

At the lower tip of Key Largo is the sprawl of Tavernier, a vestige of the Key's original outpost. It's said that Tavernier takes its name from a small nearby island that the Spanish dubbed Cayo Tabona—Horsefly Key.

Tavernier is a laid-back, colorful town, and it makes a good base for exploring, with plenty of accommodations and restaurants. The town is bordered by Tavernier Creek and Plantation Key to the south, offering boaters easy access to both ocean and bay waters.

During the 18th century the island was a base for reef hunters in search of booty from shipwrecks. In the 1860s Bahamian farmers from Key West moved in and established Tavernier as a fishing and farming village. The arrival of Flagler's railroad brought a demand for pineapples, coconuts and other fruits that could be grown here. A packing house, from where the produce was once shipped, has been restored near the railroad tracks.

The town proudly claims a historic district of sorts—a neighborhood where wooden, early 20th-century buildings survive, and stolidly built decades-old Red Cross houses squat in defiance of hurricanes and, to all appear-ances, artillery shells. After the devastating Labor Day Hurricane of 1935 denuded the Matecumbe Keys (drowning hundreds; see pp. 173–174), the Red Cross built these four-room bunkers of reinforced concrete, with steel window sashes anchored in foot-thick walls. The structures symbolize a basic fact about Keys residents then and now: They are in denial of what another great hurricane, which some predict will bring 20-foot tidal surges, will do to an archipelago whose highest point, on Windley Key, is 18 feet.

Harry Harris County Park:
Harry Harris was a onetime county commissioner and local wheeler-dealer. His influence is emphasized by the name of Tavernier's pleasant public green on the Atlantic Ocean side of the road, at MM 93.5 via Burton Drive, which angles right and left en route to the beach. Just follow the signs—you can't get lost here—to a nice little lagoon with a man-made beach for swimming and a boat launch ramp. You'll likely find softball and basketball games in progress and the air redolent of meat broiling on public charcoal grills.

Florida Keys Wild Bird Center: About a half-mile north of the turnoff to Harry Harris County Park stands the Florida Keys Wild Bird Center, opened in 1984 by naturalist Laura Quinn to provide care for injured waterfowl and shore birds. (It's easy to miss; watch

for carved wooden birds perched on the bay side of the highway at MM 93.6.) The center works with veterinary clinics to rescue injured and orphaned birds in hope of eventually releasing them back into the wild. Most injuries involve collisions with vehicles, power lines, and windows. Many birds—usually pelicans—arrive choking on half-swallowed baited fish hooks and lures or entangled in fishing line. Others have

EXPERIENCE:
Interact With Pelicans

Get up close and personal with some large birds at the Laura Quinn Sanctuary at the **Florida Keys Wild Bird Center** (see this page). Although the injured birds recuper-ate in enclosures, don't be surprised by the host of free-roaming pelicans, ibises, egrets, and herons that tend to congregate at the sanctuary. Feeding these wild birds is not part of the official daily feeding plan, but the sanctuary's workers are soft-hearted: If you're there at feeding time, ask if you may reach into the worker's bucket of herring or smelt and feed the wild birds. Then toss a fish to a particular bird to see how well it can catch or to the ground to see several birds jostle for it.

broken their wings after becom-ing entangled in fishing nets. Permanently disabled creatures are kept in the bayside mangrove wetland, among the best spots to study herons, cormorants, brown pelicans, broad-wing hawks, terns, and ospreys close-up. A short, self-guided nature trail winds through the stand of hardwood hammock adjoining the center. ■

Plantation Key

Southbound again you'll cross tiny Plantation Key, whose name commemorates banana- and pineapple-growing estates that flourished here from the 1880s until World War I, employing native Bahamians as field workers.

One of Plantation Key's popular recreation areas

Plantation Key

158 C3

There's little evidence of the plantations today—the island is densely developed and ringed with recreation beaches—nor of the Calusa, who lived here and on adjoining Windley Key (see page opposite) as far back as 4,000 years ago. Archaeologists study the refuse heaps they left for clues to the tribe's lifestyle.

Just offshore is a complex of reefs teeming with colorful and sometimes strange-looking sea creatures, including the very large but benign manta ray. The best formations are **Inner** and **Outer Conch, Davis Reef,** and **Crocker Wall**—tables, drop-offs, and coral rises cradling corridors of white sand. ■

Key Limes

Key limes are not just any lime, but a Florida hybrid. Small and round—a bit smaller than a golf ball—they are available year-round. Their thin, mottled, yellow-green skin holds juicy flesh that is high in vitamin C and tastes powerfully sweet-tart. Their most famous association is with Key lime pie—a graham cracker crust filled with yellowish lime custard and topped with meringue.

Windley Key

South across the Snake Creek drawbridge at MM 86.5 is Windley Key—originally two adjacent isles, now joined by landfill poured in during the early 20th-century railroad construction era. Extracting the fill stone from here left quarrylike pits whose walls expose a pretty formation of limestone coral rock laid down about 125,000 years ago, containing fossils of reef creatures.

Just south of the bridge, look to the bay side for these holes, now part of the **Windley Key Fossil Reef Geological State Park** *(closed Tues.–Wed.)*. The park (MM 85.5) recalls past times, when slabs of the beautiful fossil-rich keystone were quarried for building facades. Five trails meander past rusting machinery to the quarries, which amount to a dissection of the ancient reef.

INSIDER TIP:

Buildings throughout the Keys are covered with keystone—Key Largo limestone ground and smoothed into a decorative element. One example is the park visitor center.

—GERRY POWERS
Assistant park manager, Windley Key Fossil Reef Geological State Park

If you would like to explore the quarries, you must stop by the visitor center to purchase tickets *(tel 305/664-2540, $)*. You can also obtain a brochure at the visitor center that guides you along the trails. This detour and the backtrack to Long Key (MM 67.5)

are a must for devotees of fossils.

Close by there's a similar quarry, dug in 1907 by railroad construction crews and filled with seawater in 1946 to create one of the world's first marine parks. Daily shows at the **Theater of the Sea** feature a troupe of creatures led by performing sea lions and dolphins, along with other denizens of the Keys. The shows

A trainer interacts with a dolphin at the Theater of the Sea.

have a reputation for enthralling children, and the theater also offers visitors the chance to swim for a half hour in the company of dolphins, sea lions, or rays (reservation required). Among the memorable attractions here are feeding time in the shark pool and a 300-gallon aquarium containing a living reef environment. ∎

Windley Key

🗺 158 C2

Visitor Information

✉ Key Largo Chamber of Commerce, 106000 Overseas Hwy.

☎ 305/451-1414 or 800/822-1088

Theater of the Sea

🗺 158 C2

✉ 84721 Overseas Hwy.

☎ 305/664-2431

💲 $$$$$ for shows, $$$$$ for swims

www.theaterof thesea.com

Upper Matecumbe Key

Shaped like a 5-mile-long green bean, running from MM 84 to MM 79, Upper Matecumbe Key was briefly America's leading pineapple-growing center. Limes were grown here, too, although today the fruit used to make Key lime pie is grown on the Florida mainland. Cuban competition and the 1935 hurricane quashed the Keys' agricultural industry, and today Upper Matecumbe, whose commercial center is Islamorada, gets by very well by showing visitors a good time.

The Florida Keys Memorial commemorates the hundreds lost to a Category 5 hurricane in 1935.

Upper Matecumbe Key

🅰 158 C2

Visitor Information

✉ Islamorada Chamber of Commerce, 83224 Overseas Hwy., Islamorada

☎ 305/664-4503 or 800/322-5397

www.islamorada chamber.com

Islamorada

The town of Islamorada (pronounced EYE-la-mor-AH-da) claims to have more resident fishing vessels per square mile than anywhere else in the world, and bills itself as the "Sport Fishing Capital of the World." For many years, U.S. Presidents and sports celebrities have fished here with great fanfare—and the telephone directory lists more than 350 fishing charter operations. Fringed by marinas and fishing boats, its roadside sprawl lined by outfitters, bait suppliers, bistros, cafés, and a charming if sometimes funky variety of shops, Islamorada looks the part.

It is said that Spanish explorers noted the coastline's purplish color, a phenomenon created by the lavender shells of janthina sea snails, and added the name *islas moradas* (purple isles) to their charts. Local historians claim the town's 19th-century founders named it after the sailing ship that brought them there, the schooner *Island Home.* In deference to the Keys' Spanish heritage, it's said, they translated this into Islamorada, giving rise to tales of a name coined by conquistadores, not Methodist farmers. Either way, it's a pretty name.

Near MM 83 is the **Florida Keys History of Diving Museum** *(82990 Overseas Hwy., tel 305/664-9737, www.diving museum.com, $$$),* dedicated to artifacts—including the largest international collection of diving helmets—photographs, books, and oral history about the underwater sport throughout the world as well as in the Keys. Even if you're not a diving aficionado, the museum is worth a visit to see the old-time diving suits and to marvel at how far diving technology has come.

Near MM 82, look for the **red railroad caboose** that used to house the Islamorada Chamber of Commerce but today presents a good photo opportunity. Here the ill-fated Florida East Coast Railway's depot and worker's encampment stood until the hurricane on Labor Day 1935 (see p. 174) flattened it. The nearby **Pioneer Cemetery,** on the grounds of the Cheeca Lodge resort, is the final resting place for many early Keys residents.

If you're just passing through on your way to Key West, take a break at the **Islamorada Library Park** at MM 81.5 on the bay side, behind the town library. The water's clear and shallow here, although a swift current requires parents to keep an eye on children. Public restrooms, picnic tables, and patches of lawn make this little beachfront oasis a pleasant place to relax

EXPERIENCE: Stand-up Paddleboarding

Explore the Keys in a novel yet ages-old fashion aboard a stand-up paddleboard. Stand-up paddleboarding is an ancient form of surfing that in recent years has become popular on the usually calm waters off South Florida's east coast, from Oleta River State Park in North Miami to Key Biscayne and throughout the Keys. A person simply stands on the board and uses a long paddle for maneuvering. It is a great way to exercise while seeing all kinds of wildlife. And it's unlikely you will fall off as the boards are designed for stability.

If you're up for an adventure, take a paddleboard tour. Depending on which outfitter you use, your guide might lead you to a spindly mangrove forest, where you can see a mini ecosystem, and then take you over sea grass where you can look down for sea turtles and jellyfish. You might be lucky and glide over manatees or baby sharks and see dolphins in the distance. Maybe you'll pass celebrity homes and yachts.

One outfitter in the Upper Keys is **Florida Bay Outfitters** *(104050 Overseas Hwy., Key Largo, tel 305/451-3018, www .kayakfloridakeys.com).* Its guides will take you on two-hour explorations ($50) around the bay. You also can rent boards ($20/hour) for solo exploring.

Florida Keys Memorial:
Across from the library, roadside at MM 81.6, stands the pale coral limestone of the Florida Keys Memorial, known as the hurricane monument. The memorial commemorates the Category 5 Labor Day hurricane of 1935, the most devastating storm ever known to hit the Keys, and the most intense land-falling hurricane to occur in the Western Hemisphere.

In Key West on the evening of Saturday, August 31, 1935, the air was still, hot, and humid. By Monday, September 2, storm warning flags snapped downtown as citizens nailed up shutters and prepared for the worst, and by midnight windblown rain was rattling the town's tin roofs. Wires snapped, trees fell, palm fronds cartwheeled—but the storm's full fury bypassed the island, moving north to the Upper and Lower Matecumbe Keys, where it drowned more than 400 people, most of them railroad workers aboard a rescue train swept from the tracks by 200-mile-an-hour gusts and a 20-foot tidal surge.

The monument marks the grave of 423 people who died in the tempest. Key West resident Ernest Hemingway chartered a boat to carry food and water for survivors. Finding few, he later wrote that in this region there was no autumn, "only a more dangerous summer." ■

Anglers use flat-bottomed boats called flats skiffs to fish for bonefish and permit in the shallow backcountry Gulf waters—the flats—off Islamorada.

EXPERIENCE: Fishing in the Keys

South Florida is perhaps best known for offshore fishing in the deep blue waters of the Gulf Stream, where anglers in heavy harness use stout rods and reels with the diameter of coconuts to catch hard-fighting dolphin (the fish, not the mammal), dorado, sailfish, wahoo, and marlin. The Keys are also one of the world's premier shallow-water, light-tackle, spin, and fly-fishing regions, where world records are set by steely eyed experts, many of them professional fishing guides so steeped in the craft and lore they write books about it.

Most of this arcane adventuring takes place in the shallows and backwaters of the Upper Keys Florida Bay backcountry. In this wilderness of uninhabited islands, lost in watery mangrove jungles and shimmering basins carpeted with gracefully bending sea grass, the water is often a mere 2 or 3 feet deep. Here, open-sea bravado and brawn take a back seat to stealth and the deft manipulation of delicate tackle in pursuit of elusive inshore fish. The sport is characterized by slow approaches toward instinctively wary fish known for hair-trigger alertness.

Unless you're experienced in this kind of fishing, own your own gear and boat, and know your way around the backcountry, the services of a licensed professional guide are necessary, if only to make sure you don't get lost.

Backcountry fishing boats (skiffs) are in essence casting platforms from 16 to 20 feet in length, with broad flat-bottomed hulls that allow them to float in little more than a foot of water. As you approach a fishing ground, your guide will turn off the electric motor and use a long pole to push the boat along.

INSIDER TIP:

Bridge fishing is very popular from Long Key and Old Seven Mile Bridges, which serve as man-made reefs and attract lots of fish.

—JANE SUNDERLAND
National Geographic contributor

You'll stand at the bow on a raised platform, with a high-angle line of sight into the water.

A good guide's knowledge is vast. He—or she—knows the best times of day to fish for a particular species, weighing that against variables such as weather, tides, and temperatures. Depending on what fish interests you, your guide will pick a destination. In the Florida Bay backcountry the water teems with redfish, snook, pompano, tarpon, black drum, ladyfish, sheepshead, and shark.

If you'd rather fish from shore, a guide is still a valuable adviser for showing you where to cast your line, and how. In springtime, fishing for tarpon with live bait is a popular activity on bridges and along deepwater channels from Key Largo to Key West.

Regulations & Outfitters

Fishing is permitted in the national parks and wildlife refuges whose boundaries embrace the Keys; regulations are available for free at each. Biscayne National Park (see pp. 146–147) includes the north Key Largo area; Everglades National Park (see pp. 148–151) covers Key Largo nearly to Marathon; and Great White Heron National Wildlife Refuge (see p. 198) spans much of the territory between Marathon and Key West. Check on requirements for state fishing licenses, available for periods from three to seven days to five years, all for modest fees.

There are fishing supply stores throughout the Keys. One of the finest fly-fishing outfitters in the Keys is the **Saltwater Angler** (243 Front St., tel 305/296-0700, www .saltwaterangler.com) in Key West. Go online at www .fla-keys.com for listings of outfitters for Key Largo, Islamorada, Marathon, Big Pine Key and the Lower Keys, and Key West. Costs vary widely, based on length and type of outing and outfitter.

Lignumvitae Key

It is still possible to see what the Upper Keys were like in their natural state, before agricultural and entrepreneurial ventures cut, quarried, burned, buried, paved, or otherwise rendered them tame. In 1970 the Nature Conservancy and the state of Florida joined forces to buy and preserve 280-acre Lignumvitae Key and nearby Shell Key on the Florida Bay side of the Matecumbes, just south of Islamorada, and historic Indian Key on the Atlantic side.

An Unspoiled Eden

The entirety of the island is preserved as **Lignumvitae Key Botanical State Park.** A true island roughly a mile out of alignment with the Keys' coral spine, the island lies in shallow

The fruit of the lignum vitae tree, one of the many Florida Keys plants that are from the Caribbean

mangrove flats outside the sight line of railroad surveyors' transits, and was fortuitously left alone. Early in the 20th century, the hardwood hammock was purchased by Miami pioneer and financier William J. Matheson (see p. 137), who built a four-bedroom hideaway of coral rock but left the rest of his retreat unspoiled. (A windmill generated power; fresh water came from a 12,000-gallon cistern filled with rainwater captured by the house's roof.)

The result is that Lignumvitae's tropical forests still hold dense stands of the island's blue-flowered namesake evergreen tree, whose Latin name means the "wood of life." The trees flower in late spring/early summer and produce small, heart-shaped berries afterward.

The lignum vitaes—the tree name is two words, the island name one word—share the island with thickets of mahogany, mastic, strangler fig, poisonwood, pigeon plum, and gumbo limbo, and more than 120 native plants. Peaceful it is, but silent it is not, for Lignumvitae Key's isolation (and now its strict management) makes it a wild refuge for shore, wading, and migratory birds. Bring binoculars to see reclusive creatures such as white-crowned pigeons, ospreys, double-crested cormorants, and great white herons.

INSIDER TIP:

Lignum vitae is an extremely dense hardwood that will not float in water and has a waxy, self-lubricating quality. In the past, it was chosen as a bearing to house rotating bronze propeller shafts in ships.

—STANLEY SPIELMAN
Former chair, Southern Florida chapter of The Explorers Club

Visiting the Park

Don't let the fact that this piece of Eden is accessible only by private or charter boat deter you; if your schedule allows for a two-hour adventure, this is a must. You'll return with a better sense of the natural Keys than most of the 73,000 people who call them home.

Tour boat concessions operate out of **Robbie's Marina** at MM 77.5 (in Islamorada), and you can kayak or canoe from Indian Key Fill at MM 79.5. As only 50 people are permitted on the island at a time, you will need to make reservations.

Because the island's eco systems are delicate, exploring on your own is forbidden, as is

swimming within 100 feet of its shores. All visitors tour the island and the old Matheson estate in the company of park rangers, who lead 1.5-hour guided walks ($), twice daily Friday through Sunday. If you plan to arrive on your own boat, you must still notify a park ranger in advance to reserve tour space and arrange to be met at the dock. Unfortunately, the nature of the island makes access difficult for people with disabilities. Call ahead for a ranger's advice.

Finally, wear good walking shoes and make sure you're well covered with a proven insect repellent. Lignumvitae Key is a natural subtropical environment at its most pristine: In the Keys, that means swarms of aggressively biting mosquitoes. ■

Feed Tarpon

At Robbie's Marina, schools of tarpon, some weighing well over 100 pounds, congregate near the tarpon deck. To marvel at them in all their glory, show up with baitfish ($) and hold one over the water—a "silver king" will leap up to get it. Be sure to drop the baitfish in time or the tarpon might try to snack on your hand. Throw a few into the water to witness a frenzied battle for the goods between tarpon and pelicans. Feeding starts at 8 a.m. daily and finishes in the evening (the time varies by season).

Lignumvitae Key Botanical State Park

🏚 158 B2

✉ MM 78.5

☎ 305/664-2540 or 305/664-9814 (tour reservations)

🕐 Guided walks Fri.–Sun. at 10 a.m. & 2 p.m.

💲 $

www.floridastate parks.org/ lignumvitaekey

Robbie's Marina

🏚 158 B2

✉ MM 77.5

☎ 305/664-9814 or 305/664-4196
Tour boats generally depart one-half hour before listed tour times; reservations required

www.robbies.com

Indian Key

About three-quarters of a mile southeast of Lower Matecumbe Key, at the edge of the Gulf Stream, lies lushly jungled 12-acre Indian Key, named for the Calusa who once lived here. They were replaced by 19th-century Bahamian turtle hunters and fishermen, who themselves retreated in 1831 when a wealthy young New Yorker named John Jacob Housman bought the island as a base for his ship salvage business. The location offered opportunity: a supply of fresh water on nearby Matecumbe and reefs with a reputation for disemboweling ships.

Indian Key, accessible only by boat, was raided by Indians in 1840 during the Second Seminole War.

Indian Key Historic State Park

Housman turned his rocky isle into a company enterprise, building a general store, a hotel, and a cluster of cottages. The shoreline sprouted warehouses, and wharves reached out toward the wrecking grounds like greedy fingers. Housman prospered for a time, then suffered reverses in the wake of renewed accusations of wrecking misbehavior; he was forced to mortgage his island. In 1838 Housman sold out to a physician named Henry Perrine, whose true love was tropical botany. Perrine studied the cultivation of useful tropical plants and experimented with plantings until the summer of 1840, when about 100 Indians attacked his village, looted its stores, and set houses afire. Perrine was killed. His family escaped by hiding beneath the floor of their house, and later fled.

With such a somber past, it's not surprising that Indian Key has been uninhabited since the early 1900s. Visitors can still see remnants of Housman's village—there's an observation tower on the island that offers a tree-top reconnoiter—but that's about it. So why visit? Time travel: Indian Key retains its pre European wildness; visitors are transported back to a perfect semblance of the Calusa world. The vestiges of **Housman's village**—foundations and cisterns where archaeologists occasionally dig for artifacts—peek out of the undergrowth along a **self-guiding trail.**

You can take your motorboat to the recently rebuilt dock or go on a tour from Robbie's Marina (see p. 177). You also can paddle there in your own kayak or canoe or rent one from an outfitter along the Overseas Highway. Floating across the grass flats is a spectacular chance to see manatees, dolphins, sharks, and rays. And anglers can fish for a variety of species, including bonefish, tarpon, and snapper. Near shore you'll likely see wading birds such as the great heron and the snowy egret, and you might get lucky and see a magnificent frigatebird or bald eagle.

Indian Key shares a headquarters with Lignumvitae Key Botanical State Park (see pp. 176–177), where information is available. Once ashore, pick up a free brochure and use its map and historical accounts to guide yourself around the island. Be aware that the island's management plan forbids both restrooms and picnic facilities—you'll find neither here.

San Pedro Underwater Archaeological Preserve State Park

In the 1960s, divers probing an area of white sand, turtle grass, and coral 18 feet underwater in Hawk Channel, about a mile south of Indian Key, found ballast stones and cannon identifying the wreck of the *San Pedro*. This 287-ton Dutch merchantman had been sunk, along with 20 other ships in the Spanish treasure fleet, in 1733 by a hurricane.

The easily accessible site has been set aside for sport divers as an underwater archaeological preserve. The ship's original guns and timbers have been removed for preservation and study and replaced by reproductions and a period-style anchor, but divers

Indian Key Historic State Park
- 158 B2
- 305/664-2540
- Ranger-led tours 9 a.m. & 1 p.m. Thurs.–Mon.
- $
www.floridastate parks.org/indiankey

San Pedro Underwater Archaeological Preserve State Park
- 158 B2
- 1 mile S of Indian Key
- 305/664-9814 (Robbie's Marina)
www.floridastate parks.org/sanpedro

Hurricanes

On average, the Atlantic Basin generates nine tropical storms each year, six of which become hurricanes, two of them intense. Florida's hurricane season begins June 1 and ends on the last day of November. Usually born off the African coast, they are watched by the National Hurricane Center in Miami from the time they start their westward drift. If one threatens the Keys, warnings are issued several days in advance. If evacuation is ordered, visitors are given priority to leave first.

still occasionally find 18th-century coins. For more information (or to find out about snorkeling trips), call Robbie's Marina. The wreck's GPS coordinates are 24° 51.802' N, 80° 40.795' W. Be sure to tie up to mooring buoys to prevent anchor damage to the delicate bottom. ■

Long Key

The Spanish name for Long Key was Cayo Vivora—Rattlesnake Key. There are no rattlesnakes, but the isle's sinuous shape and widespread *boca* (mouth) reminded some creative conquistador of a rattler in mid-strike. Opinions differ as to whether this peaceful 965-acre state park affords an excellent idyll or merely a very good one. If you like grassy tidal flats so shallow you can walk hundreds of feet into the Atlantic before the water rises to your waist, it's excellent.

Long Key's shallow tidal flats offer a safe place for kids to swim.

Long Key
 158 A1

Long Key State Park
🏕 158 A1
✉ MM 67.5
☎ 305/664-4815
💲 $
**www.floridastate
parks.org/longkey**

Long Key State Park

Mangroves fringe the shore, providing cover for waterbirds, and you can rent a canoe to paddle their channels, or explore them on a boardwalk that angles through the wave-lapped jungle, its wildlife and flora described by interpretive panels. The elevated 1.25-mile footpath is called the **Golden Orb Trail,** named for the large red and gold spiders whose webs can be seen draped among the limbs like old lace. This is a popular camping area year-round. Check at park headquarters for ranger-led guided walks and snorkeling, fishing, and marine ecology activities. If you enjoy canoeing, paddle the **Long Key Lakes Canoe Trail.**

Across the highway on the Florida Bay side, at MM 67.7, the **Layton Trail** offers a half-hour stroll through stands of tropical hardwood. You'll see delicate blades of sea grass waving at you from underwater. There's a historical marker here noting the origins of the Long Key Viaduct, a sinuous old railroad bridge that begins a short way down the road and parallels the Overseas Highway for several miles, and Flagler's long-gone fishing retreat. ■

From tiny Conch Key at MM 65 to the southern landfall of Seven Mile Bridge at MM 40, the longest of the Keys' 42 spans

Middle Keys

A bas-relief on the copper door of the Crane Point Museum, Vaca Key

Middle Keys

Long Key Viaduct was Henry Flagler's favorite bridge, and its 180 Romanesque arches were featured on his railroad's travel literature. His trains usually puffed along at a sedate 15 miles an hour, but today motorists speed by much faster. Those who stay often have a rod and reel with them, or a mask and fins, as these islands offer superb fishing and diving. Some of the best is found within sight of the Sombrero Reef lighthouse, which watches over an extravagantly rich coral kingdom of sea life 25 feet beneath the waves.

The Keys' commercial fishing industry began here in the early 1800s. Over the years the business of hooking fish has resulted in an equally large business of enticing visitors who want to fish. An armada of charter fishing boats crowds the waterfront in Marathon, on Vaca Key, where upstanding bait poles fringe the shore like a willowy canebrake, their captains waiting to take anglers out to fish underwater canyons plunging a thousand feet. Great white herons leisurely wing their way to their namesake wildlife refuge, a vast offshore expanse of water and mangrove reaching south into the Lower Keys.

You can swim with dolphins at the Dolphin Research Center on Grassy Key. On Vaca Key, time, or at least the changes wrought in the Keys by time, has been arrested within the 63 acres of the Crane Point Hammock, the last known undisturbed stand of thatch palm, once common in the archipelago and now shrunk to this beleaguered tuft of the past. The islands' odd geology, peculiar wildlife, and dramatic human pageant are the concern of the

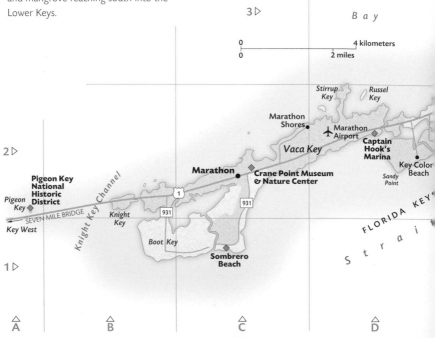

NOT TO BE MISSED:

Peaceful sunsets at Sombrero Beach, Vaca Key **185**

A snorkeling or scuba diving adventure in the Keys **186–187**

Exploring the historic Adderley House on Vaca Key **188**

Ferrying to Pigeon Key and then taking the walking tour of historic buildings **189**

The magnificent panoramas seen from Seven Mile Bridge **190**

Crane Point Museum and Nature Center. A nearby cultural trail on Crane Point loops around one of the Keys' oldest conch-style residences and the ruins of a mid-19th-century Bahamian village, whose inhabitants earned their living by producing charcoal.

On little Pigeon Key—a 2.2-mile walk on the old, now pedestrianized Seven Mile Bridge from Knight's Key—you will find what must certainly be America's loneliest national historic district. Here the study of Keys history and culture centers around a restored early 20th-century camp for railroad workers—the people who built the bridges and laid the railway track. ■

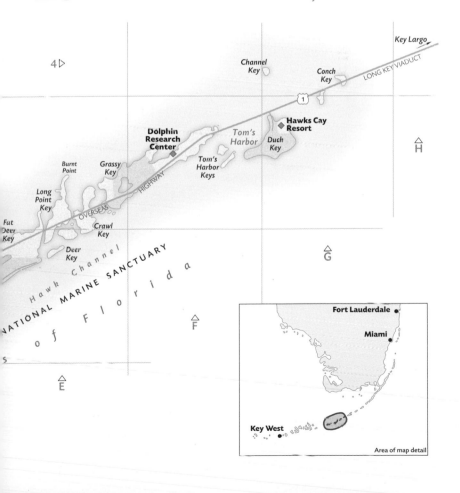

Conch Key to Grassy Key

Just before you cross Long Key Bridge to reach Conch Key and points south, turn off the highway onto the ocean side at MM 65.5 for a striking view of Flagler's old arched viaduct. Walk down the embankment to encounter its photogenic angles as it leaps off into the blue infinity.

Soft sand and palm trees—hallmarks of the Keys

Conch & Duck Keys
🏕 183 G3–G4

Grassy Key
🏕 183 E3–F3

Dolphin Research Center
🏕 183 F3
✉ MM 59, Grassy Key
☎ 305/289-1121
💲 $$$$$ for swims
www.dolphins.org

Conch & Duck Keys

Sixteen-acre Conch Key is home to retirees and fishermen and those who harvest the Florida spiny lobster. You'll see their boxlike snares, known here as "crayfish traps," stacked haphazardly all over the island.

At MM 61 of the Overseas Highway, another bridge brings you to Duck Key, site of the sprawling Caribbean-style Hawks Cay Resort (see Travelwise p. 254), the Middle Keys' most luxurious retreat. The salmon and green West Indies–style hideaway is a 1959 creation of the architect Morris Lapidus, who also designed Miami Beach's opulent Fontainebleau and Eden Roc. The resort caters to those used to being catered to, who want their golf close by, their tennis on clay, and their drinks served poolside.

Grassy Key

Few creatures are as fascinating and mysterious as dolphins, whose brains are larger and more complex than ours and, some people suspect, might possess intelligence rivaling our own. This accounts for the appeal of the nonprofit **Dolphin Research Center,** home to 19 of the sociable mammals, which may be touched under staff supervision. There's very little chance of missing the center; a 30-foot-high statue of a mother and baby dolphin fronts it on the bay side of the road at MM 59. Founded in 1984, the education and research facility offers programs on dolphin biology and communication, culminating with an opportunity to meet, touch, and "talk" with the creatures. To swim with the animals, reservations (tel 305/289–0002) may be made after the first day of any month for the following month. ∎

Vaca Key

The lion's share of 6-mile-long Vaca Key is claimed by the self-proclaimed capital of the Middle Keys, which got its name when Flagler exhorted his railroaders to make a "marathon" effort to finish the line to Key West before his impending demise.

Marathon

Marathon, whose pace is nowhere near as fast as its name implies, is an extended cluster of unadorned commerce. Just about every guidebook calls it laid-back, which it is, even though there's an airport here with a busy commuter airline schedule, along with several resorts and an enthusiastic community of concessionaires eager to rent you a boat, take you scuba diving, or get you out fishing for sailfish.

As you drive through town, stop by the venerable **Captain Hook's Marina** *(tel 800/278-4665, www.captainhooks.com),* ocean side at MM 53, for a quick immersion in Middle Keys fishing culture. Even if your notion of nirvana doesn't include deep-sea adventures, the tackle shop is an education in man's astonishing ability to produce arcane devices. If you stay on Vaca Key, check the marina's schedule for fishing charters, evening cruises, and "Heart of Darkness" voyages into the Everglades.

Come sunset, people gather wherever the subtropical sun sets. Waterside establishments like the **Island Fish Co.** *(12648 Overseas Hwy., tel 305/743-4191, www.islandfishco.com)* advertise their sundown views. Nearby,

the old Seven Mile Bridge (see p. 190), now a walkway to Pigeon Key, offers sunsets for free. (Leave your vehicle in the parking area at MM 46.8.) If you time it correctly, you can stroll south over the water, leaving the party atmosphere behind in favor of wave-lapped peacefulness, and enjoy the evening spectacle that elicits cheers and clapping up and down the Keys every sunny evening.

Crane Point Museum & Nature Center

At MM 50.5, on the bay side of the highway, incongruously surrounded by Marathon's commercial clutter, is one of the Keys' most extraordinary natural

(continued on p. 188)

Vaca Key

🅰 182 C2–D2

Visitor Information

✉ Greater Marathon Chamber of Commerce, 12222 Overseas Hwy.

☎ 305/743-5417 or 800/262-7284

Crane Point Museum & Nature Center

🅰 182 C2

✉ 5550 Overseas Hwy., Marathon

☎ 305/743-9100

🕐 Closed Sun. a.m.

💲 $$$

www.cranepoint.net

Sombrero Beach

Although it's on the wrong side of the island for sunset worship, Sombrero Beach, just south at the end of Sombrero Road at MM 50, is a lovely spot for an evening wade or swim in Hawk Channel. There's deep water here, a well-kept strand, and a verdant little park and playground where you will likely find locals playing a game of softball.

Snorkeling & Diving in the Keys

The Keys' warm water and reefs attract thousands of scuba and snorkel aficionados annually, for a recreation statistically about as safe as swimming.

How to Get Started

If you have some basic swimming skills, snorkeling is easy. It requires only a mask to see underwater, a snorkel for breathing, and fins for propulsion, all of which can be rented. (Most tours also provide buoyant vests.)

Scuba diving, however, uses sophisticated equipment and requires training by qualified teachers. The best way to learn is to take lessons from a certified member of the Professional Association of Diving Instructors, or PADI, the largest scuba training organization in the world. PADI Dive Center locations are listed on the Web (www.padi.com). The organization develops scuba programs and diver training products, monitors training programs conducted worldwide by over 135,000 professional members in more than 170 countries and territories, maintains diver certification records, and issues the credentials you must present to be allowed on open-ocean dives in the Keys without on-site instruction.

Who Can Dive?

Just about anyone over the age of 10 in normal good health can learn to dive. (Kids between 10 and 15 receive a Junior Open Water Diver certification, which requires them to dive with a certified adult. At age 15, they can upgrade to a regular Open Water Diver certification.) You'll be asked to complete a routine medical questionnaire to determine if your health requires a consultation with your physician to ensure that it's safe for you to dive. Wearing soft contact lenses poses no problem, but hard lenses should be gas permeable. Many people who take up snorkeling and diving have prescription lenses fitted into their masks.

Typically, an entry-level course begins in a pool and includes four training dives. If you'd rather try out scuba diving before committing to formal instruction, PADI offers a Discover Scuba Diving program lasting only several hours, including a shallow ocean dive supervised by an instructor after a short pool session to familiarize you with your equipment. This will allow you to master some basic techniques, such as learning to adjust your ears to the surrounding pressure so they don't hurt when you descend. A shorter pool dive program is offered in places without natural open-water diving sites.

How Long Does Certification Take?

PADI courses are performance based, meaning students progress according to their demonstrated mastery of the required knowledge and skills. A beginner's PADI Open Water Diver course might consist of five or six sessions completed in three to four days, or spread over six weeks. Approximately one-third of the course can be taken online.

If you want to wait and see how the Keys look to you before taking a lesson, PADI-certified introductory resort courses can have you exploring the reefs in hours.

The Lure of Treasure

"There is not a diver, not an adventurer, not a hunter after fame and fortune, who has not, at some time, dreamed of striking it rich." So wrote French adventurer Jacques-Yves Cousteau, whose invention of the "self-contained underwater breathing apparatus"—the SCUBA—opened up Florida's shallow, treasure-strewn reefs to a postwar generation of dreamers.

Twenty feet underwater at John Pennekamp state park, the 9-foot bronze "Christ of the Deep," a 1961 gift from the Underwater Society of America, blesses those who work or play in the sea.

They don't result in certification, but they do enable you to dive in the afternoon with an instructor following a morning of classroom and pool instruction.

Is It Costly?

As a rule of thumb, scuba diving ranks with snow skiing. Dive centers and resorts rent state-of-the-art equipment, so there's no need to buy. Consider purchasing your own mask, snorkel, and fins, however, as they can be uncomfortable if not properly sized.

If you want a record of your exploits, several major companies sell inexpensive one-time-use underwater cameras that produce good shallow-water images when the sun's out (on overcast days you lose color contrast). Some dive shops rent underwater video cameras.

places, Crane Point. Many of the islands once resembled this 64-acre virgin thatch palm hammock, the last of its kind in North America.

Walk the 1.5-mile loop trail through the forest, a stroll made more meaningful if you have a copy of the self-guided brochure that identifies the red mangrove, palms, and exotic hardwoods bending over you, hiding the creatures whose unseen scuffling and odd cries add a peculiar spookiness. There's much to

The Adderley House is the Keys' oldest example of conch architecture outside of Key West.

identify here, including 160 native plants and a menagerie of creatures, some of whom, like the graceful ibis, stand at the brink of extinction. Along the way, look for rare tree snails, and don't miss an unusual pit gouged in the island's coral foundation by rainfall erosion, exposing fossil star and brain corals from the primordial sea that formed the Keys.

The trail also passes the site of a long-gone 19th-century village, established by immigrants from the Bahamas. Still standing, however, is the well-restored **Adderley House,** built in the 1890s; now a historic site, it is said to be the oldest example of the Keys' quaint gingerbread conch architecture north of Key West. Its rough-textured walls are made of tabby, a mixture of limestone and crushed sea shells.

Crane Point Museum:

Archaeologists working on Vaca Key have uncovered a rich cache of pre-Columbian artifacts, including weapons, tools, a dugout canoe, and pottery. The oldest vessels, possibly 5,000 years old, are handsomely displayed at the Crane Point Museum. Among the most popular of the museum's 20 major exhibits (supplemented by a half dozen changing displays) is one on the many shipwrecks that brought wealth to these once isolated isles. Bronze cannon, gold and silver from the Spanish main, and everyday items commemorate the anonymous fortune seekers who found only watery graves on the reefs here. The museum also focuses on the natural history and wildlife of the Keys, featuring a simulated coral reef cave and more.

If you're traveling with kids, set them loose at the **Children's Activity Center,** an outdoor facility with touch tanks and a galleon complete with pirate clothes and treasure. ■

Pigeon Key

Pigeon Key is an idyllic and historically unique 5-acre island located 2.2 miles from the northern end of the old Seven Mile Bridge. Like the old Florida East Coast Railroad causeway that casts a shadow line across the little key, Pigeon is listed on the National Register of Historic Places, with the entire island being designated a national historic district.

From 1908 to the infamous 1935 Labor Day hurricane, the island was a workers' community, home to painters, maintenance crews, and bridge tenders. Children attended a one-room school and everyone bought staples from the company store. After the storm caused the railroad's demise, the town (whose population once rose above an overcrowded 400) set to work converting the railroad to a two-lane vehicle causeway, which opened in 1938.

A view of Pigeon Key, as seen from Seven Mile Bridge

INSIDER TIP:

On Pigeon Key, walk up the ramp to the old Seven Mile Bridge to see sharks, rays, turtles, manatees, tarpon, and ospreys.

—KELLY McKINNON
Executive director,
Pigeon Key Foundation

Visiting the Key

Park at the visitor center, situated in a vintage red and silver Florida East Coast Railway coach located at the west end of Marathon, just north of the new Seven Mile Bridge near MM 47. Beginning at 10 a.m., a boat shuttles visitors (four times daily) 2.2 miles south, near the old Seven Mile Bridge, to Pigeon Key. A walking tour guide accompanies each boat. Though the price of admission includes round-trip boat passage, many people opt to stroll to the island via the old Seven Mile Bridge and return by boat. The key's main structure, now the island's administrative headquarters, served as a dormitory for 64 railway workers in the 1920s. The restored early 20th century village includes a small museum that documents the half-century struggle to link the Keys by rail, ferry, and auto. Locals, however, come here mainly for day-long getaways on a picnic blanket with a good book. ∎

Pigeon Key
🗺 182 A2

Pigeon Key National Historic District
✉ Visitor center and boat to island at MM 47
☎ 305/743-5999
💲 $$ (Includes shuttle)

Seven Mile Bridge

To be precise, the new span stretches 35,830 feet—6.7 miles—but when viewed from its northern end, it looks as if it runs to Cuba. The bridge's opening in 1982 meant the retirement of its predecessor, which still runs alongside it. Though the old span is missing sections here and there, and in places appears to be little more than a guano-spattered pelican roost, it's plain to see why, upon its completion in 1912, newspapers proclaimed it the Eighth Wonder of the World.

The old Seven Mile Bridge (right) is sometimes described as the world's longest fishing pier.

Seven Mile Bridge
🅰 182 A1–B2

The bridge was in fact one of the most ambitious endeavors of its time, for swift-running tides and an unstable sea bottom challenged the skills of Flagler's engineers. The tycoon personally exhorted his managers to attack the project as if on a military campaign and spared no expense. Historical photographs in Pigeon Key's museum (see p. 189) document the intensity of the effort: large warehouses, four dormitories, a kitchen and dining hall, and an encampment of military-style tents for the construction crews, with building materials piled up almost everywhere else.

Still impressive, the bridge runs southwest atop 546 concrete piers and 210 arches, some of them reaching nearly 30 feet underwater to anchor on limestone bedrock. It was one of the few man-made things to withstand the force of the 1935 hurricane.

Time was when you had to stop at a drawbridge over Moser Channel at MM 43.5 while boats and small ships passed below. The new bridge simply vaults the channel, clearing the high tide mark by 65 feet. ∎

A stretch of the islands with a wilder appearance and feel than the other Keys, less developed and more densely wooded

Lower Keys

A ship anchor and rope, vital elements aboard the Keys' fleet of boats

Lower Keys

As travelers near Key West, they tend to drive faster, particularly after crossing Seven Mile Bridge, as if that were the last point of worthwhile interest before heading for Jimmy Buffett's Margaritaville and ordering a margarita to celebrate their arrival at Mile Zero. But while it is understandable, it would be a mistake, at least if you value natural places and opportunities to wander in them—which in the Lower Keys are numerous and memorable.

You'll find one of the Keys' few truly sandy beaches at Bahia Honda State Park, which also encloses a mangrove forest and a hardwood hammock stippled with West Indian exotics like the sanguine red bougainvillea, the buttery alamanda, the Jamaican morning glory, and the Geiger tree, whose startling flowers resemble small orange artillery bursts.

Florida Keys Wildlife Refuges

A good portion of the Lower Keys falls within three designated refuges that protect hundreds of thousands of acres, the vast majority of which are open water, but there are still thousands of acres of pristine sub-tropical pineland, mangrove, and hammock habitats, virtually all of which lie marooned on islands accessible only by boat. The Great White Heron National Wildlife Refuge sprawls from the latitude of Marathon as far southwest as Key West. From there, the great watery rectangle of

the Key West National Wildlife Refuge takes over, extending west to embrace uninhabited islands full of red, white, and black mangrove in the Marquesas Keys.

The third refuge, National Key Deer Refuge, encompasses most of Big Pine Key as well as 25 other islands, where several hundred miniature versions of the Virginia white-tailed deer dart through slash pine. The tips of these tiny, skittish deer's ears barely reach the level of your belt. You can wander here, too, under a 50-foot canopy of hardwood trees in Watson's Hammock, another remnant of the primordial Keys, filled with gumbo limbo, Jamaican dogwood,

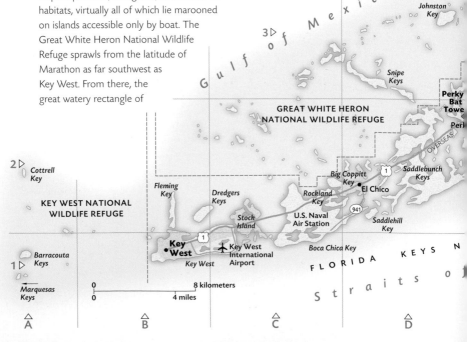

NOT TO BE MISSED:

The abandoned railroad bridge at Bahia Honda State Park **195**

Seeing wild Key deer at National Key Deer Refuge, Big Pine Key **196–197**

Getting served at No Name Pub, infamous since the 1930s **199**

Ferrying from Little Torch Key to Little Palm Island Resort for an exquisite oceanfront lunch **202**

Perky's Bat Tower, a historical oddity, on Sugarloaf Key **204**

century plants (despite their name they usually bloom every decade or so), orchids, and ferns.

Other Delights of the Lower Keys

Due south of Big Pine Key, about 7 miles out in shallow, remarkably clear Gulf Stream waters, sits Looe Key, site of a coral reef prized as the most vibrantly healthy and biologically diverse reef in the entire island chain. The other Lower Keys—No Name, Summerland, Ramrod, Cudjoe, Sugarloaf, Saddlebunch, Big Coppitt, and Boca Chica—are distinguished more by their histories and man-made eccentricities than by nature. All it takes to experience them is a bit of time and a willingness to spend it here. ■

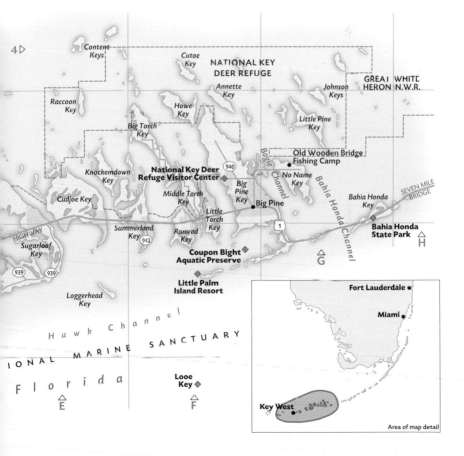

Bahia Honda Key

Environmentalists treasure Bahia Honda ("deep bay") because most of the island is claimed by Bahia Honda State Park and thereby protected from commercial development. Most day-trippers, from Key West and Greater Miami, come here for the park's graceful Atlantic-facing beach, the Keys' longest naturally sandy strand, which has been rightly described as one of America's most appealing and has excellent snorkeling just offshore.

Away from its Atlantic-facing shoreline, much of Bahia Honda remains rugged and untrammeled.

Bahia Honda Key

 193 G3

**Bahia Honda
State Park**

✉ 36850 Overseas
Hwy., Big Pine
Key

☎ 305/872-2353

💲 $$

**www.floridastate
parks.org/
bahiahonda**

Bahia Honda State Park

Although most of the 524-acre state park remains in a wild state, Bahia Honda is nevertheless one of the most accommodating parks in the Florida Keys, with such unusual amenities as a half dozen two-bedroom waterfront housekeeping cabins (each sleeping eight) rising on stilts to take in a paradisiacal ocean view. Tucked away elsewhere are 80 campsites (half of which are offered on a first-come, first-served basis) in three campgrounds, a marina (where you can rent windsurfers), a

boat-launching ramp, and a dive shop where you can rent scuba and snorkeling gear.

Treat yourself to a half-hour respite at a shaded picnic table on **Sandspur Beach,** or a stroll along Bahia Honda's northeastern shore. A self-guided nature trail flirts with a lagoon and winds through a hardwood hammock dense with exotic Caribbean trees and bushes: gumbo limbo, the Jamaica morning glory, the West Indies yellow satinwood (found nowhere else in the Keys), Geiger trees, sea lavender, bay cedar, and thatch and silver palm. Resident birds include pelicans, white-crowned pigeons, laughing gulls, ospreys, herons, and smooth-billed anis, joined seasonally by migratory birds such as ibis, willets, sandpipers, and terns. Look for a caboose that has authentic historic items for the park's interpretive program, and ask a ranger to point out the remnant of Henry Flagler's railroad rusting in the undergrowth.

INSIDER TIP:

Experiencing the Keys is best done by diving in, floating on, and flying over the shallow seas. The natural beauty of Bahia Honda is stellar from a Keys Hopper helicopter.

—BILL KEOGH

National Geographic contributor & guide, Big Pine Kayak Adventures

Diving & Snorkeling: The Bahia Honda Channel between the old and new Bahia Honda bridges is one of the deepest in the Keys, attracting divers to the bridge pilings, which create a habitat for coral, sponges, spiny lobsters, and myriad varicolored fish species. Check at the Bahia Honda Dive Shop *(tel 305/872-3210)* in the concession building for current conditions and advice, which will certainly include a warning to beware stinging fire coral, sea urchins, and the channel's powerful currents, the swiftest in the Keys.

Ask at the park headquarters about daily snorkeling programs on the reef at nearby **Looe Key** (see p. 203). The dive shop is the place to inquire about snorkeling and scuba diving trips to offshore reefs. You can also rent a small boat or kayak here.

Fishing: Bahia Honda's waters teem with snapper and grouper (best fished near the old Bahia Honda bridge) as well as bonefish, permit, and barracuda (in the shallow flats of the Atlantic). The tarpon fishing in this area is especially good, so consider trying the recreation that Ernest Hemingway credited with renewing his energy and creative powers between intensive days of writing. Charter boats operate from here—the fee provides everything except the tarpon. ■

Keys Hopper

✉ Flights depart from Florida Keys Marathon Airport, at MM 52.2

☎ 305/619-9603

💲 Flights start at $129 per person for a 25-minute flight, two-person minimum

www.ravenair.net/ keys.html

The Deceptive Lower Keys

Most of the larger islands in the Lower Keys, such as the Torches, Sugarloaf, and Saddlebunch, have convoluted shorelines that can create the illusion that they're small. Big Pine Key, for example, runs to nearly 8 miles in length, and at one point is 2 miles wide. Where the Overseas Highway negotiates an isthmus, however, it's easy to underestimate the possibilities lying alongside the road and down humble lanes that wander off into woods. Follow a dirt road here or there, and if you do not find yourself in a cul-de-sac of gates to private hideaway retreats, you'll probably wind through brush and scrub and slash pine, past explosions of scarred cactus to a rocky beach of broken shells and coral, or perhaps a mudflat, or a mangrove wilderness stretching west to the horizon.

Big Pine Key

On Big Pine Key—the second largest key after Key Largo—pinelands once shared much of the island with tropical hardwood and shoreline mangrove forests. Today, however, development has gone dangerously far, encouraged in part because Big Pine is one of the few keys with a natural year-round supply of fresh water. Houses, condos, shopping centers, marinas, and parking lots claim more of Big Pine than is desirable, but you can still sense the natural order of things.

Once considered a unique species, Key deer are now believed to be related to white-tailed deer.

Big Pine Key

🅜 193 F3

National Key Deer Refuge

🅜 193 F3

✉ Visitor center, 179 Key Deer Blvd.

☎ 305/872-0774

www.fws.gov/ nationalkeydeer

National Key Deer Refuge

What acreage that does not lie beneath some improvement belongs mainly to the pine, palm, and hardwood hammocks of the 8,900-plus land acres of National Key Deer Refuge, found on Big Pine and 25 nearby islands. The refuge was established in 1957 to protect the dwindling population of Key deer.

The largest (usually the males) among these odd creatures might stand 34 inches at the shoulder and weigh more than

100 pounds. Biologists have listed them as a pint-size subspecies of the Virginia white-tailed deer, rendered small by eons of environmental stresses, including limited water and forage, and a small habitat. They exist nowhere else in the wild but in the Keys, and are further distinguished by their ability to drink brackish water. It is supposed that their ancestors ranged south before the melting of the ancient Wisconsin ice age glacier, which elevated sea levels and turned what had been a tenuous peninsula

into an archipelago. Whatever produced these carefully stepping miniatures, whose newborns weigh 2 to 4 pounds and leave a postage-stamp-size hoofprint, their numbers were reduced by hunting and poaching to a mere 50 or so in the 1940s, from which the herd has slowly grown to something near 800. That's a peak population for the size of the habitat. A substantial number of the Key deer live on Big Pine and neighboring No Name Key. (As you drive across Big Pine, observe the slow speed limit in order to decrease your chance of hitting a Key deer, should it stray onto the roads.)

In addition to the Key deer, the refuge protects other wildlife, including alligators, Eastern diamondback rattlesnakes, hognose snakes, and raccoons; some species are unique to the Lower Keys, such as the marsh rabbit and silver rice rat.

Visiting the Refuge: To get to the refuge, turn west off the Overseas Highway just south of MM 31 onto Key Deer Boulevard (Fla. 940), where you'll soon see a sign pointing the way. Turn right into a shopping center for the refuge's **visitor center**; stop to pick up information, a map, and brochure for the self-guiding Jack Watson Nature Trail.

The **Jack Watson Nature Trail** (named for the refuge manager who strongly enforced the ban on hunting Key deer) lies 1.5 miles farther up Key Deer Boulevard, near a former quarry known

Don't Feed the Key Deer

What should you feed the Key deer that you're bound to encounter on Big Pine Key? Nothing.

Every day, dozens of people feed the little Bambi look-alikes food from their cars. But this act not only disrupts the animals' natural healthy diet, it also teaches them to walk more openly on roads, increasing their chances of being hit by a vehicle.

In 2010, 108 Key deer were killed by vehicles, further reducing the endangered species' population. Near the National Key Deer Refuge's visitor center, look for the two signs reporting how many deer have been killed by vehicles so far in the year.

as the **Blue Hole,** now naturally filled with fresh groundwater and alligators of various sizes. You can leave your car here, take a look at the torpid reptiles, and then stroll a very short paved path to the head of the mile-long loop of the nature trail, which cuts through a hardwood forest of mostly gumbo limbo and Jamaican dogwood that rise 50 feet to create an oasis of shade. Along the path you'll find water-filled sinkholes and stands of thatch and silver palm rising above a riot of subtropical plants. Come evening, you might see a Key deer lurking in the shadows. Without a doubt it will see you first. Be aware that feeding Key deer is against the law.

Next, walk or drive to the nearby quarter-mile **Mannillo Nature Trail.** Additional short walking trails in the refuge are on nearby No Name Key (see p. 199), reached via Watson Boulevard, off Key Deer Boulevard.

No Name Boat Rentals

✉ 1791 Bogie Dr., Big Pine Key

☎ 269/569-4195

www.nonamekey boatrental.com

Big Pine Kayak Adventures

✉ Big Pine Key

☎ 305/872-7474

www.keyskayak tours.com

Great White Heron National Wildlife Refuge

You probably won't see a sign announcing this federal sanctuary, the only nesting place in the United States for great white herons and the endangered white-crowned pigeon. Glance at your map, however, and you'll notice ruler-straight boundary lines embracing much of the bay side of the Lower Keys nearly to Key West.

INSIDER TIP:

On Big Pine, don't miss the obscenely cheesy pizza at No Name Pub [see p. 199], just before the bridge to No Name Key.

—JEREMY BERLIN
Editor, National Geographic
magazine

These nearly 117,700 backcountry acres of shallow water, fringe and scrub mangrove wetlands, low hardwood hammocks, and salt marsh also provide a haven for ospreys, reddish egrets, mangrove cuckoos, black-whiskered vireos, green- and blue-winged teal, red-breasted mergansers, and coots. Birdwatchers consider themselves especially fortunate to record sightings of the gawky-beautiful roseate spoonbill, the ibis, and the double-crested cormorant, among many other uncommon species.

Visiting the Refuge: You can't drive to the 6,500 acres of land included in the refuge, but you can explore them by boat, and if you have at least a half day you ought to consider it. There is profoundly affecting primordial beauty here, and local fishing guides offer day trips aboard shallow-draft boats for those who simply want to observe. Within the refuge you'll find a fertile world where native seabirds and migratory waterfowl breed, many roosting on floating nests. You're also likely to encounter sea turtles and bottlenose dolphins. Once you wander into its maze of mangrove islands, you get the pleasant sense of entering a magical kingdom. And it is—a place where the Earth abides simply by being left alone. Be sure to take binoculars.

If you're reasonably good at handling a canoe or kayak (Big Pine Kayak Adventures rents kayaks and offer guided kayak tours of the refuge), it's a fairly easy paddle from Big Pine Key (see p. 196) or the Torch Keys (see p. 202) out into the **Content Keys,** inside refuge boundaries.

If you motor out (you can rent a boat from No Name Boat Rentals, on Big Pine Key), keep your noise and speed at a minimum to avoid frightening birds from their nests or creating wakes that swamp low-lying and floating nests. Stay about 200 feet away from the islands—causing a roosting bird to flee its nest leaves eggs or nestlings unshaded in the sun's killing glare.

There aren't any facilities within the refuge, so be sure to take water and food. ∎

No Name Key

This island once hosted a secret training base for anti-Castro Cuban guerrillas. The base failed, as did No Name's only settlement. This small village was served in the 1920s by a ferry from Marathon, then a tortuous route of dusty roads and wooden bridges jumping between Big Pine, Ramrod, and Summerland Keys. Today, Watson Boulevard connects No Name to Big Pine.

A tackle and bait shop on No Name Key serves locals and tourists alike.

The only vestige of the community era is the **Old Wooden Bridge Guest Cottages & Marina** (1791 Bogie Dr., tel 305/872-2241, www.oldwooden bridge.com), a cluster of one- and two-bedroom cottages. The local hangout is the humble beer- and pizza-serving No Name Pub on Big Pine Key, just across the Bogie Channel bridge that links No Name Key to Big Pine Key.

Though some back roads here—some paved, others not—lead to the remnants of failed enterprise and broken dreams, you can explore scenic areas in and around the National Key Deer Refuge (see pp. 196–197), which encompasses much of No Name. The Big Pine Bicycle Center (tel 305/872-0130) at MM 31 on the ocean side of the highway rents single-gear, fat-tire bikes for adults and children with safety helmets included. A pleasant bike route departs from MM 30.3 on US 1's bay side and follows Wilder Road across the Bogie Channel bridge to No Name. Or pedal along Key Deer Boulevard into the refuge on Big Pine. Avoid walking trails leading through wetlands, as bike tires cut into their loam, causing damage and encouraging erosion. ■

No Name Key
 193 G3
✉ Reached via Watson Blvd., off Key Deer Blvd., at MM 31, Big Pine Key

No Name Pub
✉ N. Watson Blvd., Big Pine Key
☎ 305/872-9115
www.noname pub.com

Tropical Hardwood Hammocks

The image is appealing: drowsing in a hammock in the shade of a tropical glade to the rustle of palms and the lapping of gentle waves. In the Keys, however, there are hammocks (a word adopted by 16th-century Spanish explorers from the language of native Caribbeans, who invented them for more comfortable sleeping in their humid clime) and there are hammocks, a term that first appeared in English among 18th-century mariners who used it to designate a low rise or hillock on a sea coast.

Visitors walk through tropical hammock found in John Pennekamp Coral Reef State Park, Key Largo.

Along the coasts of southern Florida, throughout the Everglades, and in the Florida Keys, hammocks refer to the dense, vine-entangled forests that geologists believe arose here between 120 and 110 thousand years ago, after the Keys' coral reef foundation was left high and dry when ancient seas receded. A curious mix of plant and animal communities evolved along with them and competed with populations of hardy South Florida slash pines that thrive atop fossilized coral limestone and are known as pine rocklands.

A Riot of Plant & Wildlife

The hammocks support more than 20 species of broad-leafed trees, shrubs, and vines, most of them native to the West Indies. Biologists assume their seeds were washed ashore, arrived on driftwood, or were left in the droppings of migratory birds. Those exotics able to cope with scant rainfall and thin soil eventually landscaped the once barren coral knobs, forming a low canopy of live oak (their deeply furrowed bark fringed with lacy resurrection fern), red mulberry, mahogany (only in a few locations), and palm over a dense, often impenetrable tangle of vines and shrubbery whose names are whimsically charming: catbrier, Virginia creeper, pepper vine, possum grape, beautyberry, shiny sumac, red bay, Simpson's stopper, marlberry, wild coffee, wild lime, coralbean, torchwood. And below these, Spanish moss, ball moss, quill wild pine, the cardinal air plant, the green wild pine, and, if you're lucky, butterfly orchids.

The lack of a primordial physical connection between the landmasses of Florida and the West Indies barred most earthbound West Indian wildlife from colonizing the Keys. The hammocks drew their roster of animals from mainland North America, the creatures arriving in improbable ways—clinging to trees washed out to sea by flooding, arriving as captives of the Calusa Indians, or as tiny stowaways on their dugout canoes. The West Indies white-crowned pigeon made the crossing as well, and so did the Jamaican fruit bat and its Caribbean cohort, the Wagner's mastiff bat, the latter two thriving on the mosquitoes that swarmed here then.

Poke around long enough in a tropical hardwood hammock and you are likely to come nose to nose with raccoons, rough green snakes, green tree frogs, red-bellied woodpeckers, cotton mice, and white-tailed deer. If you chance across a Florida tree snail—you'll know it from the dazzling variety of colored bands covering its whorled shell—let it be. Until recently the ranks of this little spectral riot were decimated by collectors. Should you spot a flutter of blue, brown, and orange overhead, that's the Schaus' swallowtail butterfly, another living rarity. (An officially designated endangered species, its populations were unintentionally depleted by pesticides sprayed for mosquito control.)

Many hammock plants bloom in the springtime.

A Community Under Threat

Tropical hammocks sprang up as far north as Cape Canaveral on the Atlantic shoreline, and as far west as the mouth of the Manatee River on the Gulf Coast. Most of these have been destroyed—logged for valuable timber (mahogany) and the production of charcoal—leaving just a few beleaguered, scattered remnants. The tropical hammock is now one of the rarest plant communities in Florida.

Several good-size pockets of hammock remain in the Keys, however, protected in state parks and national wildlife refuges. But while these stands may never fall to the lumberjack's ax, they still face threats. Rising sea levels, storm surges and high winds from hurricanes, invasive plant and animal species, dropping water tables, and even extreme cold weather at times all exact a toll on this fragile ecosystem.

Good places to experience hammocks in all their glory are Dagny Johnson Key Largo Hammock Botanical State Park (see pp. 166–167) and John Pennekamp Coral Reef State Park (see pp. 163–165), both on Key Largo; Lignumvitae Key Botanical State Park (see pp. 176–177); and the National Key Deer Refuge on Big Pine Key (see pp. 196–197).

Torch Keys

The Torch Keys—Little, Big, and Middle—were named for the torchwood tree found here. The arrival of the Overseas Highway in the late 1930s concentrated traffic along the new road, spelling the end for the Torches' little communities, especially those on Big Torch, which is not crossed by the highway. Scenic Dorn Road, which slaloms for some 8 miles across Big Torch's swamp interior, proves this before coming to its end among a mixed mangrove jungle.

Peace and quiet are the main attractions of the somnolent, mangrove-blessed Torch Keys.

Torch Keys
⚏ 193 F3

Little Palm Island Resort
⚏ 193 F2
☎ 305/872-2524
www.littlepalmisland.com

It is this out-of-the-way atmosphere that boosts the appeal of the **Little Palm Island Resort** (see p. 255), a private 5-acre retreat with a reputation for luxury and privacy located south of Little Torch Key. Coconut palms sway above open-air thatched-roof huts set up on stilts. Beds are draped in mosquito netting; overhead ceiling fans stir the balmy air. There are no televisions, and no telephones, save the one at the front desk. The islet is accessible only by a private launch shuttling back and forth hourly from the Dolphin Marina on Little Torch Key at MM 28.5.

Many people make the effort to visit because the resort's Dining Room at Little Palm (see Travelwise p. 255), whose tables overlook the water, is consistently rated the Keys' premier dining spot outside of Key West. It serves modern tropical cuisine, has a very respectable wine list, and is renowned for its level of service. The fishing and diving here are superb, as Little Palm's isle lies within **Coupon Bight Aquatic Preserve**, a 4,600-acre area of diverse sea communities. ■

EXPERIENCE: Diving at Looe Key

To experience what many underwater enthusiasts rate as North America's premier dive spot, head to Looe Key, part of the extensive Florida Keys National Marine Sanctuary *(tel 305/292-0311, www.floridakeys.noaa.gov)*. Ramrod Key, a smallish limestone knob, is the best known staging area for eager scuba divers; from here, Looe Key is about 5 nautical miles out.

The 5.3-square-mile area around Looe Key *(map 193 F1)* encloses the most diverse coral community in the Lower Keys, a wonderland teeming with fish and other sea creatures, with shallow depths suitable for snorkelers and divers of all skill levels.

Looe Key—not really a key but a reef—commemorates the H.M.S. *Looe,* a British warship that foundered here in 1744. (Look for some of the frigate's ballast stones on the seafloor.) From the air the key sprawls darkly atop pale coral sand in the shape of a bent Y, roughly 800 yards long and 200 yards wide. Its massive accretions, or spurs, of pillar coral rise up from depths

as great as 35 feet nearly to the surface. Lying in sandy grooves between these great spurs are dome-shaped brain corals, patrolled by skulking lobsters and bottom-skimming sea rays. Varicolored fish by the thousands move in precision-swimming schools and dart among the branches of elkhorn coral. Purple sea fans sway languidly in the Gulf Stream, which surges above clusters of sponges and sea urchins. The blue-tinted scene is otherworldly.

Virtually every dive shop in the region offers half-day excursions to Looe Key twice daily, providing all equipment; a two-tank dive usually runs about $75.

The **Looe Key Dive Center** *(27340 Overseas Hwy., Ramrod Key, tel 305/872-2215, www .diveflakeys.com)* offers a three-tank reef trip for $84. The sanctuary encourages using operators dedicated to education and coral reef conservation; a list of these so-called Blue Star operators can be found on the sanctuary's website.

Although the water is comfortably warm, you will slowly lose body heat as you explore the reef. For many, a wet suit vest rented at a nominal additional cost prevents the weakness, shortness of breath, and occasional nausea that some experience after an hour underwater.

Dive boats hover over the brilliantly colored spur-and-groove coral formations of Looe Key.

Sugarloaf Key & Beyond

Anglo-American settlers first staked out homesteads on these two small isles in the late 19th century. Then in 1912, an English-born entrepreneur named Charles Chase established a sponge farm on Sugarloaf Key's shore. Chase soon owned most of the island and named its first town in honor of himself. Two years later, beset with troubles, Chase's Florida Sponge & Fruit Company failed. He sold out to R. C. Perky, a real estate man who dreamed of developing Sugarloaf. Perky renamed his newly acquired hamlet Perky, but his fortunes foundered like Chase's.

Sugarloaf Key
⚏ 193 E2

Saddlebunch Keys
⚏ 192 D2

Big Coppitt Key
⚏ 192 D2

Boca Chica Key
⚏ 192 C2

Rockland Key
⚏ 192 C2

It's easy to imagine why Chase and Perky had big dreams. Sugarloaf's pleasant somnolence tends to clear the mind and allow you to think. To experience the serenity along the island's shaggy, overgrown back roads, leave US 1 at MM 20—the turnoff is hard by Mangrove Mama's *(tel 305/745-3030; see p. 254)*, a charming, funky restaurant and bar—and take either Fla. 939 or 939A, which loop back to the highway at MM 17. A turn onto Old State Road (Fla. 4A) wanders through mangrove thickets broken by bright blue-jade flashes of the tropical

Atlantic, crosses a narrow channel, and delivers you to Upper Sugarloaf Key and a dead end at Sugarloaf Boulevard. This is how the Keys looked to motorists in the early 1930s.

South of **Perky's Bat Tower** (see sidebar this page), at MM 17, are the popular Sugarloaf Lodge resort and restaurant *(tel 305/745-3211)*, and marina and airstrip.

Beyond Sugarloaf Key

A mere 11 bridges now separate you from Key West. The longest runs a half-mile; the shortest and last—the bridge from Stock Island to Key West—a mere 159 feet. Six of the spans are necessary to complete a crossing of the low-lying **Saddlebunch Keys,** which are little more than coral mounts topped by mangroves.

South of the Saddlebunch Keys lies **Big Coppitt Key,** most of which is a bedroom community for the naval air station on adjoining **Boca Chica Key** farther south, whose beaches are mostly off-limits. Like Boca Chica, **Rockland Key** has been claimed by industry, namely a cement plant. Ahead lies Key West and the terminus of the Overseas Highway at Mile 0. ∎

Perky's Bat Tower

Real estate salesman R. C. Perky dreamed of turning Sugarloaf into South Florida's finest resort, but there was a problem—mosquitoes. He read a book by a Texas health official named Dr. Charles Campbell, who claimed to have developed a system by which bats could be enlisted to rid the Earth of mosquitoes. Following instructions, Perky built a 35-foot-tall bat tower, using Campbell's secret-formula bat bait to entice the creatures into adopting the tower as their home. They didn't, and Perky went bankrupt, leaving his empty obelisk bat tower as an exotic monument to his entrepreneurial dreams.

A beguiling, eccentric, raffishly charming end-of-the-road outpost set apart from all others, plus idyllic desertlike isles

Key West & Dry Tortugas

A six-toed feline, a descendant of one of Hemingway's polydactyly cats

Key West & Dry Tortugas

Key West is the southernmost city in the continental united States and is South Florida's oldest, established in 1829. Many find its isolated island setting irresistibly exotic. The town's slow-paced, shorts-and-sandals lifestyle has compelled more than a few travelers to read the house rental ads in the Key West *Citizen*.

Key West's day-to-day reality is so different from mainstream American life that it defies any glib summing up. Even locals will, at times, shake their heads and mutter, "Key Weird."

Many first-timers to the island are put off by its apparent disregard for notions of

conventional behavior. The prim consider it dissolute, despairing of its never-quite-correct ways: Its sidewalks are broken by banyan tree roots; its houses overgrown with vines and bowers of orange-petaled royal poinciana trees, suggesting a local law against painting. Whether

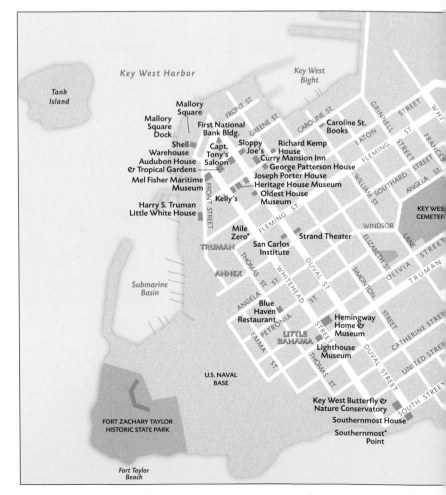

you will like it depends largely upon your expectations, and your willingness to sample the unfamiliar and indulge the eccentric.

Nineteenth-century Cubans called the island Stella Maris, "star of the sea." It was for them a prosperous place, where fishing and cigarmaking offered a good living and an escape from Cuban sugarcane fields and heavy-handed Spanish colonial rule. Early Spanish explorers found it littered with bleached human skeletons, and charted it as Cayo Hueso, "island of bones." Why these remains were there, no one knows. Some speculate Key West was a Calusa Indian burial ground, or perhaps a battlefield.

> ## NOT TO BE MISSED:
>
> Watching sunsets and street performers at Mallory Square **214–215**
>
> The myriad salvaged goods from shipwrecks at the Mel Fisher Maritime Museum **215, 218**
>
> The elegant Audubon House & Tropical Gardens **218–219**
>
> Truman's custom-made poker table at the Little White House **221–222**
>
> Kayaking around the Keys **224**
>
> Touring the Hemingway Home and Museum **225–226**
>
> Quenching your thirst at Captain Tony's Saloon **228**
>
> Colossal Fort Jefferson on Garden Key, in the Dry Tortugas **234–236**

Whatever it was once called, Key West is still a place of mystery and contradiction, of extremes and contrasts.

A World Apart

A hedonistic, self-absorbed island, it has no natural fresh water, yet lies within a vast watery wilderness. It is by turns refined and tawdry: For every fine art gallery, bookstore, and antique showroom, there are a dozen T shirt shops. For every linen-covered restaurant table, there is a much-beloved greasy spoon shoveling conch fritters and french fries onto paper trays for patrons crowding picnic tables under tin roofs. Parts of the downtown Mallory Square area, full of glitzy tourist attractions and gimcrack vendors, resemble a theme park. But look beyond that, to the untrammeled and gorgeous subtropical sea shimmering below a pollution-free sky, and you reconnect with the natural setting that underlies all that is here. Wander away from Old Key West's

The Key West Kite Company fits right in with the character of the Conch Republic.

gentrified 19th-century houses and mansions, and its new condos, and you'll find overgrown lanes and bungalow neighborhoods that are downright shabby, survivors of the wild dream-busting swings of the island's historically mercurial economy. In old Cuban and Bahamian neighborhoods only a few blocks from the bustle of Duval Street's retail bazaar, chickens scratch and cluck amid modest cottages where Caribbean families sit on porches to talk and watch life go by.

Key West's Conchs

Pronounced "konk," the term Conch today refers to a person born on Key West, and implies a free-thinking, prickly, independent-minded political sentiment. The nickname traces to 1646, when a group of British subjects established a Bahamian colony, declaring themselves exempt from royal taxation and free to worship as they pleased. When the crown tried to tax them, they defiantly declared themselves more willing to eat conch meat (which they did anyway) than pay it. Thereafter they were known as Conchs. The creature for which they are

named, however, is no longer plentiful. The conch meat served in the Keys is shipped in from the Bahamas, Belize, or the Caribbean.

Today, native Conchs are outnumbered by so-called freshwater Conchs, people who have adopted the town with a vengeance. Key West particularly attracts those who find comfort in knowing that they live in a place as unconventional as they are. It has a significant cadre of artists, writers, musicians, lifestyle devotees, and others who are probably best described as eccentric. The island is also home to a sizable gay community, credited for leadership roles in civic improvements, historic preservation, and the revival of the town's hospitality industry. A good many Key Westers are embarked on new lives—urban professionals turned innkeepers, entrepreneurs, or artists—encouraged by the island's air of isolation that produces a bracing sense of personal freedom and possibility.

A Feast for the Senses

Above all, Key West engages the senses. Come evening, the subtropical light off the water boosts colors to a fabulous intensity, and crowds gather at Mallory Square for

INSIDER TIP:

You can find tasty Key lime
pie just about anywhere, but
the Key lime fudge at Kermit's
Key West Key Lime Pie Shoppe
(200A Elizabeth St.) is amazing.

—JEROME COOKSON
Cartographer, National Geographic magazine

the nightly Sunset Celebration to applaud
as the sun eases into the sea. The air is
redolent of brine, perfumed by flowering
vines and wild orchids, laced with the scent
of old wood and damp gardens, and humid.
The island's temperature averages a balmy
79°F, and the ocean is warm and clear blue,
like old glass. Smoke from the braziers
of open-air backyard restaurants fills the
streets with the burnt spices of Bahamian
and Cuban fare, often served to the strum
of guitars. There are menus for every taste,
bistros for every mood.

Seeing the Sights

Old Key West is best (and most easily)
explored on foot, its streets lined by a
picturesque collection of indigenous architecture and historical monuments, tropical
gardens, arcane museums, and a waterfront
that is always interesting. A raffish maritime
heritage accounts for an abundance of
saloons. The variety of catches brought in by
the town's fishing fleet enables local chefs
to create fresh seafood dishes almost impossible to find elsewhere. Out-of-the-way
places like the beach and tree-shaded picnic
area inside Fort Zachary Taylor Historic State
Park, the old Key West Lighthouse, the town
cemetery, and the Audubon House gardens
offer quiet respites from the bustling downtown. There are districts, however, where
you probably ought not wander at night. By
day and in the evening, the Little Bahama
neighborhood south of downtown is charming. Locals, however, advise against strolling
its unlighted back streets later at night.

Surrounding all is the sea. A fleet of charter
boats offers day-long snorkeling trips to the
reefs that garland Key West. There are quiet
beaches to drowse on, and busy ones where
you can rent sailboats. And though a marker at
the corner of Whitehead and Fleming Streets
proclaims this Mile Zero on the Overseas
Highway (US 1), the Keys do not really end
here, but rather 70 miles west in the Dry
Tortugas. This lonely scattering of small atoll-
like islands among sandy shoals and coral reefs
is watched over by a colossal Civil War fortress
and a 19th-century lighthouse whose beacon
sweeps the sea at night. ∎

The Florida Keys Arts Scene

The Keys have a vibrant and growing
art scene. Working with an eclectic mix
of people living on the islands south of
Miami, the **Florida Keys Council of the
Arts** (*www.keysarts.com*) aims to connect
225 local galleries, theaters, museums,
festivals, and performing arts centers to
audiences around the world.

Founded in 1996 and based in Key
West, the heart of the Keys' colorful arts
scene, county commissioners designated the nonprofit council as its local
arts agency. In this role, FKCA makes
grants, supports art in public places, and
promotes the archipelago as an arts and
culture destination. It also provides services and support to visual and performing
artists, arts organizations, and students.

FKCA maintains an artist registry and
publishes a quarterly cultural calendar
and gallery guide. To find out what arts-
related events are going on when you're
in the Keys, visit the Your Visit page of the
FKCA website.

Entering Key West

On approaching Key West from the Overseas Highway, just past the commercial clutter of Stock Island—marine supply and sporting goods stores that give no hint of the older, far more charming city ahead—drivers are given the option of two routes to reach Old Key West: Stay on US 1 or take Fla. A1A. Opt for Fla. A1A. It's more scenic and interesting than the other way.

A lazy afternoon on Smathers Beach, a popular spot for sailing Hobie Cats and windsurfing

Just after you cross the bridge from Stock Island to Key West, you'll reach a T-shaped intersection with Roosevelt Boulevard. Look for highway signs indicating Fla. A1A and pointing left (south) to "Beaches/Airport." Turn left and follow S. Roosevelt Boulevard's palmy corridor south past the Key West International Airport and then west along the Atlantic Ocean side of the island. This part of Key West lying east of White Street is considered its New Town, much of it created by filling wetlands. Officially speaking, the neighborhoods west of White Street constitute Old Town.

Beaches & Wetlands

Inland, as you drive along S. Roosevelt, are the marshy **Salt Ponds,** used commercially in the mid-1800s to evaporate water and create sea salt. The ponds nowadays teem with crustaceans and small fish, attracting seabirds, especially in the early morning hours when avid birdwatchers gather here. Part of the grassy wetland is enclosed by the **Riggs Wildlife Refuge**—look for a green gate—which has a nicely designed observation platform. Across the briny bog is another wildlife sanctuary known as **Little Hamaca Park,** located just off Flagler at Government Road. This unusual preserve encloses a pristine enclave of living biological history. A boardwalk lets you examine and explore the sanctuary without disturbing the delicate wetlands.

The 2-mile-long strand opposite is **Smathers Beach,** popular among windsurfers and Hobie Cat sailors. You can rent two-person catamarans here. They're inexpensive, easy to sail, and quite stable unless the wind is whipping up whitecaps, but you're not allowed to take them out of sight of the vendors.

Fort East Martello

Florida A1A also takes you past Fort East Martello, one of the oldest brick structures on the island, a cylindrical Civil War–era fort that houses the eclectic collection of the **Fort East Martello Museum and Gardens** (3501 S. Roosevelt Blvd., tel 305/296-3913, www.kwahs .com/martello.htm, $$). Besides being a singularly pleasant place, it also gives human faces to the historical eras that make up the branches of Key West's complex family tree of pirates, soldiers, railroaders, spongers, rumrunners, shipbuilders, cigarmakers, shrimpers, and Caribbean political refugees who survived the crossing. The museum features exhibits of local artists' work, and a room devoted to Key West's lengthy roster of accomplished writers, including seven honored with the Pulitzer Prize. Be sure to climb the 48 steps to the tower's observation platform, an exertion that rewards with a splendid ocean view.

INSIDER TIP:

Wander the trails at Little Hamaca Park. It's next to a former Hawk missile battery that evokes the Cuban missile crisis. You can walk up to its earthworks, towers, and buildings.

—COREY MALCOLM
Archaeologist, Mel Fisher Maritime Museum

Entering Old Town

After traveling the length of Smathers Beach, S. Roosevelt Boulevard turns inland, becoming Bertha Street. A little ways along, turn left (west) on Atlantic Boulevard to enter a neighborhood of condominium apartments. Atlantic ends at White Street, which is considered the northern boundary of Key West's Old Town district. ∎

Key West
▲ Map pp. 206–207

Fort East Martello
▲ Map p. 207

Key West's Historic Old Town

Key West's historic center isn't its geographic center, but rather it lies hard alongside Key West Harbor and the old city's commercial moorage, Key West Bight (whose revitalized docks area is now called the HarborWalk). The official center of downtown is Mallory Square, where the Mallory Steamship Company once boarded Cuban-bound travelers.

The old First National Bank Building, at Duval and Front Streets, in the heart of Old Town

Key West

 Map pp.
206–207

History of Key West

History states that in 1822, a U.S. Navy party led by a lieutenant named Matthew Perry (who later as a commodore opened Japan to American commerce) raised the Stars and Stripes over the island for the first time. The swampy, malarial place had been purchased that year by an Alabama speculator named John Simonton from Spanish land grantee Juan Pablo Salas for $2,000. Simonton got real estate, and the U.S. got its southernmost deepwater anchorage, something rare on Florida's shallow coastline. Key West became the forward base of the Navy's pirate-hunting West India Squadron, which mounted a brutal eight-year campaign to root the murderous buccaneers from their hideaways deep in mangrove creeks up and down the Keys. Meanwhile, a few hundred settlers, mostly New Englanders and English

Bahamian whalers, merchant mariners, and marine salvagers, began to build houses and a multicultural community.

As America's merchant fleet grew and its reach extended, the reefs around Key West claimed an ever increasing number of ships. In calm weather and bright sunlight these jagged coral rasps are virtually invisible until the moment before impact. In the hurricane season, howling gales make evasive maneuvering impossible. Then, as now, this was one of the busiest sea lanes in the Western Hemisphere. As a result, hundreds of sailing ships came to grief on the reefs. Their cargoes, often strewn along Key West's shores, produced a phenomenal economic boom. American maritime salvage law, fundamentally based on the notion that finders are keepers, was largely written by Key West judges. The island's "wreckers" literally furnished their ornate mansions with the spoils of disaster.

This run of luck ended in the 1850s with the installation of lighthouses. As wrecking declined, the harvesting of sponges picked up, followed in the late 19th century by the arrival of Cuban immigrants skilled in the art of cigarmaking. Commercial fishing began to pay, and by 1890 Key West was Florida's wealthiest city, with a population of 25,000.

That all ended during the Great Depression. The sponges were gone, the cigar companies had moved north to Tampa, and ships bypassed the harbor for points north. Even the Navy had closed its base here. By 1934, four out of every five Key Westers were on the dole. The town fathers declared Key West a ward of the State, which promptly handed the starving waif over to the federal government. It was decided that Key West would be made over with public funds and volunteer work into a tourist destination.

A Town Revitalized: Some 4,000 islanders labored for half a year to smarten up the town. Trees were planted, houses repaired, mountains of trash removed, and beaches raked clear of seaweed. Federal grants reopened hotels staffed by grad-

Key West in Literature

Ernest Hemingway's novel *To Have and Have Not*, published in 1938, tells the tragic story of a Conch fisherman and smuggler named Henry Morgan, evoking the desperation of Key West's Depression years and the self-reliance Hemingway admired in his fellow townsfolk. Another Pulitzer Prize–winning Key Wester was poet and writer Elizabeth Bishop, who lived at 624 White Street from 1938 to 1942. Much of her work is set here and elsewhere in the Florida Keys.

uates of the government-funded Key West Maids' Training School. Unemployed musicians were hired to form the Key West Hospitality Band, which serenaded travelers as they stepped from trains and ships' gangways. Other locals were trained in handicrafts, including weaving sun hats from coconut palm fronds. (Stroll Duval Street

Mallory Square

🅰 Map p. 206

www.mallory
square.com

and you'll see sidewalk vendors still weaving them.)

A tourist guide was written, and nearly everything of remotely possible interest to a visitor was pointed out. A "Typical Old House" was Sight No. 12, the "Abandoned Cigar Factory" No. 35. Number 18 was Ernest Hemingway's house at 907 Whitehead Street. In "A Key West Letter" written for the April 1935 *Esquire,* Hemingway declared himself besieged by sightseers, situated as he was "between Johnson's Tropical Grove (No. 17) and Lighthouse and Aviaries

---

EXPERIENCE:
Mallory Square's Sunset Celebration

The nightly ritual of gathering at Mallory Square Dock to cheer the sun's descent into the Gulf of Mexico began in the 1960s. The sunsets are indeed spectacular—Audubon even rhapsodized over them in his journal, nearly running out of adjectives. People gather two hours before sunset—locals and tourists alike—to take in the Carnival-like scene and await the sunset.

(No. 19)." It was "all very flattering to the easily bloated ego of your correspondent," he allowed, "but very hard on production."

So began Key West's career in tourism, with this recommendation to travelers, which was written by the federal agent in charge of the island's makeover: "To appreciate Key West with its indigenous architecture, its lanes and byways, its friendly people

and general picturesqueness, the visitor must spend at least a few days in the city; a cursory tour of an hour or two serves no good purpose. Unless a visitor is prepared to spend at least three full days here, the Key West Administration would rather he did not come."

Mallory Square

Hundreds of cruise ships ease up to Mallory Square Dock every year. Legions of voyagers are met here by purveyors of ice cream, sea shells, T-shirts, balloons, and baubles of every kind. In open-air bars, bartenders working rows of blenders pour bright-colored slurries of ice, fruit juice, and alcohol—Key West versions of the daiquiri and the piña colada—into goblets. There are magicians, jugglers, tap dancers, mimes, portrait artists, flame-eaters, musicians, fortune-tellers—even an occasional tightrope walker.

The square commemorates Stephen Mallory, a Key Wester who, in 1861, served as secretary of the Confederacy's short-lived navy. Set back off Front and Greene Streets is the red and terra-cotta brick Customs House, Florida's premier example of Romanesque Revival architecture. Now home to the **Customs House Museum** *(tel 305/295-6616, www.customshousemuseum.org, $$),* it was built in the 1880s and served as a post office and federal courthouse, where Key West's judges set salvage law precedents. A permanent exhibit opened in 2012 showcases the 100th anniversary of the Florida East Coast Railway reaching Key West. The florid **First National Bank Building** nearby owes its gaudy brickwork and intricate facade to the tastes of the 19th-century Cuban cigarmakers who commissioned it.

late Mel Fisher, whose quest for a pair of Spanish treasure galleons sunk in a 1622 hurricane is part of local folklore.

Fisher found a portion of the *Santa Margarita's* cargo in 1980, but the *Nuestra Señora de Atocha* still eluded him. Finally, after more

Mel Fisher Maritime Museum

🅰 Map p. 206

✉ 200 Greene St.

☎ 305/294-2633

💲 $$

www.melfisher.org

Crowds gather nightly at Mallory Square to watch the sun dip beneath the Gulf of Mexico.

Fronting the square is Key West's oldest commercial edifice, built of coral rock quarried from the site it occupies. Originally used for storing ice, it's now the Shell Warehouse, a bazaar-in-a-building filled with the delicate cacophony of wind chimes for sale within.

Mel Fisher Maritime Museum

Captain Geiger (see p. 218) wasn't the only Key West entrepreneur to become wealthy through salvage. In recent times the most successful salvor, albeit at bitter personal cost, was the

than 16 years of searching, on July 20, 1985, his divers found the *Atocha*—and treasure valued at $100 million.

It's a short walk from Mallory Square to the museum at the corner of Whitehead and Greene Streets, where newly recovered loot is exhibited. Here you'll find a modest sampling of the gold, silver, jewelry, and rare nautical artifacts recovered from the two shipwrecks, which lay scattered at depths nearing 60 feet. There are gold and silver ingots, intricate gold chains stretching

(continued on p. 218)

Exploring Old Key West

The best way to see Old Key West is on foot—so that all of your senses get to take in all of the sights, sounds, and smells. But there are also other ways to experience Key West first-hand.

The popular Conch Train makes a 14-mile sightseeing trip around the island.

Self-guided Walking Tours

The most popular self-guided tour is the 25-block **Pelican Path,** mapped out by the Old Island Restoration Foundation, which acquaints you with a dozen streets and 50 architecturally significant and historic buildings. Pick up "A Guide to Historic Key West on the 'Pelican Path'" at the Key West Chamber of Commerce (510 Greene St., tel 305/294-2587, www.keywestchamber.org) where the walk begins and ends. The free brochure is also available at the Oldest House Museum (322 Duval St.), or contact the Old Island Restoration Foundation (tel 305/294-9501, www.oirf.org) for more

information. The walk takes several hours, including a stop for lunch along the way. Most buildings are privately owned and not open to visitors; however, January through March, during the Old Island Days celebration, the foundation offers several guided themed house and garden tours.

The **Cuban Heritage Trail** is another intriguing walk featuring nearly 40 houses, buildings, and locales, all of them historical footnotes to the history of the island's Cuban connections. For this you'll need the guide and map, available free from the Historic Florida Keys Foundation (510 Greene St., tel 305/292-6718, www.historicfloridakeys.org). While you are

A themed trolley waits till nighttime to take its passengers on a tour of Key West's macabre side.

here, have a look at the excellent annotated map of Key West's historic district, a well-researched guide to the relics of island history, which includes a driving tour of the Overseas Highway up to Key Largo. Included are evocative descriptions of Pigeon Key and the Bat Tower on Sugarloaf Key. You'll also find a brochure you can use to visit the historic Key West Cemetery (see p. 231).

Another fine walking tour is the **Key West Historic Marker Tour** (*www.keywesthistoric markertour.org*). Start by printing a copy of the tour map from the website, or have a map on your smart phone. When you reach one of the tour's 68 historic sites, marked by a numbered sign, either go to the website or call the automated tour phone number (*tel 305/507-0300*) and enter the site number to learn about it.

Tram & Trolley Tours

As an alternative to walking, board the **Conch Train** (*9 a.m.–4:30 p.m., tel 305/294-5161, www.conchtourtrain.com, $$$$$*) for a 90-minute, 14-mile narrated island tour. This open-air faux train, pulled by a Jeep fancifully disguised as a miniature locomotive, leaves from Mallory Square at 303 Front Street every half hour. You can also board at Flagler Station at 901 Caroline Street.

Similar to the Conch is the **Old Town Trolley** (*9 a.m.–4:30 p.m., tel 305/296-6688, www.trolleytours.com/Key-West, $$$$$*), small, trolleylike buses that depart from the square at Roosevelt Boulevard on the half hour. The 90-minute tours take a somewhat different route, and allow you to disembark at any stop, and continue later aboard another trolley.

The Conch Republic

On April 20, 1982, the U.S. Border Patrol, seeking to catch undocumented aliens and drug runners, blocked the Overseas Highway below Florida City. Motorists were asked to prove U.S. citizenship, and their vehicles were searched. The resulting traffic jam was a public relations disaster, and Keys residents were outraged at being treated like criminal suspects. After three days, Key West officials announced the island's secession from the Union.

A raucous Mallory Square rally proclaimed Key West an independent nation to be known as the Conch Republic. A Conch flag was raised, visas and border passes were issued, and Conch currency was printed. The rebel nation then promptly "surrendered," requested U.S. foreign aid, and partied for a week. The Conch Spring is commemorated every April during the week-long Conch Republic Independence Celebration.

Audubon House & Tropical Gardens

🅰 Map p. 206

✉ 205 Whitehead St.

☎ 305/294-2116

💲 $$

www.audubon house.com

nearly 9 feet, uncut emeralds of colossal size, and ornate jeweled crucifixes. One exhibit showcases a 77-carat raw emerald, while others display anchors, tools, cannon, and other items from everyday seafaring life. Historical exhibits tantalize with promises of greater finds yet to come, while others present the sobering reality of treasure hunting: breathtaking expense, years of backbreaking labor, and the innate perils of working underwater. (Early in the quest, Fisher lost a son and daughter-in-law when their ship capsized.)

The house of the Audubon House & Tropical Gardens museum was once the home of a wealthy sea captain.

Audubon House & Tropical Gardens

On Whitehead Street, just off Mallory Square, is a handsome, white-painted, three-story house, situated amid a lush, neatly tended garden of trees, plants, and flowering bushes—a tropical garden some insist is Florida's finest.

It is arguably the most elegant historic house on the island, filled with a marvelously attractive mix of period domestic furnishings and decorative pieces—paintings, porcelains, clothing, children's dolls, and toys. Its name, however, is misleading; the house's connection with the famed ornithologist and painter of wild birds is sentimental, not historical.

John James Audubon, who briefly visited Key West and the Dry Tortugas in 1832, never stayed here; the house was home to John Geiger, a sea captain who, like many Key West residents, made a fortune salvaging cargo from ships wrecked on the Florida Reef. He built this residence for his family some time in the 1830s. His heirs lived here until 1958. Its proximity to Mallory Square brought the threat of demolition, thwarted by local preservationists who refurbished the building and its garden as a museum to commemorate Audubon's stay in Key West.

Visitors may wander at will in the spacious manse. The children's room on the second floor is filled with toys from the 1830s, including two pairs of antique roller skates. Throughout the house are original Audubon engravings

Caroline Street

▲ Map p. 206

INSIDER TIP:

John James Audubon took cuttings from the Geigers' garden to use in his bird paintings, including "The White-Crowned Pigeon" that still hangs in the Geiger home, now the Audubon House.

—MARTHA RESK

Gallery manager, Audubon House & Tropical Gardens

and paintings, and, on the third floor, Audubon's field notes on 22 birds from the Keys. The brick-laid garden, stippled with orchids and with a nursery maintained in the style of the 1840s, is a lovely spot in which to linger.

Caroline Street

There are many fine reasons for strolling this picturesque core sample of old Key West, which runs from the Truman Little White House (see p. 220–222) on Front Street to the waterfront clutter of Key West Bight.

Across the street from the ceremonial entrance to the old Navy base (opened only for the Commander in Chief and ranking dignitaries) is a white-painted, much renovated clapboard house that once headquartered Aeromarine Airways. In the early 1920s the pioneering airline flew passengers and bags of mail aboard ex-Navy Curtiss F5-L coastal patrol flying boats to Cuba. Each carried a homing pigeon

in the event of a ditching at sea. Aeromarine's inaugural hop to Havana, on November 1, 1920, established one of America's first officially recognized international air mail routes. The seaplane company located here as it was near the waterfront—Navy landfill eventually extended the island several hundred yards to the old Navy submarine pens, now a posh marina and promenade. Aeromarine charged $50 for the 105-mile flight to Havana, which, depending upon winds and weather, took from 90 minutes to two hours. (Passage aboard a Mallory Steamship ferry took all day and cost $19.) In 1921 Aeromarine added the 185-mile route to Nassau in the Bahamas, changing its name to Aeromarine West Indies Airways, and charging $85. Within two years it had carried close to 20,000 passengers in perfect safety, but at a financial loss that forced the airline to shut

Conch Architecture

Really a subtle mixture of 19th-century styles, sometimes called Bahamian, Key West's conch-style buildings reflect the techniques of the ships' carpenters who constructed them. They were built to deal with subtropical heat, humidity, and stormy weather, and include top-hinged shutters, ventilated attics, steep galvanized steel roofs (for collecting rainwater that was diverted to cisterns), columned shade porches, and piers instead of foundations to protect against flooding and rot. Most were built of Georgia heart pine and, until Key West's tourism-inspired makeover in the 1930s, were seldom painted, instead being allowed to "silver" under the sun.

Harry S. Truman Little White House

- 🅰 Map p. 206
- ✉ 111 Front St.
- ☎ 305/294-9911
- 💲 $$$

www.trumanlittle whitehouse.com

down in 1923. Few remember Aeromarine, but the restaurant that now occupies the building, **Kelly's** (tel 305/293-8484; see p. 258), is popularly associated with the fledgling years of the almost mythical Pan American Airways Inc., which took over the pioneering route in 1927, four years after Aeromarine failed. Pan Am's distinctive blue globe logo lies atop the restaurant's roof.

Next door to Kelly's is the appealing little **Heritage House** (410 Caroline St.). Not open to the public, it houses an archive of Key West history, in a conch residence dating from the 1830s and occupied by seven generations of an old Key West clan. Behind the house, in a lovely tropical garden, is a cottage where the poet Robert Frost sometimes stayed.

The area around Caroline Street's 500-block is arguably Old Town's handsomest residential neighborhood, lined with imposing homes—none more so than the 28-room **Curry Mansion Inn** (511 Caroline St., tel 305/294-5349; see p. 256), built in 1905 by a son of William Curry, Key West's most successful 19th-century entrepreneur. (Upon his death in 1898, the elder Curry was reputed to be Florida's wealthiest citizen.) The house, inspired by the French town house look of the lavish and aristocratic "cottages" in Newport, Rhode Island, is open for self-guided tours ($). Climb to the manse's rooftop widow's walk for a splendid view of Old Town.

In 1886 a devastating fire destroyed many of the neighborhood's early manses. From their

ashes grander ones rose, including the **George Patterson House** (522 Caroline St.), an exuberant interpretation of the Queen Anne style, and the **Richard Kemp House** (601 Caroline St.) on the corner of the next block, regarded as a splendid example of conch details mixed with beaux arts notions of classical revival—the mélange assembled by ship's carpenters. Kemp, an English Bahamian, founded Key West's sponge industry.

Along the next two blocks to the waterfront you will pass more interpretations of the classical revival style, all proud dowager houses that seem a bit out of place so near the laid-back, barefoot, beer-and-conch-fritters style of the Key West Bight docks.

INSIDER TIP:

Leave some time to wander around the lush grounds of the Little Truman White House. A brochure helps you identify the myriad tropical plants.

—JANE SUNDERLAND
National Geographic contributor

Harry S. Truman Little White House

For all its comic-opera antipathy to the federal government, Key West has played gracious host to the military since the 1820s, and is one of the few American towns drafted into service as a working annex of the Executive

Formal furnishings in the Little White House tended to gather dust; Truman preferred to work at a poker table.

Branch. It happened in the wake of President Harry Truman's ascent to the Oval Office upon Franklin Roosevelt's death in 1945. Truman's public face was one of steely resolve and confidence, but he was being pushed to his limits. After presiding over the Allied victory in World War II, he faced the daunting task of advancing American interests in the postwar world. By late 1946 he was so worn out his doctors were concerned. A true vacation was impossible—there was too much to be done. He needed a secure retreat away from Washington's winter chill, where he could work, exercise outdoors, relax with advisers and friends, and from which he could quickly return to Washington if necessary.

Southern White House:

The Key West Naval Base fit the bill, and the Commandant's Quarters were conveniently vacant. An extensive two-story duplex built in 1890, with shade porches, tropical shutters, and spacious rooms for casual socializing, it more resembled a country clubhouse than a military residence. A U.S. Marine hospital was steps away, and within base boundaries was Key West's finest swimming beach (now part of Fort Zachary Taylor Historic State Park, see p. 223). In November, Truman and his staff flew down and commandeered the house, which had been converted to a single residence, and commenced to run the country from there. In

the party room, a poker table did double duty as a presidential desk, while the bar was manned by a sailor from morning to midnight. Security was such that only one Secret Service agent was deemed necessary, and his activities mainly revolved around answering the telephone.

Truman took up a regimen of work mixed with poker playing, ocean swims, fishing, and social drinking starting at seven in the morning with a shot of whiskey and a chaser of orange juice. His strength and spirits revived. "I've a notion," he confessed half-seriously, "to move the capital to Key West and just stay." He started a craze for Hawaiian shirts after a Miami publicist gave him one. During his six remaining years in office he returned ten times, occasionally walking downtown where he was known to pay for cups of coffee with autographed dollar bills. Presidents Eisenhower and Kennedy also availed themselves of Truman's winter White House.

Things have changed so much, particularly in regard to how Presidents must behave today, that the half-hour tour of the

---

EXPERIENCE: Eat Your Own Catch of the Day

While in Key West, you likely will want to sample fresh seafood, and there's nothing better than eating your own catch at a restaurant. After your day out fishing on a charter boat—try to snag a yellowtail snapper, grouper, or mahimahi, which many locals consider the tastiest—ask the crew to fillet and wrap your catch in ice, then take it to a restaurant that you know will serve it up. Your chef will suggest options for your particular fish, such as grilled, blackened, or pan fried, and serve it with side dishes like baked potato and steamed vegetables.

Restaurants that will cook your catch include **Sun Sun** *(1500 Reynolds St., tel 888/303-5717)*, **Conch Republic Seafood Company** *(631 Greene St., tel 305/294-4403)*, and **Blue Heaven** (see Travelwise p. 257), but many others will too. Most restaurants charge $10–$15 to cook your fish, but call ahead to confirm. Also ask if the chef has any instructions, such as deboning or filleting the fish before you arrive.

Little White House is wistfully evocative of an era far simpler and slower-paced. Truman's felt-covered poker table, built by Navy carpenters and still on view, features artillery shell casings for ashtrays, and cigar holders fashioned from .50-caliber machine-gun cartridges. Sensitive to propriety, Truman had them build a matching bare wood tabletop, enabling him and his poker partners to quickly conceal games in progress when outsiders were admitted. In one such moment, he signed the Marshall Plan, a post–World War II recovery program of American financial aid to Western European countries, on it.

Truman Annex: Surrounding Truman's retreat is the Truman Annex, an upscale, tropically landscaped complex of condominium apartments, town houses, and cottages built in conch style on roughly 100 acres of what was, until the 1980s, Navy property. The hospital where malaria-stricken U.S. Marines once convalesced is now occupied by apartments overlooking a marina and quaylike promenade.

The annex is a gated community, open from 8 a.m. to sunset, and a walk along its charming sidewalks loops back to the sights on and around Whitehead Street—the **Hemingway Home and Museum** (see pp. 225–226) and the old **Key West Lighthouse** (see p. 226), the Little Bahama neighborhood along Thomas Street, where at No. 729 the **Blue Heaven** restaurant *(tel 305/296-8666; see p. 257)* occupies a venerable house and yard and wins raves for its West Indian menu—and to Southard Street, which ends at the adjoining **Fort Zachary Taylor Historic State Park** (see page opposite) and the inviting tree-shaded coral beach where Truman swam in presidential seclusion. ∎

Fort Zachary Taylor Historic State Park

As you head toward the beach on the southwest side of Key West, you'll see on your right the low-lying Army redoubt that gave this 87-acre park its name.

The grassy parade ground where troops once drilled now hosts picnics and concerts.

Construction began in 1845, in an attempt to discourage foreign adventurers in the Gulf and Caribbean. The site was then 1,200 feet offshore—drifting sand and landfills eventually joined it to the island, requiring that its bedrock foundation be built up with granite blocks. Yellow fever periodically decimated the ranks of brick-laying African-American slaves and the German and Irish masons who supervised them. In the end the project took 21 years and many more lives, producing a 500-man battery with nearly 200 guns, some able to hurl 300-pound shells 3 miles.

Modernizations kept the fort in service through World War II. In 1968 an archaeological dig uncovered gun rooms, cannon, and munitions sealed up since 1898, giving the bastion's museum the most extensive collection of Civil War–era arms in the United States.

The fort, rising from a sunken parade ground in three tiers, is architecturally striking. Tour on your own, or join the free, 30-minute guided tour offered at noon.

Fort Taylor Beach

The only drawback to this exceedingly pretty strip of beach at the southern tip of the state park is its coral gravel, which is rough on bare feet; bring sturdy water shoes. Once in the water, however, it's dreamy. There are picnic tables, cooking grills, bathhouses, outdoor showers, and a small concession stand. ∎

Fort Zachary Taylor Historic State Park
- Map p. 206
- End of Southard St., on Truman Annex
- 305/292-6713
- $$

www.floridastate parks.org/forttaylor

EXPERIENCE: Kayaking in the Keys

Along with diving and fishing, kayaking rounds out the Keys' adventure trifecta. Paddlers enjoy ample access to calm water, undulating sea-grass meadows, hidden mangrove tunnels, garish sunsets, magnificent birds taking flight and splashing down, and aquatic wildlife like dolphins, manatees, young sharks, and upside-down jellyfish. Off Key West you can even stare down a giant cruise ship and arrive at tourist sites.

Kayakers paddle across Florida Bay's shallow flats.

Hard-core paddlers can take multiday trips, guided or not, with island campouts at night, while novices can learn a few feet offshore and then take half-day guided tours. Costs vary by outfitter and tour. Each region offers kayakers something a little different.

Upper Keys

Uninhabited islands here hide mangrove-shrouded tunnels you can paddle down. Search for Indian burial mounds, pieces of broken ships, and all sorts of wildlife. Manatees sometimes congregate in the deep, warm waters of Dusenberry Creek. Dolphins frolic everywhere but you won't always find them. Outfitters include **Florida Bay Outfitters** (MM 104, Key Largo, tel 305/451-3018, www.kayakfloridakeys.com),

John Pennekamp Coral Reef State Park (MM 102.5, Key Largo, tel 305/451-6300, www.pennekamppark.com/ rentals), **Backcountry Cowboy Outfitters** (MM 82.2, Islamorada, tel 305/517-4177, www.backcountrycowboy.com), and the **Kayak Shack** (at Robbie's Marina, MM 77.5, Lower Matecumbe, tel 305/664-4878, www.kayakthefloridakeys.com).

Middle Keys

The Middle Keys present more natural and man-made treasures for paddlers to discover. But here there's more open water, which means more challenging currents. There aren't many outfitters in the region. **Marathon Kayak** (Marathon, tel 305/395-0355, www .marathonkayak.com), which has no physical address, is

your best bet. Call ahead and Kayak Dave will meet you with kayaks on the water.

Lower Keys

The waters of the Lower Keys' backcountry teem with sea cucumbers, upside-down jellyfish, and young sharks, while the land, of which there's more here, features a wealth of birds in trees and mangrove flats. At low tide, miles of sandbars present hours of recreation for kayakers and motorized boaters. Check out **Big Pine Kayak Adventures** (Watson Blvd., Big Pine Key, tel 305/872-7474, keyskayaktours .com) and **Bahia Honda State Park** (MM 37, Big Pine Key, tel 305/872-3210, www.bahia hondapark.com/kayak-rentals) for rentals and/or tours.

Key West

Paddling around Key West is slow through the calm, shallow waters of the backcountry; however, if you choose to kayak to tourist sites like Smathers Beach and Mallory Square, the ocean can be congested and choppy. **Lazy Dog Island Outfitters** (MM 4.2, Stock Island, tel 305/295-9898, www.lazydogadventure.com) and **Clearly Unique Charters** (631 Greene St., Key West, tel 305/747-8651, www.clearly uniquecharters.com) both offer good service.

Hemingway Home & Museum

When Ernest Hemingway and Pauline Pfeiffer set up housekeeping in December 1931, this was the only house in Key West with a basement, created when the coral bedrock for its walls was quarried there. Set back a hundred feet on a deep 1-acre corner lot among banyan trees, date palms, sago, and palmetto, it is one of the island's most distinctive houses, a two-story villa with thick limestone walls, mansard roof, French windows, tall green shutters, and encircling iron-railed balconies.

When the Hemingways bought it (for $8,000), it was a decrepit ruin known as the Asa Tift House, named for the shipbuilder who built it in 1851. Hemingway—or more accurately his wealthy spouse—set to restoring the house into a servant-staffed domestic enclave and a creative sanctuary for a mercurial genius, whose application to his craft was so intense that the writing of 500 words could leave him physically drained. Hemingway needed undisturbed quiet, and found it in a study installed above the backyard carriage house. Pauline (a former Paris correspondent for *Vogue*) spent $20,000 to create a 65-foot-long saltwater swimming pool out of the site's limestone bedrock, a breathtaking extravagance in Depression-era Key West.

He lived in the house until his divorce from Pauline in 1940. During his 12 years in Key West (eight of them at this address) his life of writing, famously mixed with interludes of fishing, hunting, drinking, travel, war reporting, and romance, produced much of his best work, including *Death in the Afternoon*, *The Green Hills of Africa*, *To Have and Have Not*, and an enduring collection of extraordinary short stories, most notably "The Short Happy Life of Francis Macomber" and "The Snows of Kilimanjaro."

For those fascinated by Hemingway's prose and near-mythic life, there's magic in the air as they pass through the brick wall surrounding the house. Guided half-hour tours roam the house, which holds some of Hemingway's furniture and fixtures, including

Hemingway Home & Museum

- 🅰 Map p. 206
- ✉ 907 Whitehead St.
- ☎ 305/294-1136
- 💲 $$$

www.hemingway home.com

Hemingway's stylish second wife added formal furnishings and decorations to their Key West mansion.

From its observation deck, the old Key West Lighthouse offers panoramic views over the city.

Key West Lighthouse

 Map p. 206

✉ 938 Whitehead St.

☎ 305/295-6616

💲 $$

www.kwahs.com/ lighthouse.htm

ornate Venetian glass chandeliers that Pauline installed in the dining room to replace ceiling fans she considered unattractive. There is a small bookstore featuring Hemingway's work and a souvenir shop. These additions give the downstairs a slightly institutional look that disappoints some fans. Better, perhaps, to wander the grounds on your own and ponder the master's red-tiled, book-lined, backyard aerie, little changed from his days of solitary labor seated on a cigarmaker's chair at a small circular drop-leaf table. The period Smith Corona typewriter, however, is misleading; Hemingway wrote almost exclusively in longhand and had others type his manuscripts. ∎

Key West Lighthouse

At night, the treetops in Hemingway's yard would catch the light from the old Key West Lighthouse, just down White-head Street. The stocky tower, originally 57 feet tall, went on duty in 1848, tended by a lighthouse keeper who lived with his family in a pretty clapboard cottage near its base. (Local salvors, however, were not amused; the navigational aid meant fewer wrecks and the decline of their trade.) As the island's trees and buildings grew taller, masons returned to increase the tower's height. It was eventually raised to 92 feet, allowing mariners to see it from every compass point.

The light went out in 1969, replaced by automated beacons installed elsewhere, but you can climb the 88-step steel spiral staircase inside the tower to its encircling catwalk. The 360-degree panorama is splendidly photogenic, even though it's not the highest in town. That honor belongs to the Top, a lounge on top of the seven-story Crowne Plaza Key West La Concha (*430 Duval St., tel 305/296-2991*).

The keeper's 1887 house, now a museum, is so thoroughly refurbished it looks brand-new. It is filled with ship models, nautical charts, old photographs, and antique equipment from retired lighthouses throughout the Keys. There are a few artifacts from the U.S.S. *Maine*, which took on coal in the Dry Tortugas before steaming south to its explosive fate in Havana Harbor in 1898. The beacon's original Fresnel lens is here as well, demonstrating the ability of its ingenious geometry to amplify a lantern's flicker into a lifesaving beacon visible far out at sea.

Duval Street & Around

Named for the first governor of the Florida Territory, Duval Street has everything, from Spanish silver pieces of eight and jewels salvaged from sunken galleons to designer sunglasses and cookies. There are probably more T-shirts and bikinis for sale along its Old Town stretch than on any other six blocks in the United States. There is fast food and there are attempts at haute cuisine, but most eateries fall somewhere in between, made pleasant if not memorable simply because they are in Key West.

Until the 1920s, Duval Street was dirt. Bricks were laid during the islanders' Depression-era campaign to dress up the town for tourism. When the street was finally paved in the 1930s, many of the bricks ended up in the wall around Hemingway's home. Older Conchs remember when Duval was a street of raucous bars. They speak fondly of vanished flophouse hotels and Cuban cafés and cigarmakers' homes, and of seeing movies at the old **Strand Theater** *(527 Duval St.),* built by Cuban artisans in 1918. The theater's facade remains as the front of a Walgreen's. Conchs remember the days when Duval was a street that intimidated more visitors than it amused.

Today Duval is a street of friendlier but no less noisy bars, filled mainly with tourists and vacationing students instead of out-of-work railroaders, sun-burned fishermen, and merchant mariners looking for a ship. You can drive Duval in minutes, but opt to walk it, from Mallory Square to Truman Avenue, where the retail frenzy peters out. Depending on your mood, Duval will strike you as either horribly fascinating or fascinatingly

horrible. During spring break, college students swarm into town, buzzing around on mopeds whose tiny, snarling two-cycle engines are the bane of the island. If you want to be treated with respect by anyone over the age of 19, rent a bicycle not a moped.

INSIDER TIP:

For a convivial nightlife scene, head to the outdoor bar at Bagatelle. You might sit next to a fellow tourist who came for vacation and never left.

—ANNE MARIE HOUPPERT
*Index manager, National Geographic
Libraries & Information Services*

Sloppy Joe's

Between Greene and Caroline Streets, Duval is a street of bars, saloons, pubs, and more bars. Sloppy Joe's, at 201 Duval Street, is beat-up, popular, and usually crowded with tourists examining the many photographs of Hemingway, long ago a regular of the original Sloppy Joe's around the corner at 428 Greene Street—a location now

Duval Street

🅰 Map p. 206

Bagatelle

✉ 115 Duval St.

☎ 305/296-6609

**www.bagatelle
keywest.com**

Sloppy Joe's

🅰 Map p. 206

✉ 201 Duval St.

www.sloppyjoes.com

Joseph Porter House

🏛 Map p. 206

✉ 429 Caroline St.

occupied by **Captain Tony's Saloon** (www.capttonyssaloon.com), another vintage spirit house. Sloppy Joe was Joe Russell, a sometime rumrunner described by Hemingway biographer Carlos Baker as a "tough little slab-faced man," locally nicknamed Josie Grunts. Russell and Hemingway hit it off, and the author took to chartering Russell's 32-foot cabin cruiser for fishing trips. On one of these Hemingway had his first taste of marlin fishing, a sport that would enthrall him ever after. The author's observations of Russell eventually distilled into the tragic hero of one of Hemingway's short stories that evolved into the novel *To Have and Have Not*.

Joseph Porter House

On the southwest corner of Duval and Caroline Streets stands the Joseph Porter House (*No. 10 on the Pelican Path home tour; see p. 216*), one of the island's best examples of conch architecture's peculiar blend of New England, Bahamian, and creole styles. Though part private, the lower level is occupied by a pair of boutiques, permitting you to linger outside on the veranda. The graceful home is named for a physician, born here in 1847, who did pioneering work in the prevention and treatment of yellow fever, and was Florida's first public health officer. He died here at the age of 80, in the same room in which he was born.

Under the roof of the original Sloppy Joe's, Hemingway met his third wife, Martha Gellhorn.

Oldest House Museum

Just down the street is the Oldest House Museum, which occupies a conch classic that, as its name implies, is Key West's oldest house. This white clapboard building is a classic example of an early resident's home. (Its original occupant was a sea captain, Francis Watlington.) Built in 1829 on Whitehead Street, it was moved here three years later (something done fairly often in those days), and set atop 3-foot-high pier posts to keep it dry when storm surges flooded the downtown area. The little museum occupies six rooms, displaying 18th- and 19th-century antiques, model ships, and exhibits explaining how "wrecking" became not only a respectable trade here but, for a time, a fabulously lucrative one. Be sure to visit the backyard, where you'll find Key West's last outdoor kitchen, once common here.

San Carlos Institute

Until 1961, when Cuba and the United States severed diplomatic relations, Havana supported the San Carlos Institute, a political and social center. In its youth it was also an opera house, with what some insist is the South's most acoustically perfect hall. The Cuban patriot José Martí (see p. 231) spoke words from its balcony that still arouse Miami's expatriate Cuban community. The San Carlos is now a museum and archive whose focus is the role

Guayabera

Beat South Florida's summer heat and humidity by wearing a guayabera, the traditional Cuban smock shirt, often short-sleeved, seen in Miami, even in business settings, and in the Keys. Typically made from sheer white linen and cut generously large, the guayabera also makes a practical souvenir. In Key West, the gift shop of the El Meson de Pepe restaurant (410 Wall St., tel 305/295-2620) comes highly recommended as the best place to purchase a guayabera.

of Cubans in Key West history and culture.

The institute's first permanent building went up in 1884 on Fleming Street, named for Carlos Manuel de Cespedes, a Cuban plantation owner credited with the revolutionary slogan "Cuba libre!"—now more associated with a tall iced glass of rum and coke. On weekends the stirring hour-long documentary *Nostalgia Cubana*, about Cuba from the thirties to the fifties, is screened. The social unrest that led to Castro's overthrow of the Batista regime is obscured by the film's gorgeous images of Cuba's still vibrant culture. Be sure to look into the theater, whose backdrop paintings have been painstakingly restored to their original splendor. The lobby is decorated with beautifully detailed, hand-painted Spanish majolica tiles. There are

Oldest House Museum

▲ Map p. 206

✉ 322 Duval St.

☎ 305/294-9502

🕐 Closed Wed. & Sun.

💲 $$

www.oirf.org

San Carlos Institute

▲ Map p. 206

✉ 516 Duval St.

☎ 305/294-3887

🕐 Closed a.m. & Mon.–Thurs.

💲 $

www.institutosan carlos.org

Cuba lies some 90 miles beyond the United States' iconic Southernmost Point in Key West.

Southernmost Point

 Map p. 206

also exquisite hand-colored prints of Cuban wildfowl and fascinating historical exhibits.

Southernmost Point

If you peer south down Duval Street, you will see at its end the bright blue of sea and sky. Duval dead-ends beside a large, buoy-shaped, concrete marker proclaiming this the southernmost point of the United States. Across the intersection stands a magnificent turreted Queen Anne–style manse, an inn flanked by palms and known as the **Southernmost House** (*1400 Duval St.*).

The house and the marker make for memorable and dramatic photographs, but Southernmost Point isn't really what it claims to be. Key West's farthest reach toward Cuba is a knob of land about a half-mile west, inside the U.S. Naval Base and thus off-limits to the public.

That this distinction is claimed by a part of the island denied to most citizens of the Conch Republic offends local sensibilities. And as the difference between fact and fiction is a matter of only a few hundred feet, it strikes most as a technicality only the hopelessly unromantic would raise. Never mind that a far humbler house at the intersection of Whitehead and South Street one block west is itself more southerly than the handsome inn.

The actual southernmost point on American soil is far, far from here in the Hawaiian Islands, on a latitude shared with Mexico City. However, we are speaking of the continental United States. Yet, on days when the surf runs high, seawater surges onto the street, wetting the tires of passing vehicles and adding an aura of credibility to the notion that this is where America ends and the Caribbean begins. ■

Key West Cemetery

Like many things originally located elsewhere in Key West, the city's burial ground was moved (a consequence of an 1846 hurricane that flooded the grounds and opened graves) to the edge of Old Town, in a quiet neighborhood of cottages, some elegantly refurbished, others untouched by a paintbrush in decades.

Because the "new" cemetery lies atop coral rock and a shallow water table, its graves are above-ground vaults reminiscent of New Orleans' crypts. Key West's mordant humor is evident in

INSIDER TIP:

A stroll through the historic cemetery reflects as much about Key West's quirky character as any history lesson.

– SHARON WELLS
Author of Key West Walking *&* Biking Guide

its epitaphs: "I told you I was sick," one scolds. Mourning stone angels, downcast swans, and melancholy lambs grieve over untimely ends: "The Day is Gone and Tomorrow Shall Never Be Mine." Within a small fenced enclosure, surrounding a flagpole styled like a ship's mast and a stalwart stone sailor with oar held at the ready, are the graves of 22 Navy tars who died when the U.S.S. *Maine* exploded in Havana Harbor in 1898, igniting the Spanish-American War.

There is a separate monument commemorating Cubans who

died fighting for their island's independence from Spain, and a section of Jewish graves, the diversity of monuments revealing chapters of Key West's cultural history not evident elsewhere. If your schedule permits, take a guided tour *(offered Tues. & Thurs. at 9:30 a.m.)* with one of the knowledgeable volunteer members of the

> ### Key West's Cuban Heritage
>
> By 1890 Key West was Florida's wealthiest city. Among its leading citizens were Cuban bankers, shippers, and cigar manufacturers. They were joined by hundreds of self-exiled Cubans opposed to Spain's colonial rule and led by the charismatic José Martí, who adopted Key West as the base of his Partido Revolucionario Cubano. In early April 1895, Martí and Gen. Máximo Gómez set off from Santo Domingo for their homeland's coast, sparking Cuba's War of Independence. All but forgotten after decades of antipathy between Washington and Havana is the fact that Key West was once known as the Cradle of Cuban Independence.

Historic Florida Keys Foundation, starting from the sexton's office at the Margaret Street entrance. The walk takes 90 minutes and is wisely conducted before the sun begins to broil the unshaded gravel lanes. Gates are open sunrise to sunset. ■

Key West Cemetery

🅜 Map p. 206
✉ Angela, Frances, Olivia, & Windsor Sts.
☎ 305/292-6718

West Martello Tower

West Martello Tower has a rather tumble-down appearance that stems from a time when Army artillerymen at Fort Zachary Taylor across the island used the construction for target practice. Built as a coastal lookout and battery in 1861, it survived this not-so-friendly fire to serve again as a lookout during the Spanish-American War, and is now in the kinder hands of the Key West Garden Club.

Where coastal defenders once kept watch, a garden grows.

Higgs Beach, site of the African Cemetery (see sidebar this page).

Playwright's Retreat

From the tower, White Street leads inland to Old Town, a pleasant route through vintage neighborhoods. En route, take a four-minute side trip off White Street by turning right onto Duncan Street for a drive-by look at the unassuming but inviting two-story Bahamian-style house at No. 1431, once the home of Tennessee Williams *(closed to the public)*. The writer of *A Streetcar Named Desire* owned it from 1949 until his death in 1983. Williams added a writing studio and a swimming pool to the backyard, and lived and wrote enjoyably and productively here. The house was used as a set during the filming of Williams' play *The Rose Tattoo* (1955), which starred Burt Lancaster and Anna Magnani. ∎

West Martello Tower

- Map p. 207
- Atlantic Blvd. & White St.
- 305/294-3210

www.keywestgarden club.com

The club has filled the tower with plants, books on horticulture, and artworks, and every spring hosts an orchid show here. The old sentinel's greenery is a living encyclopedia of tropical plants and orchids that adjoins pleasant

African Cemetery

In the shadow of West Martello Tower lies the African Cemetery, although there are no tombstones. A plaque describes how 294 African slaves died in 1860 en route to Cuba and were buried on Higgs Beach. In 2002, approximately 15 grave sites were rediscovered and in 2011 ground-penetrating radar found more. When the Civil War fortification was built in the early 1860s, most of the cemetery's bones were removed. Today, their whereabouts are unknown. A fence encloses part of the area, which features African maps, symbols, and pillars.

Dry Tortugas National Park

In 1928, Ernest Hemingway went on a fishing trip to the Dry Tortugas, a 7-mile-long archipelago of seven low-lying sandy coral isles about 68 miles west of Key West. He became captivated by the Tortugas' desert-island wildness, star-filled nights, swirling seabird populations, and vivid, clear waters teeming with fish. There was also the astonishing ruin of Fort Jefferson, started in 1846 and never completed, still the largest brick fortress in the Western Hemisphere.

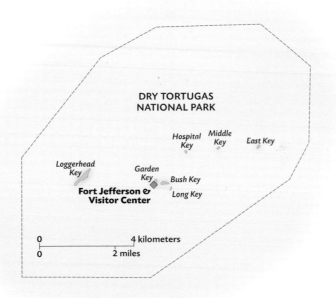

In 1930, Hemingway, his editor Maxwell Perkins, and three others spent 17 happily storm-bound days casting lines in the blue lagoon lying beneath the fort's mammoth guns. There is a photograph of the writer and the editor standing near the old fort's entrance, the gun ports behind them as empty as the eyes of a skull. If you stand there today, nothing in the background will have changed much, nor for that matter anything within the vast blue line of the encircling horizon.

In 1992 the islands were made the centerpiece of one of America's newest and most unusual national parks, a bird and marine life sanctuary whose 100 square miles enclose some of the healthiest coral reefs remaining off North American shores. Unless you take the 40-minute hop by seaplane, a visit to the Tortugas requires a full day, about half of it spent aboard one of the excursion boats that make the three-hour voyage from Key West. Either way, it will be a day you will not forget.

**Dry Tortugas
National Park**
☎ 305/242-7700
$ $
www.nps.gov/drto

NOTE: Dry Tortugas National Park is administered by Everglades National Park (40001 Fla. 9336, Homestead, tel 305/242-7700). There is currently no park office in Key West.

It should be noted that only 85 acres of this 65,000-acre park are above water, and that your visit will land you on 16-acre **Garden Key,** 11 acres of which are claimed by Fort Jefferson's massive hexagon. Three easterly islands are little more than sand spits, and the two isles adjoining Garden Key, **Bush Key** and **Long Key,** are both wildlife refuges, Long being permanently off-limits. (In recent years, a sandbar has connected Bush and Garden Keys). The Tortugas end 3 miles west with 30-acre **Loggerhead Key,** where, since 1858, a 151-foot-high lighthouse has warned mariners away from reefs and shoals known to have claimed more than 200 ships since the 1600s.

Garden Key

Garden Key is the place to be. Its tree-shaded picnic area adjoins a lovely swimming beach of soft white sand that slants gently down into crystalline shallows, deep enough near the shore to invite those who haven't snorkeled before. Behind the fort's seawall, depths increase to about 6 feet, supporting sea-grass "meadows" where brightly colored tropical fish dart about.

Allow at least an hour to wander around ghostly **Fort Jefferson,** built to anchor American control of the Straits of Florida. Proclaimed the Gibraltar of the Gulf, the 16-million-brick colossus still looks the part: 8-foot-thick walls rising 50 feet, forming a

Construction of the mid-19th-century Fort Jefferson increased Garden Key's area nearly by half.

EXPERIENCE: Snorkeling off Garden Key

It would be a shame to make the long journey to the Dry Tortugas and deny yourself the experience of snorkeling around Garden Key. The ferry services try to keep a few goggles, snorkels, and flippers on hand for loan, but bring your own if you have them.

The island's best close-to-shore snorkeling is on the **sea side of the 0.6-mile-long brick wall** enclosing Fort Jefferson's defensive moat. Here, chest-deep water covers a sandy shoal thick with sea fans, brain coral, and turtle grass and patrolled by many of the 442 species of fish identified here. If you have a companion or can enlist one for mutual safety, consider paddling from the campground's swimming beach along the wall, where fish tend to congregate. Watch for barracuda, which, though seldom aggressive, are territorial and should be given a wide berth.

If you prefer not to go in the water, stroll the seawall and look into the **moat**. Wayside exhibits detail this sheltered habitat adopted by the queen conch, yellow stingray, gray snapper, and other creatures.

hexagon whose 2,000 massive brick arches support three tiers of gun emplacements running a half mile around and designed for 450 guns, including huge Rodmans able to heave a 300-pound shell 3 miles. But the fort was a fiasco in almost every sense, literally cracking apart under its own weight as the island's crumbly coral rock gave way underneath. Fortunately, the citadel's intimidating bulk spared it from being tested in battle.

Undermanned, and with only one gun operational when the Civil War broke out, the garrison answered a Confederate navy demand to surrender with a threat to blow it out of the water. A 450-gun barrage would have certainly been lethal, had the dark gun ports concealed anything but a few soldiers peering out apprehensively at the rebel fleet. The Confederates prudently retreated, then sailed away forever, leaving the lonely outpost to serve mainly as a

INSIDER TIP:

About 2 miles northwest of Loggerhead Key lies Loggerhead Forest, a spectacular, amphitheater-like coral reef terrace of large platy corals that teems with fish.

—JERALD S. AULT
Professor of marine biology and fisheries, University of Miami

prison for Union deserters. After the war, the inmates included four men convicted of complicity in Abraham Lincoln's murder. One was the hapless physician Samuel Mudd who—unknowingly, he insisted—set the broken leg of the assassin John Wilkes Booth.

After 30 years of intermittent construction, the citadel fell in 1874 to yellow fever, the ravages of a hurricane, and the new rifled cannon, which rendered even those 8-foot-thick walls obsolete. Revived in 1898 as a Navy coaling station, the fort was permanently abandoned in 1907.

When you arrive, take a look at dockside announcement boards for ranger-led activities. If you intend to camp, check campground availability immediately (see sidebar below). The unmanned **visitor center** is just inside the fort entrance, and a Florida National Parks and Monuments Association bookstore *(1 p.m.–3 p.m. only)*. Take a few minutes to view an orientation film you can operate, then follow interpretive signs on a self-guided tour of Fort Jefferson's impressive architecture and parklike parade ground. Or join a ranger- or concessionaire-led tour.

Granite spiral staircases lead to open-air battlements and a 360-degree panorama that's ideal for binocular-aided bird-watching.

(The Dry Tortugas' populations of terns, cormorants, gulls, boobies, plovers, pelicans, peregrine falcons, and twin-tailed frigatebirds induced ornithologist and painter John James Audubon to sail out from Key West in 1832 to study them.) If you stroll the grassy parapet you will find several burly Civil War–era coastal guns on display near the fort's long-

INSIDER TIP:

Look for the shallow trenches in the floor of Dr. Samuel Mudd's cell. He cut them to drain the rainwater that would flood his cell, making it damp.

—JEROME COOKSON
Cartographer, National Geographic *magazine*

retired 19th-century lighthouse. To sit up here and watch dark frigate birds swoop by, riding the wind currents on graceful, slender wings, is a sublime experience.

Bush Key

Thanks to a sandbar that has developed in recent years, you can walk to Bush Key's primordial garden of bay cedar, seagrape, mangrove, sea oats, and prickly pear cactus—a landscape exactly like the one Spanish explorer Juan Ponce de León encountered when he first dropped anchor here in 1513. Ponce de León found the waters teeming with turtles—greens, hawksbills,

Camping

Garden Key has ten primitive tree-shaded sites with picnic tables and grills, available on a first-come, first-served basis. There are compost toilets on the public dock. The park charges a small camping fee per person per night, with a 14-day limit. Groups of ten or more must obtain a special use permit in advance from the Dry Tortugas administrative center in Everglades National Park (see p. 237).

Fort Jefferson's 19th-century iron-plate lighthouse, now retired, rises above the visitor center.

leatherbacks, and loggerheads—and so named these *cayos* las Tortugas. The turtles are now scarce, decimated by four centuries of overhunting, but every year between March and September an estimated 100,000 sooty and noddy terns return to Bush Key to roost in sandy nests. (During these months, Bush Key is closed to visitors.)

Visiting the Tortugas

How to Get There: Access to Dry Tortugas National Park is by boat or floatplane and is subject to weather conditions. Call park headquarters *(tel 305/242-7700)* for current information and a list of authorized air taxi and charter boat companies serving the islands.

Boat passage from Key West takes about three hours. Private boaters should refer to NOAA (National Oceanic and Atmospheric Administration) Chart No. 11434 ("Sombrero Key Dry Tortugas") and Chart No. 11438 ("Dry Tortugas"). There are no public boat moorings or slips; private boats must anchor offshore in designated areas. Only seasoned, fully equipped mariners in appropriate and seaworthy craft should attempt the crossing, as these waters are often shallow and subject year-round to strong winds that can bring rough seas.

The high-speed catamaran *Yankee Freedom II* serves as the main public transportation to the Tortugas; it costs $160 round-trip, plus $5 for park admission. Charter boat tours to the Tortugas are more expensive.

Yankee Freedom II
✉ Lands End Marina, Key West
☎ 305/294-7009
**www.yankee
freedom.com**

The crystal clear waters surrounding the Dry Tortugas are perfect for snorkeling.

When to Go: The park is open year-round. Visitation peaks in spring, when advance boat or airplane reservations are advised. Beware that the seas can be choppy November through April, resulting in rough sea crossings and poor visibility for snorkeling. Only Garden Key is open for overnight stays. Bush Key is closed mid-January through September (the migratory terns' nesting season).

Special Advice

The dock, the visitor center, and the ground level of Fort Jefferson are wheelchair accessible, as is the campground; however, brick pathways in the fort and sandy soil in the campground may impede mobility. Confirm charter boat and departure dock accessibility when you make reservations.

The Dry Tortugas are indeed dry: There is no fresh water available for campers or day visitors. If you plan to camp, you must bring water, fuel, food, and supplies. Day-trippers should bring plenty of water, a swimsuit and towel, a sweater or jacket for the evening (the boat trip back can be breezy, damp, and cool), snorkeling equipment, and binoculars for bird-watching and scouting nearby islands.

A final note: For however long you choose to linger in this excellent little fragment of subtropical paradise, you will be beyond the reach of worldly cares, as there is no public telephone service to the Tortugas, and there is no cell phone reception either. ∎

Traveling by air to the Tortugas is much quicker than by boat—the flight takes about 40 minutes each way—but you should expect round-trip fares of about $265 per person for a half-day idyll (which is rushing it), and around $465 for a day-long stay *(Key West Seaplane Adventures, tel 305/293-9300, www .keywestseaplanecharters.com)*.

Travelwise

Beach-bound in Miami Beach

TRAVELWISE

PLANNING YOUR TRIP

Miami has a strong image as a sunny, water-oriented resort with 354 square miles of coastal waters, 60 marinas, some 90,000 registered boats, nearly 12,000 acres of parks, and a mean annual temperature of 75°F.

The climate is extremely tropical with hot muggy summers balanced by warm winters—70°F January days are quite common. But in winter cold snaps can plunge temperatures to a low of 50°F.

The period from November to mid-May is considered high season, when South Beach is at its most active with film and fashion shoots scheduled, and many of the major events take place. The weather is at its best, with hot days, cool evenings, and low humidity, but many hotel and car rental prices shoot up during this time, lowering by the end of May. May to October brings hotter, more humid weather, with frequent, heavy showers, but these are usually brief. Most tropical storms and hurricanes occur between August and November.

The average daytime temperature in the Keys is 78°F, with night temperatures about 66°F. Cool winds across the Atlantic and Gulf keep the heat down. Key West is also the driest city in Florida and sunny nearly year-round, although December and January are the coldest months of the year and temperatures can drop to the 50s.

GETTING TO MIAMI
By Air
Miami International Airport (MIA), tel 305/876-7000, www .miami-airport.com Centrally located about 7 miles northwest of downtown Miami. Tourist information counters are located outside the customs exits at the main information counter on the upper level on Concourse E, and on Concourses D and G on the lower level of the terminal.

By Train
Although Henry Flagler opened up Florida with the railroad, visitors are only now rediscovering the ease of rail travel, primarily on the east coast, with Amtrak's Silver Service (www.amtrak.com) from New York to Miami.

GETTING TO THE KEYS
By Air
There is frequent air service to both Key West and Marathon municipal airports from Miami International Airport, Orlando, Tampa, and Fort Lauderdale. Flights between Miami and Key West take 45 minutes.

By Bus
Visitors arriving at Miami International Airport can take a Greyhound bus to Key West, which stops at various points throughout the chain of islands. The trip to Key West takes about 4.5 hours. Departures from Miami International Airport are scheduled daily at 12:15 p.m. and 5:55 p.m. The round-trip costs around $68 to and from Marathon and around $100 to and from Key West. Or bus down and fly back.

Greyhound
Tel 800/410-5397, www.grey hound.com

By Car
From Miami International Airport, take LeJeune Road south to Fla. 836 west. This connects with the Fla. 821 west tollway, which will take you south to Florida City, where it leads into US 1. (See below for car rental details at Miami International Airport.)

It can feel as if you're on a ship as you cruise down US 1 over the 42 bridges linking the Keys with the mainland. On the driver's side are the turquoise waters of the Atlantic; on the passenger's side the bold blue of Florida Bay. From Key Largo to Key West this Overseas Highway is the only road to the Keys, and includes the famous Seven Mile Bridge.

Mile markers (MM) are small green signs beside the road, which start in South Miami at MM 126 and end at Key West at MM 0. Addresses along the way are frequently followed by their mile marker location.

GETTING AROUND
By Car
Car Rentals
Most rental companies operate off-site branches that are reached by shuttle from the airport terminals. If you are arriving at night, take a taxi to your hotel and arrange for the car rental firm to deliver a car to the hotel the next day.

Pick up a guide at the airport information kiosks, car rental counters in baggage claim, or off-airport car rental facilities. The guide features special amplified maps and multilingual instructions that are designed to help get you to your destination. You can also direct your smart phone to www.miamiandbeaches.com/visitors/maps.asp.

Alamo Rent A Car
4322 Collins Ave., Miami Beach, FL 33139, tel 305/532-8257 or 800/327-9633, www.alamo.com

Avis Rent-A-Car
2318 Collins Ave., Miami Beach, FL 33139, tel 305/538-4441 or 800/331-1212, www.avis.com

Budget Car and Truck Rental
Miami International Rental Car Center, 3900 N.W. 25th St., Miami, FL 33142, tel 800/527-0700, www.budget.com

Dollar Rent-A-Car
Miami International Airport, 3670 N.W. S. River Dr., Miami, FL 33142, tel 866/434-2226, www.dollar.com

Enterprise Rent-A-Car
Miami International Rental Car Center, 3900 N.W. 25th St., Miami, FL 33142, tel 305/633-0377 or 800/325-8007, www.enterprise.com

Excellence Luxury Car Rental
Miami International Rental Car Center, 3900 N.W. 25th St., Miami, FL 33142, tel 305/526-0000, www.excellenceluxury.com

Hertz Rent-A-Car
Miami International Rental Car Center, 3900 N.W. 25th St., Miami, FL 33142, tel 305/871-0300 or 800/654-3131, www.hertz.com

National Car Rental
Miami International Rental Car Center, 3900 N.W. 25th St., Miami, FL 33142, tel 305/423-2104, www.nationalcar.com

Royal Rent-A-Car
Miami International Rental Car Center, 3900 N.W. 25th St., Miami, FL 33142, tel 305/871-3000 or 800/314-8616, www.royalrentacar.com

Wheelchair-accessible Van Rentals
Wheelchair Getaways, 8 Bay Harbour Rd., Tequesta, FL 33469, tel 561/748-8414, www.wheelchairgetaways.com

Parking
The fine for an expired meter is $18; $45 if not paid within 30 calendar days.

Contact the Miami Parking Authority, 40 N.W. 3rd St. (downtown Miami), for locations, rates, and hours of parking garages. (Open Mon.–Fri. 7:30 a.m.–5:30 p.m., tel 305/373-6789.)

If your car has been towed, contact the municipality where it was parked for further details. In Miami Beach call Beach Towing, tel 305/534-2128.

Transportation To & From Airport
Public transportation is not recommended for getting from the airport to your hotel. Buses heading downtown from the arrivals level are hourly, with poor connections.

Super Shuttle
2595 N.W. 38th St., Miami, FL 33142, tel 305/871-2000, www.supershuttle.com.
A shared-ride van service to and from Miami International Airport. Reservations are required only for services to the airport. Per-person rates from MIA to hotels/

attractions in the greater Miami area range from $15 to $20.

Taxis
From the airport to downtown Miami, the trip is approximately 8 miles and costs about $20; Miami Beach is 14 miles and costs about $25; northern Miami Beach costs about $40. Telephone 305/375-2460 with any concerns, complaints, or comments about the taxi service.

Flamingo Taxi
198 N.W. 79th St., Miami, FL 33150, tel 305/759-8100

Florida Keys Taxi Dispatch
6631 Maloney Ave., Key West, FL 33040, tel 305/296-6666, www.keywesttaxi.com

Friendly Cab Co.
800 14th St., Key West, FL 33040, tel 305/292-0000

Metro Taxi
1995 N.E. 142nd St., North Miami, FL 33181, tel 305/888-8888

Transportation In & Around Miami
Metro–Dade Transit runs Miami's public transportation system. For information on Metrobus, Metromover, and Metrorail routes and schedules, telephone 305/770-3131. Information is also available on the website: www.miamidade.gov/transit. Tickets and tokens can be bought at any Metrorail station.

Metrobus
More than 90 routes serve Greater Miami. One-way fares are $2; $1 for seniors, persons with disabilities, and students with a bus permit or Medicare card; exact change only.

Metromover

Miami's high-tech electric mono-rail with individual motorized cars runs atop a 4.4-mile elevated track looping around downtown Miami and on to the Brickell and Omni business districts. It offers great views of Biscayne Bay, and a cool, clean, comfortable ride. Metromover operates every 90 seconds daily, 5 a.m.–12 a.m. The Metromover is free of charge. It connects with Metrorail at Government Center and Brickell Avenue stations.

Metrorail

Miami's very underused rapid transit system is a 22-mile ele-vated rail system. Stations include Coconut Grove, Vizcaya, Brickell Avenue, and Government Center. Trains operate approximately every 20 minutes (5 minutes dur-ing peak hours), 6 a.m.–12 a.m. The fare is $2; exact change only. Passengers can transfer directly onto Metromover free of charge at Government Center and Brickell Avenue stations.

South Beach Local O

The South Beach Local, operated by Miami–Dade Transit, is a bidirectional circular bus service to the entire South Beach area. Mon.–Sat. 7:45 a.m.–12 a.m. Sun. 10 a.m.–12 a.m. For a map, visit www.miamidade.gov/transit.

Tri-Rail

www.tri-rail.com
A commuter rail line to West Palm Beach at the Tri-Rail/ Metrorail Transfer station, near the Hialeah end of the Metrorail. All trains and stations are wheel-chair accessible.

Key West Transportation

Driving can be more trouble than it is worth, especially around the narrow streets of Key West's Old

Town. It is far better to explore on foot, or rent a bike or moped. Trolleys and trains are another way of getting around and seeing the sights.

Old Town Trolley Tours

200 Simonton St., Key West, FL 33040, tel 305/296-6688, www.trolleytours.com/Key-West The Old Town Trolley fleet pro-vides narrated tours of the city's historic landmarks.

Conch Tour Trains

1805 Staples Ave., Key West, FL 33040, tel 305/294-5161, www.conchtourtrain.com The Conch Tour Trains consist of small canvas canopied cars that are pulled by Jeeps disguised as miniature locomotives, and tour all the historic sites.

Port of Miami Cruises

Miami is known as the Cruise Capital of the World. The Port of Miami (tel 305/371-7678, www.miamidade.gov/portofmiami) is the embarkation point for 15 cruise ships operated by ten cruise lines—the world's largest year-round fleet. The port's 12 air-conditioned terminals offer duty-free shopping, wheelchair access, and ground-level customs clearance.

The port's website lists cruises that are available from three to eleven days.

FURTHER READING

South Florida has been the source of inspiration for many writers. The following are just a few of the authors who have set all or some of their work in South Florida:

John D. MacDonald, The Deep Blue Goodbye (Florida-based thriller); Elmore Leonard, La

Brava (South Beach mystery); Carl Hiaasen, Striptease (by the famous Miami Herald columnist); Jimmy Buffett, Where Is Joe Merchant? (rock guitarist missing in the Keys); John Hersey, Key West Tales (short stories set in Key West); Tom McGuane, 92 in the Shade (set in Key West); Ernest Hemingway, To Have and Have Not (famous Keys resident); and Marjorie Kinnan Rawlings, The Yearling (classic novel set in central Florida).

PRACTICAL ADVICE

Communications
Newspapers

The Miami Herald (www.miami herald.com) is South Florida's main newspaper. The Friday edition includes a good section on weekend events, restaurants, movies, music, and night life. Miami's alternative newspaper is the free weekly New Times (www.miaminewtimes.com) with a comprehensive listing of restau-rants, arts, and entertainment.

Post Offices

General Mail Facility 2200 N.W. 72nd Ave., Miami, FL 33126, tel 305/470-0222 or 800/275-8777. Call for postal information and branch locations.

Fishing Licenses

Florida Fish and Wildlife Conser-vation Commission, tel 888/347-4356, www.myfwc.com/license

Fishing licenses (for both fresh and saltwater) are required (with some exceptions) and are avail-able at the Florida Fish and Wild-life Conservation Commission website, and some tackle shops, discount retail stores, and sport-ing goods stores. Nonresident licenses are valid for three to ten days; freshwater and saltwater licenses are valid three to seven days or for one year.

Travelers With Disabilities
Miami–Dade Transit Agency, Special Transportation Service
2775 S.W. 74th Ave., Miami, FL 33155, tel 786/469-5000. Mon.–Fri. 8 a.m.–5 p.m.

Miami Lighthouse for the Blind
601 S.W. 8th Ave., Miami, FL 33130, tel 305/856-2288, www.miamilighthouse.com. Mon.–Fri. 8 a.m.–5 p.m.

Visitor Information & Reservation Services
GREATER MIAMI
Art Deco Welcome Center
Miami Design Preservation League, 1001 Ocean Dr., Miami Beach, FL 33139, tel 305/672-2014, www.mdpl.org

Greater Fort Lauderdale Convention & Visitors Bureau
100 E. Broward Blvd., Ste. 200, Fort Lauderdale, FL 33301, tel 954/765-4466 or 800/227-8669, www.sunny.org

Greater Miami and the Beaches Hotel Association
1674 Meridian Ave., Ste. 420, Miami Beach, FL 33139, tel 305/531-3553, www.gmbha.com

Greater Miami Convention & Visitors Bureau
701 Brickell Ave., Ste. 2700, Miami, FL 33131, tel 305/539-3000, www.miamiandbeaches.com

Miami Beach Chamber of Commerce
1920 Meridian Ave., #3A, Miami Beach, FL 33139, tel

305/674-1300, www.miami beachchamber.com

Miami–Dade Gay & Lesbian Chamber of Commerce
1130 Washington Ave., Miami Beach, FL 33139, tel 305/673-4440, www.gogaymiami.com

Sunny Isles Beach Visitor Center
18070 Collins Ave., Ste. 219, Sunny Isles, FL 33160, tel 305/792-1952

Surfside Tourist Bureau
9293 Harding Ave., Surfside, tel 305/864-0722, www.visitsurfsidefl.com

Tropical Everglades Visitor Association
160 US 1, Florida City, FL 33040, tel 305/245-9180, www.tropicaleverglades.com

FLORIDA KEYS
Monroe County (Florida Keys) Tourist Development Council
1201 White St., Key West, FL 33040, tel 800/352-5397, www.fla-keys.com

Key Largo Chamber of Commerce/Florida Keys Visitor Center
106000 Overseas Hwy., Key Largo, FL 33037, tel 305/451-1414 or 800/822-1088, www.floridakeys.org

Islamorada Chamber of Commerce
83224 Overseas Hwy., Islamorada, FL 33036, tel 305/664-4503 or 800/322-5397, www.islamoradachamber.com

Marathon Chamber of Commerce
12222 Overseas Hwy., Marathon, FL 33050, tel 305/743-5417 or 800/262-7284, www.floridakeysmarathon.com

Lower Keys Chamber of Commerce
MM 31/Overseas Hwy., Big Pine Key, FL 33043, tel 305/872-2411 or 800/872-3722, www.lowerkeyschamber.com

Key West Chamber of Commerce
510 Greene St., Key West, FL 33040, tel 305/294-2587, www.keywestchamber.org

Key West Information Center
201 Front St., Ste. 108, Key West, FL 33040, tel 888/222-5590, www.keywestinfo.com

EMERGENCIES

Call **911** in case of police, ambulance, or fire emergency. Nonemergency police inquiry: 305/595-6263.

Emergency Road Service
AAA Emergency Road Service
Members receive free towing and roadside service. Nonmembers can join over the phone, but existing members have priority. Tel 800/222-4357, or 800/618-8734 in Miami.

Lost Credit Cards
To report lost or stolen credit cards or travelers' checks, contact the following:

American Express, tel 800/528-4800
Diners Club, tel 800/234-6377
Discover, tel 800/347-2683
MasterCard, tel 800/826-2181
Visa, tel 800/336-8472

Hotels & Restaurants

Accommodations listed below range from small bed-and-breakfast establishments with the emphasis on personal attention rather than, say, room TVs or phones, to full service hotels that are usually multistory buildings and include a coffee shop and restaurant.

All hotels and restaurants are listed alphabetically by price category. Unless otherwise stated, all the following hotels have private bathrooms with shower and/or bathtub. Prices quoted do not include taxes. Most municipalities levy special taxes on hotel rooms and food and beverages served in hotels and restaurants, on top of the 6 percent sales tax and 0.5 percent local sales tax. In South Beach and Miami–Dade County combined hotel taxes are 12.5 percent, in Surfside 10.5 percent, in Bal Harbour 9.5 percent. Most hotels charge extra for breakfast.

Reservations are recommended for restaurants, but a special note has been made of those places where it is essential. Few restaurants offer fixed-price menus, but some do so for Sunday brunch, or offer "early bird" specials (between 4 p.m. and 6 p.m.). Many restaurants open early for dinner (5 p.m.) and close late.

Water defines the Keys, and whether you're staying in a glitzy resort or a simple bed-and-breakfast, all Keys' accommodations offer access to some of the best water sports facilities in South Florida. Vacationers down for the fishing may like to get to bed early, but for others, late-night bars and restaurants are part of the Keys way of life. The Keys always give a feeling that they are perched precariously on the edge of the world, and that seems to boost appetites for food and drink.

Not all of the hotels and restaurants listed are readily accessible to people with disabilities. Many buildings, especially in South Beach and Key West, may have one or more steps to negotiate before entering. Visitors are advised to check when booking to make sure the hotel or restaurant meets their specific needs

Abbreviations Used

AE = American Express
DC = Diners Club
MC = MasterCard
V = Visa
L = lunch
D = dinner

■ MIAMI'S CENTRAL DISTRICTS

From the fountains of the cultural center to the excitement of the commercial district, the downtown area of Miami has benefited from the multicultural population. Some bay side restaurants here offer the freshest fish in the city.

Little Havana's Calle Ocho (8th St.) is noted for restaurants specializing in mojito-laced *lechón* (rum and lime marinated pork) and *carne asada* (roast meats). Although high-style Cuban SoBe (South Beach) experiences such as Yuca, or Larios on the Beach, are making waves with their innovative cuisine, the more traditional eateries still offer good value for the dollar with traditional dishes of pork, chicken, or seafood, and yellow or white rice, with yucca, black beans, plantains, or fried bananas on the side. The residential area of North Miami

offers some of the city's better restaurants and shops.

DOWNTOWN MIAMI

🏨 INTERCONTINENTAL
🍴 MIAMI
$$$$$
100 CHOPIN PLAZA, FL 33131
TEL 866/396-7606
FAX 305/577-0384
www.icmiamihotel.com
Deluxe high-rise on Biscayne Bay, adjacent to Bayside Marketplace and Bayfront Park. Elegantly appointed rooms, full range of first-class services. This is the place to stay downtown.
🛏 675 rooms & suites
🅿 Valet 🔄 🈁 🈁 🈁 🈁
🈁 🈁 All major cards

🏨 HOLIDAY INN PORT OF
🍴 MIAMI – DOWNTOWN
$$
340 BISCAYNE BLVD., FL 33132
TEL 305/371-4400
www.holidayinn.com
An economically priced hotel minutes from all the activity.
🛏 200 rooms 🅿 🔄 🈁 🈁
🈁 🈁 All major cards

🏨 RIVER PARK HOTEL
🍴 & SUITES
$$
100 S.E. 4TH ST., FL 33131
TEL 305/374-5100
www.booking.com
In the heart of downtown, next to the Metromover, the River Park reflects Miami's international sophistication. Spacious rooms and suites feature cable, data port, voice mail, and coffeemaker.
🛏 149 🅿 🔄 🈁 🈁 🈁
🈁 All major cards

PRICES

HOTELS

An indication of the cost of a double room in the high season is given by $ signs.

$$$$$	Over $280
$$$$	$200–$280
$$$	$120–$200
$$	$80–$120
$	Under $80

RESTAURANTS

An indication of the cost of a three-course meal without drinks is given by $ signs.

$$$$$	Over $80
$$$$	$50–$80
$$$	$35–$50
$$	$20–$35
$	Under $20

🍴 BRISA BISTRO

$$–$$$

HILTON MIAMI DOWNTOWN
1601 BISCAYNE BLVD.
TEL 305/374-0000
High standards in an elegant mirrored, marbled dining room tucked away in a corner of the hotel lobby. Seafood seldom comes better than this with dishes such as seared swordfish with Oriental vinaigrette.
🛏 100 🅿 Valet 🕐 Closed Sun. & L Sat. 🚭 ❄ 💳 All major cards

LITTLE HAVANA 33130

🏨 MIAMI RIVER INN BED & BREAKFAST

$$

118 S.W. SOUTH RIVER DR.
TEL 305/325-0045 or
800/468-3589
FAX 305/325-9227
www.miamiriverinn.com
Historic inn made up of five restored clapboard buildings dating from 1906. Charming rooms, styled individually but retaining a traditional look. Lush garden.
ⓘ 40 rooms & suites 🅿 🚭 ❄ 🏊 💳 All major cards

🍴 EXQUISITO RESTAURANT

$

1510 S.W. 8TH ST.
TEL 305/643-0227
www.holidayinn.com
Owned by a Cuban whose family owned a Havana restaurant confiscated by the communists, it sits next to the historic Tower Theater. Specialties include tamales and pork chunks.
🛏 50 ❄ 💳 All major cards

🍴 LA CARRETA

$

3632 S.W. 8TH ST.
TEL 305/444-7501
Old-style Cuban restaurant, part of a chain. Large portions of classic dishes, and a backroom cafeteria for strong coffee, sweet pastries, and sugarcane juice.
🛏 300 ❄ 💳 All major cards

🍴 VERSAILLES

$

3555 S.W. 8TH ST.
TEL 305/444-0240
www.versaillesrestaurant.com
Famous Cuban landmark with kitsch decor and wall-to-wall mirrors—a must for tourists. Menu offers every Cuban dish imaginable in hearty portions.
🛏 400 ❄ 💳 All major cards

NORTH MIAMI 33180

🏨 TURNBERRY ISLE RESORT & CLUB

$$$$$

19999 W. COUNTRY CLUB DR.,
AVENTURA
TEL 305/932-6200 or
800/327-7028
FAX 305/933-6554
www.turnberryislemiami.com
This is the grandest of the grand Miami resorts, a stunning Mediterranean-style hotel set in a secluded oasis of 300 tropical acres by the bay. Oversize rooms, large terraces, two golf courses, and moorings for 117 boats.
ⓘ 392 rooms & suites 🅿 ❄ 🚭 ❄ 🏊 💳 All major cards

🍴 PASHA'S

$

19501 BISCAYNE BLVD.,
AVENTURA
TEL 305/917-4007
www.pashas.com
This Miami chain serves fast, casual, healthy Mediterranean meals including hummus wraps, kebabs, and tatziki soup.
🛏 90 ❄ 💳 All major cards

■ MIAMI BEACH

SoBe (South Beach) offers an entirely new world of sleek, chic cuisine, backed by cool art deco hotels and hyper-designed fantasies—the undoubted king of which is Ian Schrager. His showpiece Delano Hotel opened in mid-1995, just as a major renovation project began on the Lincoln Road pedestrian mall between Washington Avenue and Lenox Street.

MIAMI BEACH 33139

HOTELS

🏨 CASA GRANDE

$$$$$

834 OCEAN DR.
TEL 305/672-7003
FAX 305/673-3669
www.casagrandesuite
hotel.com
At this deluxe, all-suite hotel, ocean views are standard, and stunning contemporary amenities such as carved teak and mahogany furnishings and Indonesian batiks capture the

SoBe look exactly.

(i) 34 **P** Valet ⊟ ⊕
⊗ All major cards

🏨 DELANO
🍴 $$$$$

1685 COLLINS AVE.
TEL 305/672-2000 or
800/697-1791
FAX 305/532-0099
www.delano-hotel.com
Understated luxury is reflected
in designer Philippe Starck's
blinding white decor, offset
by billowing curtains, antique
pieces, and the Granny Smith
apple, replaced daily, in every
one of the rooms. See **Bianca**
restaurant, p. 247.

(i) 194 rooms, suites & lofts
🛏 200 **P** Valet ⊟ ⊕ ⊗
⊠ 🔲 ⊗ All major cards

🏨 NATIONAL HOTEL
🍴 $$$$$

1677 COLLINS AVE.
TEL 305/532-2311 or
800/327-8370
www.nationalhotel.com
A beachfront landmark, the
National has been restored
to its chic art deco glamour.
Complimentary poolside
yoga and luxurious amenities,
including flat-screen TVs.

(i) 151 rooms & suites
P Valet ⊟ ⊕ ⊠ 🔲
⊗ All major cards

🏨 SEA VIEW
$$$$$

9909 COLLINS AVE.
BAL HARBOUR, FL 33154
TEL 305/866-4441 or
800/447-1010
FAX 305/866-1898
www.seaview-hotel.com
European-style beachfront
hotel and resort with Mediterranean cabanas directly across
from the famous Bal Harbour
shops. Attracts a conservative clientele who want the
beach but not South Beach.

(i) 220 rooms & suites
P ⊟ ⊕ ⊗ ⊠ 🔲 ⊗ All
major cards

🏨 THE TIDES
$$$$$

1220 OCEAN DR.
TEL 305/604-5070
FAX 305/604-5180
www.tidessouthbeach.com
One of the most beautiful
hotels that South Beach has to
offer, The Tides features suites
overlooking the ocean; those
on the ninth and tenth floors
are among the highest points
on Ocean Drive.

(i) 45 rooms & suites **P** Valet
⊟ ⊕ ⊗ ⊠ 🔲 ⊗ All major
cards

🏨 HOTEL IMPALA
🍴 $$$$

1228 COLLINS AVE.
TEL 305/673-2021
www.hotelimpalamiami
beach.com
Diminutive, discreet
celebrity hideaway, offering
Mediterranean flair, custom
furnishings, original artwork, and European-style
service. Rooms are small
but elegant. **Spiga** is a note-
worthy restaurant, see p. 249.

(i) 17 rooms & suites
🛏 100 **P** Valet ⊟ ⊕ ⊗
⊗ All major cards

🏨 HOTEL OCEAN
$$$$

1230 OCEAN DR.
TEL 305/672-2579
FAX 305/672-7665
www.hotelocean.com
A full renovation has resulted
in a French Riviera feel to this
hotel. The owners and managers
are French, as is the food.

(i) 27 ⊟ ⊕ ⊗ All
major cards

🏨 ALBION
$$$

1650 JAMES AVE.
TEL 305/913-1000
FAX 305/531-4580
www.rubelhotels.com
White-sand beach, a poolside
outdoor living room, and
contemporary deck and

rooftop solarium suites define
this trendy hotel, attracting a
cosmopolitan crowd.

(i) 96 **P** Valet ⊟ ⊕ ⊗ ⊠
🔲 ⊗ AE, MC, V

🏨 CARDOZO
$$$

1300 OCEAN DR.
TEL 305/535-6500 or
800/782-6500
FAX 305/702-5437
www.cardozohotel.com
Classic art deco hotel, the
informal headquarters of
owners Gloria and Emilio
Estefan. Stylish and modern
rooms featuring handcrafted
furniture. Great location.

(i) 43 **P** Valet ⊟ ⊕ ⊗ All
major cards

🏨 CAVALIER
🍴 $$$

1320 OCEAN DR.
TEL 305/531-3555
www.cavaliermiami.com
This renovated and redeco-
rated prime deco building is
popular both for its hotel and
the Crab Shack restaurant
and bar.

(i) 45 rooms & suites **P** Valet
⊟ ⊕ ⊗ ⊗ All major cards

🏨 DADDY O HOTEL
$$$

9660 E. BAY HARBOR DR.
BAY HARBOR ISLANDS, FL 33154
TEL 305/868-4141
www.daddyohotel.com/
miami
Waterfront inn on scenic
Indian Creek in a quiet neigh-
borhood. Walking distance
to fishing and scuba charters.
Close to Bal Harbour shops.

(i) 38 **P** ⊟ ⊕ ⊠ ⊗ AE,
MC, V

🏨 ESSEX HOUSE
$$$

1001 COLLINS AVE.
TEL 305/534-2700
FAX 305/531-3953
www.essexhotel.com
European charm, modern

🏨 Hotel 🍴 Restaurant **(i)** No. of Guest Rooms 🛏 No. of Seats **P** Parking ⊕ Closed ⊟ Elevator

conveniences, and affordable luxury at this Hohauser-designed deco hotel. The pastel-colored rooms are stylish and soundproof. Complimentary continental breakfast and Wi-Fi.

[i] 74 rooms & suites 🔲 [S] 🌀 🔑 All major cards

🏨 GREENVIEW HOTEL
$$$

1671 WASHINGTON AVE.
TEL 305/531-6588
FAX 305/531-4580
www.greenviewhotel.com
Extraordinary Henry Hohauser deco building brought up to date by the Rubell family. Cool, urbane interior of exceptional tranquility from Parisian designer Chaban Minassian.

[i] 45 🔲 [S] 🔑 AE, MC, V

🏨 HOTEL ASTOR
🍴 $$$

956 WASHINGTON AVE.
TEL 305/531-8081
FAX 305/531-3193
www.hotelastor.com
Another great deco building, built in 1936 and magnificently renovated with attention to detail. Blond wood furniture, original, polished terrazzo floors, and restful colors define the look. See **Joley Restaurant & Lounge**, p. 248.

[i] 41 rooms & suites 🅿 Valet 🔲 [S] 🌀 🔑 All major cards

🏨 KENT
$$$

1131 COLLINS AVE.
TEL 866/826-5368
FAX 305/403-7592
www.thekenthotel.com
A striking deco hotel, the lobby is popular with fashion shoots, and the style is contemporary chic. An affordable retreat in South Beach.

[i] 54 rooms & suites 🅿 Valet 🔲 [S] 🌀 🔑 All major cards

🏨 PARK CENTRAL
$$$

640 OCEAN DR.
TEL 305/538-1611 or 800/727-5236
FAX 305/534-7520
www.theparkcentral.com
Authentically restored to reflect the 1940s, this Hohauser beachfront hotel boasts wraparound corner windows and sleek, modern touches. The lobby bar attracts a cool fashion crowd.

[i] 125 rooms & suites 🅿 🔲 [S] 🌀 📺 🔑 All major cards

🏨 PELICAN HOTEL
$$$

826 OCEAN DR.
TEL 305/673-3373
FAX 305/673-3255
www.pelicanhotel.com
Four-story deco-inspired frivolity with wonderful, eclectic styling in custom-designed themed rooms such as Power Flower and Best Whorehouse. The bathrooms are amazing.

[i] 30 rooms & suites 🅿 Valet 🔲 [S] 🌀 🔑 All major cards

🏨 AVALON
🍴 $$

700 OCEAN DR.
TEL 305/538-0133 or 800/933-3306
FAX 305/534-0258
www.avalonhotel.com
Classic deco-style hotel. Tidy, small rooms offer simple modern amenities, but the main attraction is that this is a friendly place to stay in a great beachside location. Complimentary continental breakfast and Wi-Fi.

[i] 108 🅿 Valet 🔲 [S] 🔑 All major cards

🏨 CLAY HOTEL
$$

1438 WASHINGTON AVE.
TEL 305/534-2988 or 800/379-CLAY

FAX 305/673-0346
www.clayhotel.com
Listed on the National Register of Historic Places, this hotel on Española Way offers single, double, and family rooms. The hallways are painted with vivid scenes of tropical Miami, while the rooms are clean and quiet. Outdoor courtyards and a patio dining area. Long-term stays possible.

[i] 106 🔲 [S] 🌀 🔑 MC, V

🏨 BEACHCOMBER
$

1340 COLLINS AVE.
TEL 305/531-3755 or 888/305-HOTEL
FAX 305/673-8609
www.beachcombermiami.com
Quaint art deco hotel in the heart of SoBe with functional, small rooms and a tropical, carefree atmosphere. The breakfast buffet is a bargain, the beach a block away.

[i] 28 🅿 🔲 [S] 🌀 🔑 All major cards

🏨 CARLTON
$

1433 COLLINS AVE.
TEL 305/672-5858
FAX 305/534-6855
www.carltonsouthbeach.com
Central location in the heart of the Art Deco District. Quaint, family-run hotel with emphasis on personalized attention.

[i] 67 rooms & suites 🅿 🔲 [S] 🌀 🔑 All major cards

RESTAURANTS

SOMETHING SPECIAL

🍴 BIANCA

Located in the famous and fashionable Delano Hotel (see p. 246), Bianca opened in early 2012 as a restaurant serving modern Italian cuisine. It features local, organic ingredients in line with the slow food movement.

$$$$
DELANO HOTEL
1685 COLLINS AVE.
MIAMI BEACH
TEL 305/ 674-6400
www.delano-hotel.com
🛏 250 🅿 Valet 🛗
🚫 D, MC, V

🍴 **ESCOPAZZO**
$$$$
1311 WASHINGTON AVE.
TEL 305/674-9450
Intimate, passionately run,
and offering some of the best
Italian food on South Beach.
Soufflés are recommended—
seafood in herb-infused *fumé*—
or there's arugula and goat
cheese risotto. Reservations
required.
🪑 90 🕐 Closed L & Mon.
🛗 🚫 All major cards

🍴 **THE FORGE**
$$$$
432 41ST ST.
TEL 305/538-8533
Classic, expensive, rococo
restaurant serving excellent
Continental American cuisine
that includes scrambled eggs
with caviar served in the egg-
shells, 16-ounce steaks, organic
arugula salads, escargots,
and soufflés. Club with disco
and cigar room every Wed.
Reservations required.
🪑 275 🅿 Valet 🕐 Closed L
🛗 🛗 🚫 All major cards

🍴 **CHINA GRILL**
$$$
404 WASHINGTON AVE.
TEL 305/534-2211
www.chinagrillmanagement
.com
Lively, upscale, new wave
Asian/Chinese restaurant
cloned from New York City's
East-Meets-West. Try seared
rare tuna with spicy Japanese
pepper and avocado sashimi,
and mushroom fettuccine in
sake-Madeira-cream sauce.
Great for celeb-spotting.

Reservations required.
🪑 500 🅿 Valet 🛗 🛗
🚫 All major cards

🍴 **GRILLFISH**
$$$
1444 COLLINS AVE.
MIAMI BEACH
TEL 305/538-9908
www.grillfish.com
Serving healthy and tasty
seafood, this eatery is popular
with locals.
🪑 130 🛗 🛗 🚫 All major
cards

🍴 **JERRY'S FAMOUS DELI**
$$$
1450 COLLINS AVE.
TEL 305/532-8030
www.jerrysfamousdeli.com
This historic restaurant, which
is open 24 hours a day, is a
great place to slow down after
an evening out.
🪑 70 🛗 🚫 All major cards

SOMETHING SPECIAL

🍴 **JOLEY RESTAURANT
& LOUNGE**
Joley is a stunning restaurant
in an innovative setting
under a glass atrium. Chef
John Suley's newest hot spot
features American cuisine with
a European influence.
$$$
HOTEL ASTOR
956 WASHINGTON AVE.
SOUTH BEACH
TEL 305/672-7217
🪑 200 (plus 80 outdoors)
🕐 Closed L 🛗 🚫 All major
cards

SOMETHING SPECIAL

🍴 **MEAT MARKET**
Most South Beach fashion
models are purported to be
vegetarians, but the ones who
aren't must be here. This fashionable steak house on Lincoln
Road is, believe it or not, sexy.
The seafood is just as beloved

as the beef.
$$$
915 LINCOLN RD.
MIAMI BEACH
TEL 305/532-0088
www.meatmarketmiami.com
🪑 160 🕐 Closed L 🛗
🚫 All major cards

🍴 **NOBU MIAMI BEACH**
$$$
1901 COLLINS AVE.
TEL 305/695-3232
A celebrity/fashion model
hangout that serves what's
considered the ultimate sushi
and sashimi, as well as the
newest cocktails.
🪑 125 🅿 Valet 🕐 Closed L
🛗 🛗 🚫 All major cards

🍴 **OSTERIA DEL TEATRO**
$$$
1443 WASHINGTON AVE.
TEL 305/538-7850
It's elbow room only at Dino
Pirola's intimate gray-on-gray

North Italian restaurant. The homemade bread is great, the pasta exceptional, the fish imaginative (try halibut with sliced garlic and olives), and the desserts a must. Reservations essential.
🔢 60 🕐 Closed L & Sun.
🅂 🅐 All major cards

🍴 SUSHISAMBA DROMO
$$$
600 LINCOLN RD.
TEL 305/673-5337
A colorful hot spot that mixes Japanese, Brazilian, and Peruvian dishes, SushiSamba Dromo is a New York transplant like so many Miamians. The caipirinhas and various sakes are great for washing down sushi and livening up the evening.
🔢 300 🅂 🅂 🅐 All major cards

SOMETHING SPECIAL

🍴 YUCA
This upscale restaurant—the name is an acronym for Young Urban Cuban Americans—serves fun Nuevo Latino food with attitude from chef Paco Francisco Rodriguez. That means Caribbean and South American influences in dishes such as sweet plantains wrapped around a savory cured beef filling and steamed yucca filled with a truffle-scented wild mushroom picadillo. Reservations required.
$$$
501 LINCOLN RD.
MIAMI BEACH
TEL 305/532-9822
www.yuca.com
🔢 190 🅿 Valet 🅂 🅐 AC, MC, V

🍴 A FISH CALLED AVALON
$$
700 OCEAN DR.
TEL 305/532-1727
www.afishcalledavalon.com

A casual restaurant/bar with indoor and outside seating, A Fish Called Avalon offers fresh local seafood and live music in an art deco hotel setting.
🔢 200 🕐 Closed L 🅿 Valet
🅂 🅂 🅐 All major cards

🍴 FRONT PORCH CAFÉ
$$
1458 OCEAN DR.
TEL 305/531-8300
www.frontporchocean drive.com
Casual dining and intense people-watching. A place where the locals come to eat, drink, and have fun.
🔢 120 🅂 🅐 All major cards

🍴 JOE'S STONE CRAB
$$
11 WASHINGTON AVE.
TEL 305/673-0365
www.joesstonecrab.com
This South Beach landmark hasn't looked back since opening in 1913 (although it did change locations a few years ago). Stand in line for stone crabs and mustard sauce (available Oct.–May), fried green tomatoes, and perfect Key lime pie. No reservations taken.
🔢 475 🕐 Closed Aug. 1– Oct. 15 🅿 Valet 🅂 🅂
🅐 All major cards

🍴 LARIOS ON THE BEACH
$$
820 OCEAN DR.
TEL 305/532-9577
www.bongoscubancafe.com/locations/larios-on-the-beach.html
Quintin Larios is backed by Gloria and Emilio Estefan at this Cuban restaurant with South Beach attitude that's crowded with Cuban Americans hungry for their grandmother's cooking. Sidewalk tables are best for people-watching.
🔢 114 🅂 🅐 All major cards

🍴 MANGO'S TROPICAL CAFÉ
$$
900 OCEAN DR.
TEL 305/673-4422
www.mangostropicalcafe.com
Pulsing with Cuban bartenders and waitresses who double as table-top dancers, Mango's has some of the best desserts on the beach. Entrees include Caribbean mahimahi and margarita chicken.
🔢 570 🅂 🅐 All major cards

🍴 NEXXT CAFÉ
$$
700 LINCOLN RD.
TEL 305/532-6643
www.nexxtcafe.com
One of the busiest spots on Lincoln Road for dining and people-watching, the portions are always large and delicious. Serves a variety of American sandwiches and entrees.
🔢 400 🅂 🅂 🅐 All major cards

🍴 SPIGA
$$
HOTEL IMPALA
1228 COLLINS AVE.
TEL 305/534-0079
Pastas, breads, and desserts are all homemade at this great Italian spot set in the tiny Hotel Impala (see p. 246). Seafood is a specialty. Reservations required.
🔢 75 🅿 🕐 Closed L 🅂
🅂 🅐 All major cards

🍴 SUSHI DORAKU
$$
1104 LINCOLN RD.
TEL 305/695-8383
Benihana owns this concept sushi spot, part of the regal South Beach movie complex. Plates of sushi roll by on a conveyor belt; you pick what you want. Best bets: South Beach roll and Spider roll.
🔢 130 🕐 Closed L Sat. & Sun. 🅂 🅂 🅐 All major cards

🅂 Nonsmoking 🅂 Air-conditioning 🅸 Indoor Pool 🅾 Outdoor Pool 🅷 Health Club 🅐 Credit Cards

🍴 BALANS

$

1022 LINCOLN RD.

TEL 305/534-9191

British-owned eatery that hits the spot. Try a tasty sampler of goat cheese and portobello, don't miss the herb-crusted Chilean sea bass, and leave room for desserts such as baked chocolate cheesecake.

🛏 140 🔲 🔲 All major cards

🍴 CAFÉ PRIMA PASTA

$

414 71ST ST.

NORTH MIAMI BEACH

TEL 305/867-0106

www.primapasta.com

Tiny budget Italian restaurant with a great combination of beach location, top-notch service, and a reputation for the best Italian food in the area. Pasta is homemade, veal dishes recommended.

🛏 150 🔲 🔲 🔲 Cash only

🍴 NEWS CAFÉ

$

800 OCEAN DR.

TEL 305/538-6397

www.newscafe.com

More Euro than American, this is the people-watching place. Wait for an outside table, choose a burger, omelette, or salad, and browse the national and international press while you wait.

🛏 150 🅿 Valet 🔲 🔲 All major cards

🍴 VAN DYKE CAFÉ

$

846 LINCOLN RD.

TEL 305/534-3600

www.thevandykecafe.com

From the owners of the News Café (see above), a jazzier version on two floors. The same Euro-American style, identical menu, and a great people-watching venue.

🛏 200 🔲 🔲 All major cards

■ KEY BISCAYNE

This former coconut plantation has been given over to rows of luxury high-rises with wonderful beaches and multimillion-dollar waterfront estates. Ocean views are paramount with restaurants and hotels offering some of the most superb settings imaginable.

KEY BISCAYNE 33149

🏨 RITZ-CARLTON, KEY BISCAYNE

$$$$$

455 GRAND BAY DR.

TEL 305/365-4500

www.ritzcarlton.com

Elegance and spectacular settings are Ritz-Carlton's hallmarks, and this hotel doesn't disappoint. It also features a 20,000-square-foot spa and salon and two oceanfront swimming pools.

ℹ 450 🅿 🔲 🔲 🔲 🏊 🔲 🔲 All major cards

🍴 CIOPPINO

$$$

455 GRAND BAY DR.

TEL 305/365-4500

You don't have to be a guest of the Ritz-Carlton to eat at Cioppino, which serves Tuscan cuisine. The lush, waterfront terrace presents subtropical dining at its finest. Sunday brunch.

🛏 234 🔲 🔲 All major cards

🍴 RUSTY PELICAN

$$

3201 RICKENBACKER CAUSEWAY

TEL 305/361-3818

www.therustypelican.com

Landmark waterfront restaurant serving continental seafood against the stunning backdrop of the downtown Miami skyline. Sunday brunch is best, or just go for a drink and soak up the view.

🛏 450 🅿 Valet 🔲 🔲 All major cards

■ COCONUT GROVE

Once a colony of artists and writers, Coconut Grove is now a base for wealthy winter and year-round residents. A few craft shops remain next to the expensive boutiques and smart restaurants. Luxurious yachts lie in Biscayne Bay, and a young weekend crowd hangs out in the CocoWalk shopping and entertainment complex.

COCONUT GROVE 33133

🏨 MAYFAIR HOUSE

$$$$$

3000 FLORIDA AVE.

TEL 305/441-0000 or

800/433-4555

FAX 305/447-9173

www.mayfairhotelandspa.com

Intimate all-suite hotel, despite its hectic Mayfair in the Grove mall setting. Most suites have private terraces facing the street, screened by plants; some have a Japanese hot tub on the balcony.

ℹ 179 🅿 🔲 🔲 🔲 🔲 🔲 All major cards

🏨 MUTINY HOTEL

$$$$$

2951 S. BAYSHORE DR.

TEL 305/441-2100

www.providentresorts.com/mutiny-hotel

This suites-only hotel presents Miami as a 3-D movie screened on your large windows.

ℹ 172 🅿 Valet 🔲 🔲 🔲 🔲 🔲 All major cards

🏨 GROVE ISLE CLUB & RESORT

$$$$

4 GROVE ISLE DR.

TEL 305/858-8300 or

800/88-GROVE

FAX 305/858-5908

www.groveisle.com

This comfortable hotel is on Biscayne Bay, over the bridge onto the island. Popular with families and for small

conferences, and with a wide range of sports facilities.
[i] 50 ⊟ ⊟ 🅲 🅰 ☒ All major cards

⊞ SONESTA BAYFRONT
❚❙ HOTEL
$$$
2889 MCFARLANE RD.
TEL 305/529-2828 or 800/SONESTA
www.sonesta.com/Coconut Grove
Your stay will be enhanced by beautifully appointed rooms (many with balconies) and bay views. Art by Lynne Golub Gelfman, Frank Stella, and Robert Rauschenberg graces public areas. Rooms have flat-screen TVs and free Wi-Fi. Enjoy dining or lounging at Panorama or Nikki Coconut Grove. This hotel stands across from the CocoWalk shopping mecca.
[i] 210 rooms & suites
[P] Valet ⊟ 🅲 🅲 🅰 ☒
☒ All major cards

❚❙ GROVE ISLE
$$
4 GROVE ISLE DR.
TEL 305/858-8300
www.groveisle.com
Wonderful waterside setting. Modern American cuisine is served in either the indoor dining area or the tented terrace, a favorite.
🔲 100 ☒ All major cards

■ CORAL GABLES
Coral Gables offers a more conservative dining experience compared to the glitzy chic of South Beach. Some of Miami's most acclaimed establishments are here, and the food offered is among the best in the city.

CORAL GABLES 33134

⊞ BILTMORE
$$$$$
1200 ANASTASIA AVE.

TEL 305/445-1926 or 800/727-1926
FAX 305/913-3152
www.biltmorehotel.com
National historic landmark that oozes Old World Mediterranean elegance. Roman columns, hand-painted ceilings, Spanish tiles, and marble floors add to the style. The pool has to be seen to be believed.
[i] 280 rooms & suites [P]
⊟ 🅲 🅲 🅰 🆅 ☒ All major cards

⊞ HOTEL PLACE
❚❙ ST. MICHEL
$$$
162 ALCAZAR AVE.
TEL 305/444-1666
FAX 305/529-0074
www.hotelstmichel.com
Sophisticated European-style hotel in the heart of the Gables. The building dates from 1926, and it's filled with antiques, dark paneling, and fresh flowers. See Restaurant St. Michel, below.
[i] 27 [P] ⊟ 🅲 ☒ All major cards

⊞ WESTIN COLONNADE
HOTEL
$$$
180 ARAGON AVE.
TEL 305/441-2600
www.westin.com/coralgables
Former home of Coral Gables founder George Merrick, now an elegant hotel with upscale decor and service. Central location between business and retail districts ensures a mainly business clientele.
[i] 157 rooms & suites
[P] Valet ⊟ 🅲 🅲 🅰 🆅
☒ All major cards

❚❙ RANDAZZO'S LITTLE
ITALY
$$$–$$$$
385 MIRACLE MILE
TEL 305/448-7002
www.randazzoslittleitaly.com
Hearty meals made from

southern Italian recipes, with a lively atmosphere. Randazzo's meats are renowned, including the meatball salad. Also popular are chicken Buoniconti and rigatoni vodka.
🔲 125 🕐 Closed Mon.
🅲 ☒ All major cards

SOMETHING SPECIAL

❚❙ LA PALMA RISTORANTE
& BAR
Serves Northern Italian delicacies like lobster La Palma and clams with fettuccine. Also try the Maine lobster sautéed with white wine and the 14-ounce veal chop.
$$$
116 ALHAMBRA CIRCLE
CORAL GABLES
TEL 305/445-8777
www.lapalmarestaurant.net
🔲 150 [P] Valet 🅲 🅲 ☒ All major cards

❚❙ RESTAURANT
ST. MICHEL
$$$
HOTEL PLACE ST. MICHEL
162 ALCAZAR AVE.
TEL 305/444-1666
Historic Gables hotel restaurant with European feel—excellent on every count. Crêpes are the best in town; fish dishes are outstanding. Romantic setting, charming service. Reservations required. Early bird specials.
🔲 92 [P] ⊟ 🅲 ☒ All major cards

❚❙ ORTANIQUE ON THE
MILE
$$
278 MIRACLE MILE
TEL 305/446-7710
www.cindyhutsoncuisine.com
Named after a hybrid fruit (orange and tangerine), this restaurant resonates with Floribbean cuisine such as candied pecans, jerk pork loin and yellowtail snapper.

🍴 120 🕐 Closed Sat. & Sun.
L 💳 💳 All major cards

■ SOUTH MIAMI

See listings under Excursions from
Miami, below.

■ EXCURSIONS

Homestead and Florida City are
both starting points for those
visiting the shallow "river of
grass," the Everglades. In both
places there are numerous shops
and small restaurants, although
accommodations tend to be of
the standard chain motel variety.

🏨 EVERGLADES MOTEL

$$

605 S. KROME AVE.,
HOMESTEAD, FL 33030
TEL 305/247-4117
Small, well-run motel with
bright contemporary look
to well-maintained rooms.
🛏 14 🅿 💳 💳 💳 💳 All
major cards

🏨 RIVERSIDE HOTEL

🍴 $$

620 E. LAS OLAS BLVD.,
FORT LAUDERDALE, FL 33301
TEL 954/467-0671 or
800/325-3280
FAX 954/462-2148
www.riversidehotel.com
The location in the fashionable
historic district with lush
gardens along the New River
is the draw. Old World charm,
some rooms with canopy
beds, plus free transportation
to beach.
🛏 217 rooms & suites
🅿 Valet 💳 💳 💳 💳 All
major cards

🍴 MICCOSUKEE RESORT

& GAMING

$–$$$$

500 S.W. KROME AVE.,
HOMESTEAD
TEL 877/242-6464
www.miccosukee.com
This huge modern complex

has plenty to do other than
eat, but if you want to play at a
casino while seeing a modern
take on one of America's
smallest Indian tribes, try the
resort's restaurant, buffet, deli,
or snack bar.
🍴 372 (in buffet) 🅿 Valet
💳 💳 All major cards

🍴 BIMINI BOATYARD BAR

& GRILL

$$–$$$

1555 S.E. 17TH ST.,
FORT LAUDERDALE
TEL 954/525-7400
www.biminiboatyard.com
This spacious waterfront
establishment and its
Caribbean-flavored seafood
will make you feel like you're
in the Bahamas. You can
even dock your yacht here.
Immensely popular among
Fort Lauderdale's famous
denizens, including 1970s pop
star David Cassidy.
🍴 350 🅿 💳 D, MC, V

🍴 EL TORO TACO

$

1 S. KROME AVE., HOMESTEAD
TEL 305/245-8182
Authentic home-style Mexican
cooking from the Hernandez
family. Expect chile rellenos,
chicken fajitas, grilled T-bone
with fiery salsa verde, and
great guacamole.
🍴 95 🅿 💳 💳 💳 💳 DC,
MC, V

■ UPPER KEYS

The 1948 film *Key Largo*, in which
Humphrey Bogart and Lauren
Bacall fought crime and hurri-
canes, put the place on the tourist
map, although only a few scenes
were shot here. Visitors can see a
bit of old movie magic by check-
ing out the famous movie prop
African Queen, memorably dragged
by Bogey in the eponymous film,
now moored in the marina of the
Holiday Inn at MM 99.7.

PRICES

HOTELS

An indication of the cost of
a double room in the high
season is given by $ signs.

$$$$$	Over $280
$$$$	$200–$280
$$$	$120–$200
$$	$80–$120
$	Under $80

RESTAURANTS

An indication of the cost of
a three-course meal without
drinks is given by $ signs.

$$$$$	Over $80
$$$$	$50–$80
$$$	$35–$50
$$	$20–$35
$	Under $20

KEY LARGO 33037

🏨 JULES' UNDERSEA

LODGE

$$$$$

51 SHORELAND DR., MM 103.2
TEL 305/451-2353
FAX 305/451-4789
www.jul.com
The only underwater hotel in
the world. Guests swim down
to the unit, comprising two
bedrooms and galley. Popular
with diving honeymooners.
Staff deliver anything to your
room—including dinner—in
waterproof containers.
🛏 2 💳 💳 All major cards

🏨 MARRIOTT KEY

🍴 LARGO BAY RESORT

$$$$

OVERSEAS HWY., MM 103.8
TEL 305/453-0000 or
800/228-9290
FAX 305/453-0093
www.marriottkeylargo.com
For island glitz, one of the

Keys' latest resorts, only 55 minutes south of Miami International Airport. Rooms are oversized, some deluxe two-bedroom suites, all with Wi-Fi. Great range of facilities. See **Gus' Grille**, below.
🛏 147 rooms and suites 🅿 🚭 🕏 🕏 ⛱ 🛡 🗠 All major cards

🏨 SUNSET COVE BEACH RESORT
$$
OVERSEAS HWY., MM 99.6
TEL 305/451-0705 or
877/451-0705
FAX 305/451-5609
www.sunsetcovebeach
resort.com
Mom-and-pop place with a feel of Old Florida. Cottages, palm-thatched chickee huts, a wooden fishing pier, canoes, and pelicans that gather twice daily for feeding.
🛏 11 🅿 🕏 🗠 All major cards

🍴 GUS' GRILLE
$$$
MARRIOTT KEY LARGO BAY RESORT
OVERSEAS HWY., MM 103.8
TEL 305/453-0000
Creative, seafood-inspired Floribbean cooking, which translates as yellowtail snapper with almond crust, topped with avocado, orange, and chive sweet-butter sauce. Pizzas are recommended. Terrific view of the Gulf.
🍴 600 🅿 🕏 🖼 🗠 All major cards

🍴 SNAPPER'S WATER-FRONT SALOON
$$$
139 SEASIDE AVE., MM 94.5
TEL 305/852-5956
www.snapperskeylargo.com
Dine on the water in an Old Florida atmosphere with Caribbean-style seafood.
🍴 200 🅿 🕏 🗠 All major cards

🍴 THE FISH HOUSE ENCORE
$$–$$$
OVERSEAS HWY, MM 102
TEL 305/451-0650
www.fishhouse.com
Spawned from the historic Fish House, Encore has a piano bar, indoor and outdoor seating, and an ultra-casual outlook. But the food is first-rate with fresh stone crab (from Oct.–May), Cayman chicken and rack of lamb.
🍴 125 🅿 🕐 Closed L 🕏 🗠 All major cards

🍴 PILOT HOUSE
$$
BAYSIDE CAY CLUB RESORT & MARINA
13 SEAGATE BLVD., MM 100
TEL 305/451-3142
www.pilothousemarina.com
A 1950s old stager, famous for Harvey's fish sandwich. Seafood takes in snapper stuffed with lobster, topped with shrimp, and served on homemade Florentine pasta, steak Diane and New York strip are just as popular.
🍴 65 🅿 🕏 🗠 All major cards

🍴 SUNDOWNERS ON THE BAY
$
OVERSEAS HWY., MM 104
TEL 305/451-4502
www.sundownerskeylargo
.com
A great eatery for watching the sun set while eating solid pub grub. Vegetarian options.
🍴 185 🅿 🕏 🗠 All major cards

PLANTATION KEY

🍴 MARKER 88
$$$
MM 88
TEL 305/852-9315
www.marker88.info
Marker 88 is a legendary,

innovative Upper Keys landmark. Banana, papaya, pineapple, mango, currant jelly, and cinnamon butter accompany fish Rangoon, or there are great Florida lobster, stone crab, and shrimp. Key lime-baked Alaska is a must-have dessert. Rustic decor, romantic sunsets.
🍴 300 🅿 🕐 Closed L 🕏 🗠 All major cards

UPPER MATECUMBE KEY 33036

🏨 CHEECA LODGE & SPA
🍴 $$$$$
OVERSEAS HWY., MM 82,
ISLAMORADA
TEL 305/664-4651 or
800 327-2888
FAX 305/664-2893
www.cheeca.com
This top-rated Upper Keys resort is noted for its first-rate fishing and diving programs. Blue-and-white plantation-style buildings on 27 lush beachfront acres. Low-key luxury in simply furnished but spacious rooms. Its **Atlantic's Edge** restaurant is wonderful (see below).
🛏 199 rooms & suites
🅿 🚭 🕏 🕏 🖼 ⛱ 🗠 All major cards

🍴 ATLANTIC'S EDGE
$$$
CHEECA LODGE & SPA, MM 82,
ISLAMORADA
TEL 305/664-4651
www.cheeca.com/atlantics
edge
A classy resort hotel serves as the backdrop for executive chef Bader Ali's cuisine, which features wild, exotic and naturally farmed meats and fish and organically grown Florida produce fused with a unique Florida Keys twist.
🍴 115 🅿 🕏 🗠 All major cards

🕏 Nonsmoking 🕏 Air-conditioning 🖼 Indoor Pool ⛱ Outdoor Pool 🛡 Health Club 🗠 Credit Cards

🏨 PELICAN COVE RESORT
$$$

84457 OLD OVERSEAS HWY.,
MM 84.5, ISLAMORADA
TEL 305/664-4435 or
800/445-4690
FAX 305/664-5134
www.pcove.com
Contemporary decor, balconies, and ocean views define the look at this pleasant, well-run resort hotel. Wide range of activities in and out of the water.
🛈 50 🅿 🅂 🕿 🅖 All major cards

🍴 ZIGGIE'S CONCH RESTAURANT
$$$

OVERSEAS HWY., MM 83.5, ISLAMORADA
TEL 305/664-3391
Memorable seafood amid laid-back 1950s decor. Stone crab; conch fritters; cracked conch; yellowtail meunière, almondine, or veronique; oysters stuffed a half dozen ways; Florida lobster in a mustard sauce. A must.
🍴 77 🅿 🕒 Closed Labor Day–Oct. 🅂 🅖 All major cards

🍴 SMUGGLER'S COVE
$$–$$$

MM 85.5, ISLAMORADA
TEL 800/864-4363
www.smugscove.com
The name lets you know you're in for colorful characters at this waterside eatery. Clams, oysters, conch, and fish—you can even bring in the fish you just caught and the chef will cook it up.
🍴 150 🅂 🅂 🅖 All major cards

🍴 LAZY DAYS OCEANFRONT BAR & SEAFOOD GRILL
$$

79867 OVERSEAS HWY., MM 79.9, ISLAMORADA
TEL 305/664-5256
www.lazydaysrestaurant.com
Directly on Atlantic shore, elevated, plantation-style property offering great water views as well as some creative Floribbean seafood dishes. Dolphin (the fish) with tropical fruit salsa and mango rum sauce sums it all up.
🍴 160 🅿 🅂 🅖 All major cards

🍴 LOR-E-LEI RESTAURANT & CABANA BAR
$$

MM 82, ISLAMORADA
TEL 305/664-4338
www.loreleicabanabar.com
Serving some of the Florida Keys' best seafood, and live rock music, Lor-e-Lei has been an Islamorada landmark for decades.
🍴 330 outside, 250 inside 🅿 🅂 🅂 🅖 All major cards

🍴 MORADA BAY BEACH CAFÉ
$–$$

81600 OVERSEAS HWY., MM 81.6, ISLAMORADA
TEL 305/664-0604
www.moradabay-restaurant.com
Outdoor dining here means peacefully sitting on white chairs on the beach while being serenaded by island music and the surf. A blend of Caribbean and American dishes is served.
🍴 100 🕒 Closed Tues. 🅖 All major cards

🍴 GREEN TURTLE INN RESTAURANT
$

81219 OVERSEAS HWY., MM 81.3, ISLAMORADA
TEL 305/664-2006
www.greenturtlekeys.com
This unpretentious dining icon, operating since 1947, prides itself on a laid-back lifestyle with gourmet flair.

Much of the seafood is caught locally, and you can even bring in your own catch to be prepared. Specialties include seared diver scallops, prime rib, and turtle chowder. Next door is an art gallery.
🍴 50 🅂 🅖 All major cards

■ MIDDLE KEYS

The Middle Keys stretch from MM 85 to MM 45 and are considered the fishing and diving capital of America, as well as a year-round refuge for South Floridians who take full advantage of the Keys' proximity to the mainland. But don't expect to find any beaches here. There are no natural ones, and sand is shipped in from the Caribbean islands to create tiny stretches near the sea.

DUCK KEY 33050

🏨 HAWKS CAY RESORT 🍴 & MARINA
$$$$$

MM 61
TEL 305/743-7000
FAX 305/743-0641
www.hawkscay.com
Spacious rooms await the guests at this West Indies-style resort on a private island. The amenities include a marina and water-sports center, plus sandy beach, saltwater lagoon, and kids' club, Dolphin Connection, offering interactive program.
🛈 193 🅿 🅂 🅂 🕿 🎥 🅖 All major cards

VACA KEY 33050

🍴 KEYS FISHERIES MARKET & MARINA
$$$

OFF MM 49.2 ON 35TH ST. MARATHON
TEL 866/743-4353
www.keysfisheries.com
Although relatively unknown, Keys Fishery is an outdoor,

📠 Hotel 🍴 Restaurant 🛈 No. of Guest Rooms 🍴 No. of Seats 🅿 Parking 🕒 Closed 🚪 Elevator

casual eatery famous for lobster reuben sandwich and coconut shrimp.
🔲 250 🅿 🅢 All major cards

🏠 SOMBRERO REEF INN & FISHING LODGE
$$
500 SOMBRERO BEACH RD.
MM 50
MARATHON
TEL 305/743-4118
www.sombreroreefinn.com
Relaxed bed and breakfast on the water's edge overlooking the Atlantic Ocean. The style is Florida casual; all rooms have private entrances and water views. Ramp and dockage for boats.
ⓘ 4 suites 🅢 🅢 MC, V

■ LOWER KEYS
The Lower Keys start at the end of the Seven Mile Bridge. Big Pine, Sugarloaf, Summerland, and the other Lower Keys are less developed and therefore more peaceful than the Upper Keys. Pride of the place goes to the Bahia Honda State Park on the ocean side of Big Pine Key; it has one of the loveliest beaches in South Florida and one of the most beautiful coastlines.

BIG PINE KEY 33050

🏠 BARNACLE BED AND BREAKFAST
$$
1557 LONG BEACH DR.
MM 33
TEL 305/872-3298
FAX 305/872-3863
www.thebarnacle.net
Caribbean-style home set off by a beautiful garden—with hot tub, hammock, and private beach—cherished eclectic furnishings and just two rooms in the main house, two in the cottage.
ⓘ 4 🅿 🅢 🅢 MC, V

SUGARLOAF KEY

🍴 MANGROVE MAMA'S RESTAURANT
$$
19991 OVERSEAS HWY.
TEL 305/745-3030
www.mangrovemamas
restaurant.com
Landmark old timer—a plain shack that survived the 1935 hurricane. You will find simple tables inside and out, shaded by a banana grove. Fresh seafood, chowders, and great Key lime pie, as well as teriyaki chicken and spicy barbecued baby back ribs.
🔲 150 🅿 🅢 🅢 All major cards

LITTLE TORCH KEY

SOMETHING SPECIAL

🏠 LITTLE PALM ISLAND
🍴 RESORT & SPA
Holiday heaven. Private island accessible only by seaplane, boat or 15-minute water taxi ride. Individual, luxury palm-thatched suites are dotted about five lush acres; all with sun decks with hammocks. There are no phones, no TV. In the dining room, open to nonguests as well, executive chef Luis Pous uses local ingredients to create mouthwatering European, Caribbean, and Asian dishes. Reservations only.
$$$$$
MM 28.5, LITTLE TORCH KEY,
FL 33042
TEL 800/343-8567 (reservations),
305-515-4004 (front desk), or
305/872-2551 (dining room)
FAX 305/872-4843
www.littlepalmisland.com
ⓘ 30 suites 🅢 🅢 🅢 All major cards

■ KEY WEST & DRY TORTUGAS
There are more guest houses, inns, and bed-and-breakfasts per capita in Key West than in any other city in the country. Quaint and eccentric inns are what Key West is known for.

KEY WEST 33040

HOTELS

🏠 OCEAN KEY RESORT & SPA
$$$$$
ZERO DUVAL ST.
TEL 305/296-7701 or
800/328-9815
FAX 305/295-7016
www.oceankey.com
For those who prefer lots of room and modern convenience, this five-story hotel at the foot of Duval Street is the place. The hotel's Dockside Bar has the best seats in town for sunsets.
ⓘ 100 suites 🅿 🗘 🅢 🅢 🅢 All major cards

🏠 PIER HOUSE
🍴 $$$$$
1 DUVAL ST.
TEL 305/296-4600 or
800/327-8340
FAX 305/296-7569
www.pierhouse.com
Stylish, deluxe, Old Town property with Caribbean flavor, discreetly screened by lush tropical gardens. Enjoy a health spa, man-made sand beach, and a choice of bars and restaurants. Highly rated restaurant, see p. 257.
ⓘ 142 rooms & suites 🅿 🗘 🅢 🅢 🆅 🅢 All major cards

SOMETHING SPECIAL

🏠 MARQUESA HOTEL
🍴 Luxury hotel converted from two 1880s private homes

(listed on the National Register of Historic Places) and two recently constructed buildings. Tasteful blend of contemporary and antique furnishings, marble baths, two pools, and a rated restaurant, **Café Marquesa** (see p. 257).

$$$$

600 FLEMING ST.
TEL 305/292-1919 or
800/869-4631
FAX 305/294-2121
www.marquesa.com
🏨 27 🛏 50 🔲 🔲 🏊 🅰 AE,
MC, V

🏨 WALDORF CASA
🍴 MARINA
$$$$

1500 REYNOLDS ST.
TEL 305/296-3535 or
800/626-0777
FAX 305/296-4633
www.casamarinaresort.com
This romantic seaside classic is the oldest hotel in all of the Keys, built in 1921 by railway magnate Henry Flagler. There are a private beach, a choice of two pools, and a restaurant, **Sun Sun,** noted for its Sunday brunch.
🏨 314 🅿 🔲 🔲 🏊 🅰 All major cards

🏨 CHELSEA HOUSE
$$$

709 TRUMAN AVE.
TEL 305/296-2211 or
800/845-8859
FAX 305/296-4822
www.historickeywestinns.com
Laid-back, relaxed gray-and-white jewel of a house, surrounded by lush tropical plants. Rooms in the main house have antique touches, and those by the pool are Mediterranean in style. The sundeck is clothing optional.
🏨 37 🔲 🔲 🏊 🅰 All major cards

🏨 CURRY MANSION INN
$$$

511 CAROLINE ST.
TEL 305/294-5349 or
800/253-3466
FAX 305/294-4093
www.currymansion.com
Rambling, historic, classy Victorian mansion, a masterpiece of belle epoque grandeur. Open to the public for guided tours. Bedrooms are in a modern wing, accented with antiques and wicker.
🏨 28 🔲 🔲 🏊 🅰 All major cards

🏨 HERON HOUSE
$$$

512 SIMONTON ST.
TEL 305/294-9227 OR
800/294-1644
FAX 305/294-5692
www.heronhouse.com
Comfortable inn, simply but tastefully styled. Generous private decks and balconies to large rooms that merge with private gardens. Detailed interiors feature walls of teak, oak, and cedar.
🏨 25 🔲 🔲 🏊 🅰 All major cards

🏨 ISLAND CITY HOUSE
HOTEL
$$$

411 WILLIAM ST.
TEL 305/294-5702
FAX 305/294-1289
www.islandcityhouse.com
Of the three converted 1880s houses that make up this unique hotel, the Arch House is the sole surviving carriage house in the Keys. There's a choice of suites and studios.
🏨 24 rooms & suites 🔲 🏊 🅰 All major cards

🏨 SIMONTON COURT
HISTORIC INN
$$$

320 SIMONTON ST.
TEL 305/294-6386

PRICES

HOTELS
An indication of the cost of a double room in the high season is given by **$** signs.

$$$$$	Over $280
$$$$	$200–$280
$$$	$120–$200
$$	$80–$120
$	Under $80

RESTAURANTS
An indication of the cost of a three-course meal without drinks is given by **$** signs.

$$$$$	Over $80
$$$$	$50–$80
$$$	$35–$50
$$	$20–$35
$	Under $20

FAX 305/293-8446
www.simontoncourt.com
Nine buildings full of character on this former cigar factory site are set into the gardens. There are four swimming pools to choose from—one is lit at night. For adults.
🏨 26 🔲 🏊 🅰 AE, MC, V

🏨 CONCH HOUSE
HERITAGE INN
$$

625 TRUMAN AVE.
TEL 305/293-0020
FAX 305/293-8447
www.conchhouse.com
One of the island's earliest historic family estates, listed on the National Register of Historic Places. Spacious, elegant bedrooms in the main house or Caribbean-style wicker rooms in the tropical poolside cottage.
🏨 8 🅿 🔲 🏊 🅰 All major cards

🏨 Hotel 🍴 Restaurant 🏨 No. of Guest Rooms 🛏 No. of Seats 🅿 Parking 🕒 Closed 🔲 Elevator

DUVAL HOUSE
$$

815 DUVAL ST.
TEL 305/294-1666
FAX 305/292-1701
www.duvalhousekeywest.com
No phones or radios,
though there is cable TV.
Simple wicker furniture, some
antiques, and a pool crowded
by luxurious hibiscus are the
keynotes to this laid-back
Victorian gingerbread house.
① 31 😠 😊 🚢 🐾 All major
cards

EDEN HOUSE
$$

1015 FLEMING ST.
TEL 305/296-6868
FAX 305/294-1221
www.edenhouse.com
Lovingly restored, well-run
1920s hotel. Reasonably priced
rooms in wicker-filled main
house; pricier private suites
in three adjoining tin-roofed
conch houses.
① 40 😊 🚢 🐾 AE, MC, V

THE MERMAID AND
THE ALLIGATOR
$$

729 TRUMAN AVE.
TEL 305/294-1894
FAX 305/295-9925
www.kwmermaid.com
A 1904 former city attorney's
home, now an unusual inn with
Oriental and art deco accents,
book-lined hallway, and lots of
open space. The Conch House
annex has more economi-
cal rooms. Breakfast served
poolside.
① 9 😊 🚢 🐾 AE, MC, V

RESTAURANTS

CAFÉ DES ARTISTES
$$$$

1007 SIMONTON ST.
TEL 305/294-7100
www.pisceskeywest.com
Long-standing French

restaurant with a reputation
for first-rate cooking. Formal,
pricey, but strong on creativity.
Try the snapper sautéed in tar-
ragon butter with shrimps and
scallops. Also has an excellent
wine list.
🍴 65 🕐 Closed L 😊 🐾 AE,
MC, V

SOMETHING SPECIAL
LOUIE'S BACKYARD

Prime piece of Atlantic ocean-
front property. Stunning out-
door dining room, exquisite
interior, new Caribbean cuisine
centered on local seafood.
Try Bahamian conch chowder
with bird-pepper hot sauce.
Reservations essential.
$$$$

700 WADDELL AVE.
TEL 305/294-1061
www.louiesbackyard.com
🍴 160 😊 🐾 All major cards

PIER HOUSE
RESTAURANT
$$$$

1 DUVAL ST.
TEL 305/296-4600 or
800/327-8340
FAX 305/296-7569
Stunning, glass-enclosed
waterfront dining room,
great backdrop for upbeat,
ambitious American cooking
with strong Caribbean accents.
Menu built around local
seafood. Good wines.
🍴 150 🅿 😊 🐾 All major
cards

BLUE HEAVEN
$$$

729 THOMAS ST.
TEL 305/296-8666
www.blueheavenkw.com
Located behind a rickety old
house, the restaurant features
fresh fish, vegetarian dishes,
and various salads. It's best to
walk or bike to this famous
restaurant, whose motto is
"Blue Heaven: You don't have

to die to get there."
🍴 85 😊 🐾 All major cards

SOMETHING SPECIAL
CAFÉ MARQUESA

One of Key West's most imaginative restaurants with the
air of a European brasserie.
Innovative cuisine and stunning presentation; try the
seared yellowfin tuna in salsa
verde, or the spicy Jamaican
barbecued prawns. Reservations essential.
$$$

600 FLEMING ST.
TEL 305/292-1244
www.marquesa.com
🍴 50 🕐 Closed L 😊
🐾 All major cards

MICHAEL'S
RESTAURANT
$$$

532 MARGARET ST.
TEL 305/295-1300
www.michaelskeywest.com
Nestled along the backstreets
of Key West's Old Town
District, Michael's Restaurant
serves island elegance both
inside and next to a fountain
outside. Meals are on the
heavy side with prime beef,
pasta and the local seafood,
as well as cheese fondues.
🍴 100 🕐 Closed L 😊 🐾 All
major cards

SQUARE ONE
$$$

1075 DUVAL ST.
TEL 305/296-4300
www.squareonerestaurant
.com
Stylish, sophisticated bistro
offering innovative New
World cooking. Signature
dishes of sautéed sea scallops
on poached spinach with mus-
tard cream sauce set the
pace. Reservations required.
🍴 85 🅿 Access Simonton St.
😊 🐾 All major cards

😊 Nonsmoking 😊 Air-conditioning 🚢 Indoor Pool 🚢 Outdoor Pool 🍸 Health Club 🐾 Credit Cards

🍴 DUFFY'S STEAK AND LOBSTER HOUSE

$$

1007 SIMONTON ST.

TEL 305/296-4900

www.duffyskeywest.com

Steaks, ribs, and lobster are always good, and reasonably priced at this art deco-style off-shoot of Café des Artistes next door (see p. 257). All dishes are simply prepared with salad, freshly baked bread, and choice of potato.

🔧 85 🅢 🕸 All major cards

🍴 KELLY'S CARIBBEAN BAR & GRILL

$$

301 WHITEHEAD ST.

TEL 305/293-7897

www.kellyskeywest.com

Set in historic old Pan Am office, and themed with flying memorabilia. Also the home of Southernmost Brewery—try Havana Red Ale with your jerk chicken. No reservations.

🔧 150 🅢 🕸 All major cards

🍴 MANGOES

$$

700 DUVAL ST.

TEL 305/292-4606

www.mangoskeywest.com

Caribbean-style seafood served indoors or out. Specialties take in pan-seared yellow snapper with passion fruit. Super-thin-crust pizzas. Great for people-watching.

🔧 175 🅿 Valet 🅢 🕸 All major cards

🍴 ORIGAMI

$$

1075 DUVAL ST.

TEL 305/294-0092

One of Key West's best Japanese restaurants, Origami is renowned for its sushi deluxe dinner and Origami super special.

🔧 50 🅿 Valet 🕒 Closed L 🅢 🅢 🕸 All major cards

🍴 CAMILLE'S RESTAURANT

$

1202 SIMONTON ST.

TEL 305/296-4811

A local favorite open from breakfast through dinner. A hefty full rack of lamb is served with garlic-oregano marinade or raspberry coulis, or try stone crab clawmeat cakes with spiced rum-mango sauce.

🔧 150 🅿 Valet 🅢 🅢 🕸 All major cards

🍴 EL SIBONEY

$

900 CATHERINE ST.

TEL 305/296-4184

www.elsiboneyrestaurant.com

Simple decor defines this great neighborhood hangout serving authentic Cuban food. Enormous portions at low prices. *Ropa vieja,* paella, *boliche,* plus an array of sandwiches and much more.

🔧 50 🅢 🕸 All major cards

🍴 HALF SHELL RAW BAR

$

231 MARGARET ST.

TEL 305/294-7496

www.halfshellrawbar.com

Old Key West-style waterside hangout, noted for casual, laid-back atmosphere, simply prepared local seafood, and reasonable prices. Stone crabs in season and Maine lobsters.

🔧 247 🅿 🅢 🕸 All major cards

🍴 HELP YOURSELF

$

829 FLEMING ST.

TEL 305/296-7766

www.helpyourselffoods.com

Serving organic fare such as spinach salad, coconut curry, and hummus wraps, this small, colorful eatery aims to make your stay in Key West healthy. All seating is outdoors, which is ideal in the relatively cool winter.

🔧 30 🕒 Closed D 🕸 All major cards

🍴 HOG'S BREATH SALOON

$

400 FRONT ST.

TEL 305/296-4222

www.hogsbreath.com

Built to resemble an authentic surfer's bar, packed with tourists and locals drawn by laid-back Keys' atmosphere. Grilled fish sandwiches are sold by the ton; also good burgers and seafood, plus the T-shirt. Happy hour 5 p.m.–7 p.m.

🔧 90 🅿 Valet L 🅢 🕸 All major cards

🍴 PEPE'S CAFÉ

$

806 CAROLINE ST.

TEL 305/294-7192

www.pepescafe.net

Established in 1909, this is the oldest restaurant in Key West for traditional American-style home cooking of steaks, pork chops, and burgers, as well as Apalachicola oysters in season. Breakfast is a Keys' tradition.

🔧 90 🅢 🕸 DC, MC, V

🏨 Hotel   🍴 Restaurant   🛈 No. of Guest Rooms   🔧 No. of Seats   🅿 Parking   🕒 Closed   🛗 Elevator

Shopping

As a result of relatively low rents and a sales tax of 6.5 percent on top of the retail price, goods are generally cheaper than in New York or Los Angeles. South Beach, Coconut Grove, Coral Gables, and downtown Miami are the few spots in Miami where walking is really encouraged. Here the shopping is diverse and individual.

Elsewhere, the majority of shopping is in air-conditioned megamalls, offering department store fare from the likes of Macy's and JC Penney, and chains such as the Gap, Banana Republic, and Victoria's Secret, as well as food courts, and possibly a movie mall of six or more screens.

But the current trend is also toward upscale, open-air shopping malls with a directory of designer names in deluxe settings. These places are popular with wealthy South Americans, lured by names such as Gucci, Bulgari, Prada, and Vuitton.

Shopping in Key West is expensive, especially for clothes. The shops worth checking out offer something more unusual than the regular close encounters with Key West's over-prolific T-shirt shops. Swimsuits, cigars, sandals, and skin-care products are all homemade in the Keys. Other bargains include paintings, sculptures, and sketches from local artists, or rarer finds such as conch pearls.

Indoor Malls
Bal Harbour Shops
9700 Collins Ave., Bal Harbour, tel 305/866-0311, www.balhar bourshops.com
Exclusive mall specializing in designer shops such as Tiffany, Chanel, Prada, Gucci, DeBeers, Hermès, and Bulgari, as well as Florida's largest Neiman Marcus and Saks Fifth Avenue.

Village of Merrick Park
Coral Gables, tel 305/529-0200, www.villageofmerrickpark.com

Neiman Marcus, Nordstrom, and 115 designer boutiques and spas.

Dolphin Mall
11250 NW 25th St., Miami, tel 305/DOL-PHIN, www.shop dolphinmall.com
One of Miami's largest shopping, dining, and tourist attractions, Dolphin Mall offers visitor-friendly shopping and family entertainment, including restaurants, a 19-screen cinema, and designer outlets, as well as retail and specialty shops.

Outdoor Malls
Bayside Marketplace
401 N. Biscayne Blvd., Miami, tel 305/577-3344, www.bayside marketplace.com
An outdoor mall on the waterfront, with sightseeing boat tours, street performers, Miami's Hard Rock Café, and a variety of shops.

CocoWalk
3015 Grand Ave., Coconut Grove, tel 305/444-0777, www.cocowalk.net
Funky, multistory, semi-outdoor mall. Lots of cafés with terrace seating and a 16-screen cinema, but retail outlets go no further than Gap and Victoria's Secret.

Downtown Miami Shopping District
Biscayne Blvd. to 2nd Ave. W. and S.E. 1st St. to N.E. 3rd St., Miami, tel 305/379-7070
More than 1,000 shops including the second largest jewelry district in the country, hundreds of electronics, sporting goods, clothing, and shoe stores.

Florida Keys Outlet Center
250 E. Palm Dr. (S.W. 344th St.), Florida City, tel 305/248-1727
Only 30 minutes' drive south of Miami, in a lush tropical village setting with more than 60 manufacturers' factory outlet stores, ranging from Nike and OshKosh B'Gosh to Levi's Outlet.

Mayfair in the Grove
2911 Grand Ave., Coconut Grove, tel 305/448-1700
Mediterranean-inspired town square in the heart of Coconut Grove, with outdoor cafés, nightspots, movie theaters, restaurants, and nationally known retailers.

Arts & Antiques
The Americas Collection
214 Andalusia Ave., Coral Gables, tel 305/446-5578, www.americas collection.com
One of the most reputable in Miami, the gallery is dedicated to contemporary Latin American art with the inclusion of some European and American works.

Gotta Have It! Collectibles
4231 S.W. 71st Ave., Coral Gables, tel 305/446-5757. Closed Sat.–Sun.
Vintage autographs and memorabilia from sport, Hollywood, and rock music.

Haitian Art Co.
600 Frances St., Key West, tel 305/296-8932
Brilliant, colorful artworks, artifacts, and sculpture from Haiti.

Lincoln Road Shopping District
Lincoln Road, Miami Beach,

tel 305/673-7010
Impressive, upscale 12-block shopping district with individual shops, fine art galleries, and artists' studios, as well as acclaimed restaurants and cafés. Individual merchants' hours vary. Home also to Miami City Ballet and New World Symphony.

Bookstores
Barnes and Noble Booksellers
www.barnesandnoble.com
5701 Sunset Dr., South Miami, tel 305/662-4770
152 Miracle Mile, Coral Gables, tel 305/446-4152
18711 Biscayne Blvd., North Miami Beach, tel 305/935-9770
12405 S.W. 88th St., Miami, tel 305/598-7727
More than 17,000 titles including subjects by local authors.

Books & Books
933 Lincoln Rd., Miami Beach, tel 305/532-3222
358 San Lorenzo Ave., Coral Gables, tel 305/442-44087
9700 Collins Ave., Bal Harbour, tel 305/864-4241
Great range of titles, plus readings by authors.

Kafka's Used Book Store
1464 Washington Ave., Miami Beach, tel 786/348-0901
Mostly used paperbacks.

Smoking Matters
Cuban Crafters
3604 N.W. 7th St., Miami, tel 305/573-0222
More than 100 different brands at five shops throughout the area.

Cuban Leaf Cigar Factory
310 Duval St., Key West, tel 305/295-9283
Everything you want to know about cigars, including watching them being made before buying.

Deco Drive Cigar East
1436 Ocean Dr., Miami Beach, tel 305/672-9032
1650 Meridian Ave., Miami, tel 305/674-1811
Buy cigars from Honduras, Nicaragua, and the Dominican Republic. You can also watch cigars being rolled in the store.

El Crédito Cigars
1106 S.W. 8th St., Little Havana, Miami, tel 305/858-4162. Closed Sun.
Cuban-owned cigar factory.

Key West Cigar
1117 Duval St., Key West, tel 305/296-1977, www.keywest cigar.com
Huge selection of cigars.

Jewelry
Carroll's Jewelers
365 Miracle Mile, Coral Gables, tel 305/446-1611
The Gables' oldest jewelry store has featured handcrafted pieces for more than 60 years.

Kirk Jewelers
142 E. Flagler St., Miami, tel 305/371-1321. Closed Sun.
Wide selection of brand-name watches, 14-carat, 18-carat, and platinum jewelry.

Local Color
276 Margaret St., Key West, tel 305/766-7959, www.local colorkeywest.com
A jewelry boutique with pure Key West pieces.

Rainbow Jewelry
101 N.E. 1st St., Miami, tel 305/371-2289. Closed Sun.
Large selection of Cartier products. Also Hermès, Carrera y Carrera 18-carat gold jewelry, and Mont Blanc pens.

Seybold Building
36 N.E. 1st St., Miami,

tel 305/374-7922
The historic downtown building has almost 300 jewelers.

Sports Equipment
Alf's Golf Shop
11805 S. Dixie Hwy., Coral Gables, tel 305/663-4653. Closed Sun.
Golf equipment, shoes, apparel, and bags.

Capt. Harry's Fishing Supplies
8501 N.W. 7th Ave., Miami, tel 305/374-4661. Closed Sun.
Wide range of fishing tackle.

Tarpoon Lagoon
300 Alton Rd., Miami Beach, tel 305/532-1445
One of Miami's oldest scuba dive shops.

South Beach Dive & Surf
850 Washington Ave., Miami Beach, tel 305/673-5900. Closed Sun a.m.
Large range of surfboards as well as scuba diving gear, and lessons available for both sports.

Specialty Shopping
Armani Exchange
760 Collins Ave., Miami Beach, tel 305/531-5900
Giorgio Armani's newest, edgiest apparel.

Key West Aloe
419B Duval St., Key West, tel 800/445-2563
More than 300 aloe products, including a line of original fragrances.

La Casa de las Guayaberas
5840 S.W. 8th St., West Miami, tel 305/266-9683
One of the best places in Greater Miami to purchase the ubiquitous guayabera.

Entertainment

During the day, Miamians have an excess of outdoor pleasure to pursue; by night the lure of some of the trendiest bars, restaurants, and nightclubs is hard to resist. And when the money runs out, people-watching from a South Beach or Coconut Grove sidewalk café can be very entertaining. Theater and classical music have surged in popularity in recent years, with several performance venues putting Miami on the arts map.

For details of performance times, complete movie listings, rock and jazz venues, and nightclubs, buy the Friday edition of the *Miami Herald* for its very comprehensive "Weekend" listing section. Or visit *www.miamiherald.com*.

Visitors to Key West should check the arts and entertainment section in the Friday edition of the Key West *Citizen* for a listing of the latest cultural events.

Cinemas

It is customary to buy tickets at the box office just prior to the start of the film, but book in advance for much-hyped opening nighters. Prices are often reduced for early afternoon showings, and most cinemas offer discounts for students (with college ID) and senior citizens.

Paragon Grove 13

3015 Grand Ave., Coconut Grove, tel 305/446-4386
Multiplex with 13 screens, and a policy of showing art-house and independent films among the new releases.

AMC Sunset Place 24

5701 Sunset Drive, South Miami, tel 888/262-4386
With 24 screens, one is IMAX, you'll miss nothing at this multiplex theater. New releases only.

Miami Beach Cinematheque

512 Española Way, Miami Beach, tel 305/673-4567

Miami Beach's best venue for alternative and foreign films.

Regal South Beach 18

1100 Lincoln Rd., South Beach, tel 305/674-6766
Although part of a chain, this giant glass-walled theater mixes big-budget studio films with low-budget art and foreign films.

Frank Theatres Intracoastal 8

3701 N.E. 163rd St., Miami, tel 305/949-0064
This theater's eight screens show big-budget, independent, and foreign films.

Clubs & Bars

GREATER MIAMI

Miami is well known for its nightlife. Indeed, Miami's clubs are often compared to New York's: nocturnal, sleep deprived, and driven by relentless energy. It is not done to be seen at a club before 11 p.m., when things really get going. This is especially true of South Beach, the epitome of cool Miami, which plays host to some of Miami's trendiest clubs.

You have to be 21 to drink alcohol, so few clubs will admit under-21s. Take photo ID even if you are much older. The law states clubs must stop serving alcohol by 5 a.m.; most clubs close between 3 a.m. and 5 a.m. Cover charges vary, and women often get in for free. Some places don't charge at all and put it on the price of drinks.

You will need cash to pay admission, however.

Note that Miami's clubs open and close at will. Always telephone first to see if they are still there, and check dress codes.

Clevelander Bar

1020 Ocean Dr., South Beach, tel 305/531-3485
This bar/restaurant has been popular for years, especially with visitors over the age of 30.

La Folie D'Amour

655 Washington Ave., South Beach, tel 954/940-0939
This SoBe club has a New York-inspired interior but local DJs play the sounds.

Glass at The Forge

432 41st St., Miami Beach, tel 305/604-9798, www.theforge.com
Sophisticated club where business suits, celebs, and chic partyers dance the night away.

The Improv

3390 Mary St., Coconut Grove, tel 305/441-8200, www.miamiimprov.com
Famous comedy club that draws nationally known comics.

John Martin's Irish Pub & Restaurant

253 Miracle Mile, Coral Gables, tel 305/445-3777, www.johnmartins.com
Day or night, this is the place to refresh yourself with heavy food and thick ale while you're on Miracle Mile.

Mynt
1921 Collins Ave., South Beach, tel 305/532-0727, www.myntlounge.com
The place to hang out with the beautiful people.

Mansion
1235 Washington Ave., South Beach, tel 305/695-8411, www.mansionmiami.com
One of SoBe's hottest clubs, with A list celebrities hanging out regularly.

Nikki Beach Club
One Ocean Dr., South Beach, tel 305/538-1111, www.nikki beachmiami.com
Hedonistic models and international businesspeople thrive at this oceanfront club.

Fat Tuesday
3015 Grand Ave., CocoWalk, Coconut Grove, tel 305/476-0202, www.fat-tuesday.com
On a hot day, grab a frozen daiquiri—Fat Tuesday has two dozen to choose from—and sit down or stroll around this New Orleans inspired locale.

Set
320 Lincoln Rd., South Beach, tel 305/531-2800, www.set miami.com. Closed Mon.–Wed.
SoBe's newest VIP club, teeming with models.

Tapas & Tintos
448 Española Way, South Beach, tel 305/538-8272, www.tapasy tintos.com
Relaxed eatery and bar that nonetheless uses gourmet ingredients. The name means appetizers and red wine.

Twist South Beach
1057 Washington Ave., South Beach, tel 305/53-TWIST, www.twistsobe.com

One of South Beach's most popular gay bars, it's actually seven bars in one complex.

KEY WEST
Eating and drinking may seem to be the main cultural activity in Key West. There is an "anything goes" attitude and the numerous bars make up the bulk of nightlife here, clamorous places that are often open until 4 a.m. with live music—folk, rock, country. The best bars are grouped at the northern end of Duval Street.

Sloppy Joe's
201 Duval St., tel 305/294-5717, www.sloppyjoes.com
Hemingway memorabilia draws the crowds, and they are kept there by a mix of live sounds and lively atmosphere.

Captain Tony's Saloon
428 Greene St., tel 305/294-1838, www.capttonyssaloon .com
The original Sloppy Joe's where Hemingway really did hang out.

Jimmy Buffett's Margaritaville Café
500 Duval St., tel 305/292-1435, www.margaritavillekey west.com
The legend in his own lifetime, Florida crooner Jimmy Buffett lent his name to this great bar. It still draws the crowds, despite the fact that Buffett moved away years ago. Live bands cater to a wide spectrum of tastes, and there is Buffett memorabilia and a tourist shop.

La-Te-Da
1125 Duval St., tel 305/296-6706
The laid-back lifestyle and tolerant attitude that is part of the Key West experience has encouraged a strong

gay community. There are a number of predominantly gay bars along Duval Street, but a more mixed attitude prevails at La-Te-Da. This place is great for poolside drinks and the occasional tea dance.

Theater, Classical Music, Opera, & Dance
GREATER MIAMI
Several excellent websites offer information on Greater Miami's performing arts palette, including **Event Guide Miami** (*www.miami.eventguide.com*), a listing of happenings in the Greater Miami area, and **Florida Theater on Stage** (*www.florida theateronstage.com*). The website of the alternative newspaper *Miami New Times* (*www.miami newtimes.com*) features reliable readers' recommendations on local bests. And the "Tropical Life" section of Friday's *Miami Herald* (*www.miamiherald.com*) offers a broad range of event notices and insights into Greater Miami's ethnic jambalaya.

Unless otherwise stated, all venues are wheelchair accessible.

Adrienne Arsht Center for the Performing Arts
1300 Biscayne Blvd., Miami, tel 305/949-6722, www.arsht center.org
This 570,000-square-foot complex, which premiered in 2006, hosts performances by the Miami City Ballet, the Florida Grand Opera, and New World Symphony.

Jackie Gleason Theater
1700 Washington Ave., Miami Beach, tel 305/673-7300, www.fillmoremb.com
2,700-seater that's home to Broadway shows, and modern, classical, jazz, and pop concerts.

Miami–Dade County Auditorium

2901 W. Flagler St., Miami,
tel 305/547-5414
Historic site now used for community performances.

New World Center

541 Lincoln Rd., Miami Beach,
tel 305/673-3331, www.nws.edu
Opened in 2011, this Frank
Gehry–designed performance
venue is the new home of
the New World Symphony, a
90-member orchestral company
under founder and artistic director Michael Tilson Thomas.

Olympia Theater at the Gusman Center for the Performing Arts

174 E. Flagler St., downtown
Miami, tel 305/374-2444,
www.gusmancenter.org
Hosts ballets, orchestras, film
festivals, and other events
throughout the year.

KEY WEST
Red Barn Theatre

319 Duval St., tel 305/296-9911,
www.redbarntheatre.com
All types of plays from classical
English/American playwrights to
modern productions.

Tennessee Williams Fine Arts Center

5901 W. College Rd., tel
305/296-1520, www.tennessee
williamstheatre.com
All things musical, from Broadway shows to classical concerts,
jazz, and opera.

Waterfront Playhouse

Mallory Sq., tel 305/294-5015,
www.waterfrontplayhouse.org
A combination of classic and
modern plays and popular
musicals.

Calendar of Events
GREATER MIAMI

Information on the following
events and more is available
from www.miamiherald.com/
calendar.

JANUARY
Art Deco Weekend

Tel 305/672-2014, www.mdpl
.org
A tribute to Miami's South
Beach art deco architecture,
when the streets are filled
with big-band sounds and
hotels are hard to find.

FEBRUARY
Annual Miami International Film Festival

Tel 305/237-FILM, www
.miamifilmfestival.com
A ten-day film show scattered
throughout the city, featuring
world and U.S. premiers of
international and domestic
productions, plus big-budget
movies and more ambiguous
fare produced during the year.

Coconut Grove Arts Festival

Tel 305/447-0401, www.cgaf
.com
Considered the number one
fine arts festival in the
country, attended by up to a
million people, with the work
of more than 300 artists on
show.

Miami International Boat Show

Tel 954/441-3220, www
.miamiboatshow.com
More than 2,300 of the
world's leading marine industry manufacturers display the
newest powerboats, engines,
and accessories at the Miami
Beach Convention Center.

MARCH
Carnaval Miami

Tel 305/644-8888, www
.carnavalmiami.com
Little Havana's week-long
celebration of Latin food,
music, drama, and dance. The
highlight is the final Sunday
night street party known as
Calle Ocho.

Sony Ericsson Open

Tel 305/442-3367, www.sony
ericssonopen.com
One of the nation's most
popular tennis tournaments
is held at the Tennis Center at
Crandon Park, Key Biscayne.
Top players compete for
more than $7.5 million.

Asian Festival

Tel 305/247-5727, www.fruit
andspicepark.com
Held over two days at
the Fruit & Spice Park in
Homestead, where South
Florida's thousands of Asian
immigrants celebrate their
food and culture.

JUNE
Miami/Bahamas Goombay Festival

Tel 305/448-9501
Coconut Grove's Bahamian
community pays tribute to
its roots. Watch Junkanoo
parades, the Royal Bahamian
Police Marching Band, and
try some of the best conch
fritters around.

JULY
Annual America Birthday Bash

Tel 305/358-7550
The state's largest Fourth of
July party, held at Bayfront
Park. Something for everyone
with an ethnic food court,
three stages, rock bands,
Latin musicians, and great
fireworks.

AUGUST
Miami Reggae Festival
Tel 305/891-2944
The entire Jamaican community turns out for local, national, and international musicians at this two-day event in honor of Jamaica's Independence Day.

NOVEMBER
Miami Book Fair International
Tel 305/237-3258, www.miami bookfair.com
Week-long literary extravaganza that features appearances and readings by authors of local, national, and international standing.

NASCAR Championship
Tel 866-989-RACE, www.home steadmiamispeedway.com
The NASCAR Ford 200, 300, and 400 Championships take place at Homestead-Miami Speedway, ending the racing season.

DECEMBER
Art Basel Miami Beach
www.artbaselmiamibeach.com
This four-day event is the American sister of Art Basel in Switzerland, perhaps the world's most prestigious annual art show. Art Basel Miami Beach showcases 1,000 artists from around the world as well as music, film, and other events. Book your tickets well ahead of time.

ING Miami Marathon
Tel 305/278-8668, www.ing miamimarathon.com
A marathon, half marathon, and smaller races plus a giant health & fitness expo at the Miami Beach Convention Center. Tens of thousands participate.

King Mango Strut
Tel 305/444-7270, www.king

mangostrut.org
Local and national events and characters are satirized in this wacky Coconut Grove New Year's Eve day parade whose theme is "Putting the NUT back in CocoNUT Grove."

KEY WEST
Conch Republic Independence Celebration
www.conchrepublic.com
A ten-day festival celebrating the Conch Republic's mock secession from the Union, based on the area's "insurrection" against a United States Border Patrol's alien and drug search road-block that jammed the Keys' roadways in 1982. This is reenacted each year on April 23, recalling the republic's motto: "We seceded where others have failed."

Fantasy Fest
Tel 305/296-1817, www .fantasyfest.net
A ten-day event held in late October, which marks the start of the autumn/winter season. It embraces Halloween, and is Key West's answer to New Orleans' Mardi Gras and Rio's Carnival. Centered around the Old Town, food festivals, street fairs, concerts, art and craft shows, a "Pretenders in Paradise" costume contest, pet masquerade, and parade, culminate in a Twilight Fantasy parade of spectacular floats and costumes.

Hemingway Days Festival
www.hemingwaydays.net
The highlight of this nearly week-long festival, which takes place around Hemingway's birthday (July 21), is the Look-Alike Contest, where dozens of square-jawed, white-haired gents turn up to vie for the

prize of being judged the most Hemingway-esque.

Sunset in Key West
Sunset at the southernmost city in the United States is renowned as a spectacular sight. Each day, as sunset draws near, crowds of locals and tourists make their way to Mallory Square, where celebrations take place as the sun seems to drop off the edge of the world into the Gulf of Mexico, to the accompaniment of entertainment, food, and music, and applause from the crowd.

INDEX

ILLUSTRATIONS CREDITS

All photographs by Matt Propert unless otherwise listed below.

4, Catherine Karnow/NGS; 8, Rudy Umans/Shutterstock; 11, Andy Newman/Florida Keys and Key West Tourism Development Council; 12, John Brooks/National Park Service; 20, Stanley Meltzhoff/NGS Image Collection; 23, Florida Photographic Collection; 25, Miami Museum of Science; 26, Stephen Ferry/Getty Images; 28, Jim Schwabel/Getty; 29, Roxy-Fer/Shutterstock; 30, Maureenpr/iStockphoto; 46, Raul Touzon/NGS; 75, Uliana Bazar; 76, Justin Dernier/EQUI-PHOTO, Courtesy Gulfstream Park; 88, Kay Hankins; 146, Pictures Colour Library; 148, Blend Images/iStockphoto; 154, Roberto A. Sanchez/iStockphoto; 162, John J. Lopinot/Silver Image; 167, Mike Theiss/NGS; 171, Courtesy Theater of the Sea; 174, Image Studios/Getty; 176, Raymond Gehman/NGS; 178, FL Stock/Alamy; 187, Stephen Frink/Florida Keys News Bureau; 200, Peter Titmuss/Alamy; 203, Doug Perrine/Minden; 224, Corey Rich/Aurora Photos; 234, Varina and Jay Patel/Shutterstock; 237, Henryk Sadura/Fotolia; 238, Scott Cramer/iStockphoto.

National Geographic
TRAVELER
Miami & the Keys

Published by the National Geographic Society
John M. Fahey, Jr., *Chairman of the Board and Chief Executive Officer*
Timothy T. Kelly, *President*
Declan Moore, *Executive Vice President; President, Publishing and Digital Media*
Melina Gerosa Bellows, *Executive Vice President, Chief Creative Officer, Books, Kids, and Family*

Prepared by the Book Division
Hector Sierra, *Senior Vice President and General Manager*
Anne Alexander, *Senior Vice President and Editorial Director*
Jonathan Halling, *Design Director, Books and Children's Publishing*
Marianne R. Koszorus, *Design Director, Books*
Barbara Noe, *Senior Editor*
R. Gary Colbert, *Production Director*
Jennifer A. Thornton, *Director of Managing Editorial*
Susan S. Blair, *Director of Photography*
Meredith C. Wilcox, *Director, Administration and Rights Clearance*

Staff for This Book
Jane Sunderland, *Editor*
Kay Kobor Hankins, *Art Director*
Matt Propert, *Illustrations Editor*
Michael McNey and Mapping Specialists, *Map Production*
Galen Young, *Rights Clearance Specialist*
Caroline Hickey, Larry Shea, *Contributors*

Manufacturing and Quality Management
Christopher A. Liedel, *Chief Financial Officer*
Phillip L. Schlosser, *Senior Vice President*
Chris Brown, *Vice President, NG Book Manufacturing*
George Bounelis, *Vice President, Production Services*
Nicole Elliott, *Manager*
Rachel Faulise, *Manager*
Robert L. Barr, *Manager*

National Geographic Traveler: Miami & the Keys (Fourth Edition)
ISBN: 978-1-4262-0953-6

First edition: Edited and designed by AA Publishing (a trading name of Automobile Association Developments Limited, whose registered office is Norfolk House, Priestley Road, Basingstoke, Hampshire, England RG24 9NY. Registered number: 1878835)

Cutaway illustrations drawn by Maltings Partnership, Derby, England

Printed in China
12/TS/1

The National Geographic Society is one of the world's largest nonprofit scientific and educational organizations. Founded in 1888 to "increase and diffuse geographic knowledge," the Society's mission is to inspire people to care about the planet. It reaches more than 400 million people worldwide each month through its official journal, *National Geographic,* and other magazines; National Geographic Channel; television documentaries; music; radio; films; books; DVDs; maps; exhibitions; live events; school publishing programs; interactive media; and merchandise. National Geographic has funded more than 9,600 scientific research, conservation and exploration projects and supports an education program promoting geographic literacy. For more information, visit www .nationalgeographic.com.

For more information, please call 1-800 NGS LINE (647-5463) or write to the following address:

National Geographic Society
1145 17th Street N.W.
Washington, D.C. 20036-4688 U.S.A.

For information about special discounts for bulk purchases, please contact National Geographic Books Special Sales: ngspecsales@ngs.org

For rights or permissions inquiries, please contact National Geographic Books Subsidiary Rights: ngbookrights@ngs.org

The Library of Congress has cataloged the first edition as follows:
Miller, Mark.
  The National Geographic traveler. Miami & the Keys / Mark Miller.
    p.   cm.
  Includes index.
  ISBN 0-7922-7433-4
  1. Miami (Fla.) Guidebooks. 2. Florida Keys (Fla.) Guidebooks.
  I. Miller, Mark. II. Title. III. Title: Miami & the Keys.
  F319.M6A78 1999
  917.59'3810463—dc21   99-40354
                                              CIP

The information in this book has been carefully checked and to the best of our knowledge is accurate. However, details are subject to change, and the National Geographic Society cannot be responsible for such changes, or for errors or omissions. Assessments of sites, hotels, and restaurants are based on the author's subjective opinions, which do not necessarily reflect the publisher's opinion.

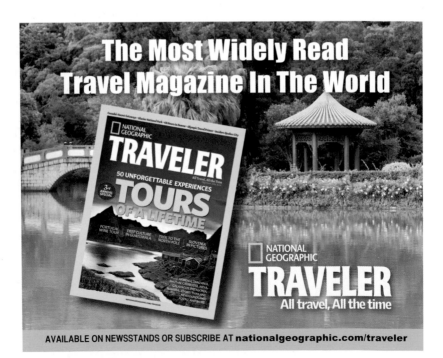